POKER ACES

POKER ACES

The Stars of Tournament Poker

Ron Rose
Winner of the First WPT Battle of Champions

Via Quinta Press

First published in 2004 by
Via Quinta Press
P.O. Box 751143
Dayton, OH 45475-1143

Library of Congress Control Number: 2004109406

ISBN Number: 0-9749724-0-1

Cover Design by Scott Hofmann
Front cover photo courtesy of the Aviation Club of France, Paris, France
Back cover photo by Image Masters Photography
Other photo credits listed on page 179

Printed and bound by Kromar Printing Limited, Canada

Acknowledgements

A book like this does not happen without the efforts of a great team. I would like to thank those who spent their days (and nights, at times!) doing the design and layout, research and writing, statistics and photographs and more.

I would like to thank my son Michael, a best-selling author in his own right, for his commitment to taking time from his own projects to interview players and hone the text of this book into something that is at the same time informative and enjoyable. My daughter Christina Rose Sprance has done everything from marketing to interviewing, and I could not have accomplished this without her unwavering assistance and willingness to respond at the drop of a hat. The layout of the book is the work of my wife, Mary Jo, who has put up with my changes from one day to the next with as much good humor as I could wish for.

My former bridge partner, Tom "Squeeze" Miller, was instrumental in providing statistics for the European players; and Eric Harkins of *Image Masters* accommodated my ever-expanding need for photos with a minimum of complaint. And my good friend, Barbara Buddendeck, was kind enough to lend an extra set of eyes for proofing.

I am grateful to all of these people for their indispensable contributions to this book. And I want to thank them for their assistance from the bottom of my heart.

Thank you all!

Contents

Foreword by Mike Sexton v
Introduction vii
World Flag Index viii
Photography Credits 180

THE POKER ACES

Joe Beevers 2
David Benyamine 4
Chris Bigler 6
Barney Boatman 8
Ross Boatman 10
John Bonetti 12
Humberto Brenes 14
Doyle Brunson 16
Vince Burgio 18
Garry Bush 20
"Miami" John Cernuto 22
Johnny Chan 24
T.J. Cloutier 26
David Colclough 28
Diego Cordovez 30
Peter "the Poet" Costa 32
Alan Cunningham 34
Bonnie Damiano 36
Paul Darden 38
"Freddy" Deeb 40
Martin de Knijff 42
Asher Derei 44
Annie Duke 46
John Duthie 48
Antonio Esfandiari 50
Chris Ferguson 52
Bruno Fitoussi 54
Layne Flack 56
Ken "Skyhawk" Flaton 58
Ted Forrest 60
Kirill Gerasimov 62
Phil Gordon 64
Barry Greenstein 66
Hassan Habib 68
Gus Hansen 70
Thor Hansen 72
Jennifer Harman 74
Dan Harrington 76
Brian Haveson 78
Phil Hellmuth 80
Juha Helppi 82
Randy Holland 84
Phil Ivey 86
Kenna James 88
Randy Jensen 90
Chip Jett 92
Christer Johansson 94
John Juanda 96
Mel Judah 98
Chris Karagulleyan 100
Phil Laak 102
Howard Lederer 104
Jim Lester 106
David Levi 108
Kathy Liebert 110
Erick Lindgren 112
Marcel Luske 114
Tony Ma 116
Tom McEvoy 118
Chris Moneymaker 120
Carlos Mortensen 122
John Myung 124
Daniel Negreanu 126
Men "the Master" Nguyen 128
Scotty Nguyen 130
Frankie O'Dell 132
Pascal Perrault 134
Young Phan 136
David Plastik 138
"Amarillo Slim" Preston 140
Greg Raymer 142
Chip Reese 144
Lucy Rokach 146
Ron Rose 148
José Rosenkrantz 150
Eric Seidel 152
Mark Seif 154
Mike Sexton 156
Charlie Shoten 158
Barry Shulman 160
Jeff Shulman 162
Dewey Tomko 164
An Tran 166
Simon Trumper 168
David "Devilfish" Ulliott 170
Amir Vahedi 172
Ram Vaswani 174
Dennis Waterman 176
Robert Williamson III 178

Some of the World Poker Tour Champions from the WPT First Season gathered at the Bellagio in 2003

Bottom row, from left: Jack McClellan (Tournament Director), Doug Dalton (Bellagio Poker Host), Chris Karagulleyan, Ron Rose, David "Devilfish" Ulliott, Steve Lipscomb (WPT Producer), and Lyle Berman (CEO Great Lakes Gaming)

Top row, from left: Paul Darden, José Rosenkrantz, Gus Hansen, Howard Lederer, Juha Helppi, and Chris Johansson

"There are few things that are so unpardonably neglected in our country as poker. The upper class knows very little about poker. Now and then you find ambassadors who have sort of a general knowledge of poker, but the ignorance of the people is fearful. Why, I have known clergymen, good men, kind-hearted, liberal, sincere, and all that, who did not know the meaning of a "flush." It is enough to make one ashamed of the species."

– Mark Twain

Foreword

Ron Rose came up and introduced himself to me a few years ago at one of the Aviation Club's poker tournaments in Paris, France. I didn't know who he was as he was a newcomer to tournament poker. As soon as he said, "Hi, Mike. I know you're from Dayton, Ohio. I'm also from Dayton and in fact, we went to the same high school," we became close friends. You don't meet many guys at a poker tournament in Paris who went to your high school!

Ron proceeded to tell me that he had retired not long ago. Knowing that I used to play bridge, he told me that he had just completed playing duplicate bridge for a year. He became a Life Master within a year and won the Mini-McKinney award—which goes to the player accumulating the most Master Points in one year. That award is the highest honor a player can achieve in the bridge world. And that impressed me! Now, having succeeded at bridge, he was considering a new venture—tournament poker—which simply meant another challenge for Ron.

Well, participating in tournament poker and becoming successful at it are two different things. It didn't take me long to realize that when Ron Rose puts his mind to doing something, he does it! He reminds me of the story involving the famous football coach, Buddy Ryan of the Philadelphia Eagles. After a loss to a team he felt they should have beaten, he was lambasting the team for their poor play. One player finally said, "But coach, we're trying." Ryan shouted back, "You're trying? You're trying? I don't want 'triers,' I want 'doers.' I could hire a bunch of truck drivers and pay them a million a year and they would try! I want doers!" I will simply say this about Ron Rose. He is a "doer."

I remember vividly the first final table Ron Rose made on the World Poker Tour. It was in November of 2002 at Foxwoods, in season one on the World Poker Tour. He made the final table for TV, but he finished in 6th place in that event, meaning he was the first one out. He seemed devastated about that and was upset with himself as to how he played. He later came over to me and said, "Mike, you can believe this. I'll be back. And the next time I make a WPT final table, I'm going to win the tournament."

Later that season, in Reno Nevada, that is exactly what happened. Ron Rose captured his first World Poker Tour title. And that victory earned him an invitation to the inaugural WPT Battle of Champions event at Bellagio which was televised on Super Bowl Sunday 2004 on NBC. There, he made poker history by defeating the WPT Champions of poker and capturing the first-ever WPT Champion of Champions title.

With *Poker Aces*, Ron gives the reader an insight as to who some of the top players are, their success stories, an in-depth look at their lives, and how they got involved in the poker world. It is a fascinating book that I'm sure you will enjoy.

Mike Sexton
Co-host of the World Poker Tour

Introduction

With the explosion of poker as a televised sport, fans of the game are clamoring for more information about their favorite players. The bookstores are full of poker advice, game strategy and how-to's for every type of poker game. But until now there was not a current book for fans to check out stories, photos, personal facts and general information about the players they admire. *Poker Aces* fills that void by presenting the fascinating stories of today's poker players, along with an abundance of photographs in one concise book.

I have put together personal stories of some of the most notable poker champions from all over the globe, along with personal facts and professional statistics. Now, you will have a valuable resource at your fingertips to find out more about your favorite players. For instance, you will find out that John Myung, the million dollar winner of the Showdown at the Sands narrowly escaped being a victim of 9/11; and how that experience changed his life and ultimately brought him into the world of poker. You will finally know how David "Devilfish" Ulliott got his infamous nickname and how "Amarillo Slim" was kidnapped by a drug lord in Colombia. You'll be riveted by the story of how Men "the Master" Nguyen and other Vietnamese players escaped South Vietnam after years of Communist oppression and amazed at how Phil Laak survived a serious motorcycle accident.

You will find more than just a compilation of statistics and facts. You'll have an opportunity to look at the human side of poker and satisfy your curiosity about what exactly lies behind those deadpan poker faces.

What you won't find is an exhaustive list of every poker player who has won a tournament. I quickly realized as I began to narrow down the list of tournament players that to list them all would require the book to be larger than an unabridged dictionary. And consequently just a bit unwieldly to carry! So, what I did was use three different lists of standout players—the Champion of the Year race compiled by poker great Phil Hellmuth, *Cardplayer* magazine's compilation of the best players of the year, and *Poker in Europe's* player of the year statistics. To that I added a few players whose histories or personalities add both color and substance to tournament play, in order to give a broad (albeit limited) view of the tournament poker community.

There are so many more players that I would like to have included, but for various reasons was not able to. I hope to continue the series with another *Poker Aces* book where you will find even more poker greats. For now, enjoy all of the fascinating stories of the most recognizable faces on the poker scene today. I guarantee you'll find some fascinating insights into the minds and lives of the players. I hope you enjoy reading the book as much as I enjoyed putting it together.

Until we meet across the green felt ......

Ron Rose

World Flag Index

THE POKER ACES

Joe Beevers

"That certainly added to the tension, knowing that so many friends, family, and other people were watching."

Personal Notes

- **Born in London, England, 1967**
- **Holds B.A. Honors degree in Finance and Accounting**
- **Formerly worked for Citibank**
- **Member of the Hendon Mob**
- **Resides in London (Hendon), England**

Joe Beevers used to play blackjack with his late father back in the 1980s. At the time, there were 23 casinos in the London area. The Beevers' father-son team was so good, Joe was banned from four casinos and his father got banned from 19. But it was Joe's blackjack habit that led him to tournament poker.

In the early 1990s Joe was playing blackjack in a casino in Luton, about 30 miles outside of London. "Two of the players got up to leave in the middle of a very good shoe," he remembers, "and I asked them where they were going." They told Joe that they were off to play in a £10 poker tournament and suggested that he come along. "I had played bragg and a little poker and thought that I knew how to play, so I agreed."

After folding the first few hands, Joe found one he liked and decided to play. By this time he had £350 in chips left from the initial £500. One player bet £100 and another raised £400 more. "I didn't know what to do," he says, "and I was told I had to put all my chips into the pot if I wanted to play." That's what Joe did—and he went bust. A £10 rebuy bought him another £500 in chips, and he returned to the same table to continue. "On receiving my £500 chip, I threw it to the last winner and asked for £350 change," he says. "I thought that I owed him £150 from the last pot! The table all burst out laughing."

Following his first tournament, Joe played a few more. Before long he noticed that the same players often made the money. "I watched them," he says, "and tried to work out what they did right. I also watched the losers and tried to work out what they did wrong." Joe also spent a fair amount of time reading poker books, and after a short time found that he was regularly making final tables and pulling in prize money.

Since then Joe has had countless memorable poker experiences including winning the Irish Open in 2003 after finishing third the year before. "Probably the highest profile moment was finishing second to professional

snooker player Jimmy White in the Poker Million-the Masters," he says. The final table action was broadcast live on Sky Television in Europe with under-the-table cameras. "That certainly added to the tension, knowing that so many friends, family, and other people were watching," he adds.

In 2004, Joe is on a world tour with his group of London-based poker players known as The Hendon Mob (named after their neighborhood in London). "We're playing in over £1 million in tournament entries sponsored by primapoker.com. For anyone who would like to keep up to date with Joe and his Mob's poker exploits, they can do so by checking out thehendonmob.com, where the Mob logs its daily reports.

"Poker is habit forming. Make sure that you get into good habits as bad ones can be hard to break."

-Joe Beevers

A visit to the website gives the reader an idea of the distinctive style of the "Mob." In an article in *Esquire* magazine, Joe Beevers and his buddies got plenty of good ink. Joe is depicted as the Armani-attired tall one with gelled hair. "You would like Joe," the article promises. "Joe is reliable, he is straight down the line and he speaks his mind. He likes nice things. He likes to drink champagne and drive his Porsche 911 with its numberplate JOE 911, but not both at the same time because he likes the car a lot," they quip. "He is focused, disciplined and disturbingly patient at the poker table. But if it was a Saturday night and you were going out drinking with some people to have a good time, you would ask Joe to come with you."

The Hendon Mob—Ross Boatman, Ram Vaswani, Barney Boatman, Joe Beevers with Bonnie Damiano (center)

Major Poker Accomplishments

2003, First place, Irish Open, No Limit Hold'em Championship

2003, First place, Poker Classics, Pot Limit Hold'em

2002, First place, British Open, Pot Limit Omaha

2001, First place, Grosvenor Grand Challenge, Pot Limit Hold'em

1997, First place, Master Classics of Poker, Limit Hold'em

David Benyamine

"I think it does matter a lot to have chance on your side when you play."

Personal Notes

- **Born in France, 1972**
- **Has never read a poker book or magazine**
- **Has no poker superstitions**
- **Married with one child**
- **His favorite movie is "Rocky."**
- **Resides in Paris**

You won't find David Benyamine playing poker on the internet, but you will find him at a lot of final tables, particularly at the Aviation Club in Paris, the city that David calls home. In the few years that David has been playing poker professionally, he finds that the club in Paris has the best service (and many of the best players in Europe)!

His foray into the world of poker began by a lucky coincidence when a friend of his who worked at a poker club brought him there to play. David played first in small games, gradually coming into his own on the European poker circuit. Now he lives by the game. Not that David has not always considered himself a "player" in life. He just saw that poker was a good way to combine business with pleasure.

His congenial smile and good looks belie the fearsome player within. This intensity at the table led him to his biggest win to date—the 2003 Grand Prix de Paris, a World Poker Tour event held at the Aviation Club. Facing five other players and even more cameras, for the taping of the event, David exuded confidence.

When it came down to heads-up play, David was pitted against a fellow Frenchman, Jan Boubli, who himself is a highly regarded player. With several all-in bets and the chip lead volleying from one player to the other, a less focused fellow may have been rattled. But not David. In the final hand, David raised to 38,000 with A-10 suited and Jan moved all in with pocket 8's. David called him and won the hand (and a cool 357,800 Euros) with a diamond flush. This gave David the first major win of his poker career and gave him the distinction of being the first winner of the World Poker Tour's second season.

With this win under his belt, David has set a formidable goal for himself—to win the World Series of Poker one day! He is determined to make a good living playing the game he loves. But winning is not everything to David. He places great importance on peace in all manner and form. If he could change anything about the world, it would be to bring about peace. He sees peace at the poker table as another critical factor.

Admired by his fellow players as a generous and appreciative player who treats players and staff with great consideration, he would like to see more cordiality among players. "I would like to see the players behave, so it would be fun to play in a nice ambiance." He also thinks that more penalties should be enforced to make sure the players really understand the importance of behaving at the table.

When it comes down to which games to play, David admits that, though he likes all games, "Hold'em and Omaha are the games where I have the best results." A look at his career poker record will attest to that.

"You have to get rid of all of your outside problems. You also need to really want to play poker, and to win. It's my recipe."

- David Benyamine

Major Poker Accomplishments

2003, First place, WPT Grand Prix de Paris, No Limit Hold'em Championship

2002, First place, Euro Finals of Poker, No Limit Hold'em event

2002, Second place, Euro Finals of Poker, Pot Limit Omaha

2000, First place, Aviation Club Autumn Tournament, No Limit Hold'em Championship

2000, First place, Euro Finals of Poker, Pot Limit Hold'em/Omaha Championship

Chris Bigler

"In two years I went from never having heard of No Limit Hold'em to making the final table at the World Series."

Personal Notes

Born in Zurich, Switzerland, 1949

Married with one son

Internet business consultant

Dislikes playing with beginners

Anti-smoking crusader

Resides in Baden, Switzerland

"Poker?—Never heard of it." That's what Swiss businessman Chris Bigler would have said before his first visit to Las Vegas's Horseshoe Casino in 1997. It just happened to be during the World Series of Poker. "I remember wondering what the hell was going on there with all those chips on the tables," says Chris. "I didn't even know what poker was."

Chris Bigler became instantly fascinated with the game. He wasted no time sitting down at the poker tables and losing a few games before he bought several "how-to" poker books that he found indispensable. "I read all the books and got very enthusiastic," he remembers. When he returned to Switzerland, he couldn't find anyone to play against. In fact, he was hard-pressed to find anyone who even knew *how* to play poker. "In Switzerland most people still think of poker in the setting of the old Western movies, where players got shot during the game."

He launched out to play at the major European tournaments in Vienna, Paris and Amsterdam, where he cut his teeth at cards. "For the first year and a half, I basically won nothing," he admits. The tables turned when he came to Atlantic City in December of 1998. Chris won his first satellite tournament, which led to his first final table at a big event. The following month he won a Pot Limit Hold'em tournament in Reno. "That was my first international tournament win," he says. "It was a huge field and great prize money."

After winning a couple more tournaments in Europe he returned to Nevada for the World Series of Poker. "My experience playing non-stop poker was incredible. In two years I went from never having heard of No Limit Hold'em to making the final table at the World Series." Chris finished fifth there, catapulting him to poker stardom.

"Don't bluff an unknown player; he might call you."

-Chris Bigler

In 2001, Chris sold his business in Switzerland to take up professional poker playing full time. "I get excited about tournament poker," he explains. "I play cash games in order to survive the tournaments, but I never really enjoy them, nor am I very successful at it. My strength is in tournament strategy."

When the WPT started taping their tournaments, Chris says he "wanted to get on TV really bad." In May of 2002 he did just that in the very first WPT event. He won his $10,000 seat at the Bellagio's Five Diamond World Poker Classic in Las Vegas and made it to the final table. "I wanted to make it onto the first WPT television show so bad that I played my hands differently than I otherwise might have." In the end, it paid off for him, and he became a TV star. Although Chris was the first to get knocked out at the final table play, later that year he placed a very respectable second in the WPT Lucky Chances Championship.

Chris kept a journal of the play at the Bellagio for his online fans, from documenting the exciting play to behind the scenes production insights. "We were taken in a limo to buy new clothes for the final table," Chris remembers, "and the film crew followed us around taping everything. Quite a new experience." Chris came away from that tournament knowing that television was going to play a huge role in promoting the legitimacy of poker. "Everything was just classy and very professional," Chris states.

When he returned to Switzerland after the tournament he was glad that his friends could now see exactly what it was that he was doing while he was away from home. "Now I can show everybody the WPT programs on DVD," he says, "and they get excited about it—as excited as the people in America, even though most of them don't understand the game, and some of them don't even understand English."

Despite all the excitement from his Swiss friends, none have yet caught the poker-playing bug. Chris still has to travel out of the country to get a good game. "There's a casino about seven miles from my house in Baden, and they just put in two poker tables, making Baden the poker epicenter in Switzerland," he says with his tongue in cheek. "But I can't even play there. I don't want to play there. The other players are so bad, it's like sitting at a table with a bunch of craps shooters. If there aren't at least three or four other good players at the table, I might as well be shooting craps."

Major Poker Accomplishments

2002, Second place, WPT Lucky Chances, No Limit Hold'em Championship

2002, Fifth place, WPT Five Diamond World Poker Classic, No Limit Hold'em Championship

2002, Sixth place, World Poker Open, No Limit Hold'em Championship

1999, Fifth place, WSOP, No Limit Hold'em Championship

Barney Boatman

"One of the worst things that happened to me was . . . win[ning] the first tournament that I ever entered. . ."

Personal Notes

- **Born in Summerstown, England**
- **Freelance journalist and budding screenwriter**
- **Member of the Hendon Mob**
- **Poker commentator in Europe**
- **Speaks Spanish fluently**
- **Resides in Archway, England**

Barney Boatman is not a man who stands alone. If it's not his brother he's associated with, it's the "Mob," the Hendon Mob, that is. But Barney is a poker player who needs no one's assistance to play the game with a daring and unreadable demeanor. It all started with the very first tournament that he entered. "One of the worst things that happened to me," Barney recalls, "was . . . win[ning] the first tournament that I ever entered—a Seven Card Stud tournament in London. I went back the next week and came in second in the same tournament." Barney just thought that it was all too easy. "Looking back," he says," I must have been incredibly lucky. Because I didn't win anything again for ages after that. But it was enough to hook me."

Along with his younger brother, Ross, who is also a topnotch poker player, Barney made some poker history. Barney and Ross were the first two brothers to ever make a final together in Omaha at the World Series of Poker. This happened in the 2002 tournament. And then, in 2003, at the Four Queens Poker Classic, the brothers Boatman came in first and second in a tournament, with Barney taking home the title.

But playing in tournaments is not the only tie that Barney has with the sport of poker. He is also a poker commentator in Europe. When Barney played in the first five series of the popular "Late Night Poker" show he did commentary as soon as he was knocked out. He got his start doing commentary at the first and only Isle of Man tournament. "I was in the final round," says Barney, "and then I got knocked out in second place and went straight into the commentary booth along with Phil Hellmuth to commentate on the rest of the tournament." This brief stint at the Isle of Man developed into a sideline career for Barney, allowing him to do the commentary for Late Night Poker, Celebrity Poker and the World Heads Up Tournament. He is hoping his next job is in the U.S.A.

Barney and Ross, along with Joe Beevers and Ram Vaswani, the other members of the Hendon Mob, have made quite a name for themselves in the poker world in a very short time. They've packed their bags and are touring non-stop, it seems, for Prima Poker throughout the world. They are making the Hendon Mob a household name through both television and on their popular internet website thehendonmob.com.

"If scientific reasoning were limited to the logical processes of arithmetic, we should not get very far in our understanding of the physical world. One might as well attempt to grasp the game of poker entirely by the use of the mathematics of probability."

-Vannevar Bush

Barney relates that the group began to be known as the Hendon Mob after they all started playing on the *Late Night Poker* show in England. Barney had the foresight to see that poker was eventually going to go into a sponsorship situation and he and the boys started a website to promote themselves as a group. When the site began to grow by leaps and bounds, they secured advertising to pay for the site and expanded it into one of the most popular poker websites around.

Because of their popularity on the web, Prima Poker approached Barney with a sponsorship deal. In just 15 minutes over coffee at Paddington Station, they shook hands on what is basically a million dollar deal. This was in 2003 and they are still going strong. The Hendon Mob has done very well on the tour.

When asked about his life aside from poker, Barney relates that he has many other interests. He loves the cinema and has even tried acting, but now he leaves that to his brother Ross, a television star in his own right. Barney loves to travel and to learn other languages, one of which is Spanish which he speaks fluently. Barney even used to invent board games; but being "ripped off" by the game companies, he gave it up. "I just didn't have the heart to do it any more."

One of the things he does like to do, however, is participate in adventurous sports. He loves such things as parachuting, snow boarding and scuba diving. "I like to give them all a go," he says. Knowing how adventurous Barney can be should give his opponents an indication of the level to which he is willing to go in a tournament. He is considered by some as "tricky, unreadable and a daring opponent, best avoided."

And Barney has a big heart, as well. When his sister was dying of breast cancer he took two years off to care for her. "She was the most amazing person," he remembers. "She had thousands of friends. As a result, I now have all those friends. My sister always had this big belief in me," he says with pride. "She always used to tell me that I could do anything." Barney Boatman has not let her down.

Major Poker Accomplishments

2003, First place, Helsinki Freezeout, No Limit Hold'em Championship

2003, First place, Christmas Cracker, No Limit Hold'em Championship

2003, First place, Four Queens Poker Classic, Pot Limit Hold'em

2002, First place, European Poker Championship, Pot Limit Seven Card Stud

2002, WSOP, Most Notable Tournament Performance

2000, Sixth place, Poker Million, No Limit Hold'em Championship

1999, Europe's top-ranked Seven Card Stud player

Ross Boatman

"My father and mother say when we're around, 'It's just luck.' But when we're not around we hear that they show off about us."

Personal Notes

Born in Archway, England

Career actor

Starred in Britain's most successful TV drama

Married with one child

Member of the Hendon Mob

Resides in Archway, England

Ross Boatman must have felt very much at home as he starred in London's West End production of *Dealer's Choice*, a comedy based around a poker game. A champion poker player several times over, Ross juggles two careers, both as actor and professional poker player, and has been successful at both.

His acting career includes eight years playing the character of Kevin in *London's Burning*, the British equivalent of America's *Hill Street Blues*. It is Britain's most successful TV drama series ever. Ross has a host of other acting credits to his name including a big screen role in the black comedy, *Hard Men*, the forerunner to *Lock, Stock and Two Smoking Barrels*. Although he enjoys his acting career and has no plans to give it up, he has spent a lot of time in the last few years playing professional poker—and playing it well!

Ignoring the fact that both of these pursuits, acting and playing tournament poker, can be full time work, one just as stressful as the other, Ross and his family take it all in stride. In fact, his wife and child love it. Though his wife leaves the poker playing to "the boys" she admits to liking the travel and lifestyle that poker tournaments allow. As to Ross's parents, he says that they do have their reservations. "My father and mother say when we're around, 'It's just luck.' But when we're not around we hear that they show off about us." He adds, "They support anything that we do. I'm sure they'd rather Barney be writing and I be acting but we're bringing home the bacon." Being Europe's top money winner in 2002 attests to this fact.

Along with Joe Beevers, Ram Vaswani and his brother Barney, Ross is a member of what has been dubbed the "Hendon Mob." Joe used to run a private game in Hendon, which is a neighborhood of London." Ross explains. "None of us is actually from there except for Joe. But that's where we all met." Ross says that the name was given to them by others and they decided to stick with it.

"We thought it was kind of funny," Ross says with a smile. "We decided to keep it and use it. It's become a business."

"Never play with your own money!"

-Ross Boatman

That business includes a comprehensive website—thehendonmob.com—where the viewer can read about the four members, learn how to play poker, scan a number of articles that relate to the Mob and even play poker with them if one dares.

Ross relates an unusual tidbit about Hendon—the neighborhood and the Mob. "The funny thing is that the only thing that Hendon is known for is their police academy, which is the most unlikely place in London that you would actually find a mob."

As to how Ross learned the game of poker, he credits his brother Barney with teaching him the basics. He recalls a time when Barney was babysitting for him and he was sitting around with his pals playing poker. "I saw these shiny coins and colorful cards," Ross relates. "I said, 'please let me play.' Sure I didn't have a clue what I was doing. Barney and his friends let me sit in. I just remember raking in these big piles of shiny coins. And that was it," Ross confesses. "[I was] hooked for a lifetime."

Ross admits to "bunking off" (playing truant) with his high school friends behind the school gym in order to play poker. His brother had a group of poker friends as well, so they "sort of merged" the groups and started playing regular games at their house.

It wasn't until 1992 that Ross began to play poker professionally. Together with his brother, he went to a club in London. "We played our first tournament. And we never looked back." Will Ross's son Buster play poker like his Dad? "Buster will be taught if he wants to, but he won't be forced into it," Ross muses. "Too early to tell."

With a stellar acting career to supplement his poker exploits, Ross says that he has managed to provide very well for everything his family needs. He admits, though, that it is stressful at times. But he has the support of his wife and his brother, and the company of the other members of the Mob to keep him going in the right direction. As a poker player, Ross is well-liked but his opponents also give him the respect he deserves as a fearsome poker ace.

Major Poker Accomplishments

2004, First place, British Open, Pot Limit Omaha Hi/Lo

2002, First place, European Poker Classic, No Limit Hold'em Championship

2002, Top money-winner on the European tournament circuit

Final table, four out of five years, at the European WSOP

2002, First place, Irish Winter Festival, Pot Limit Omaha

2002, First place, Austrian Masters, Pot Limit Omaha

John Bonetti

"It's a funny game. You can be flying high and doing everything well and then lose a $20,000 pot to a guy who had a 50-1 shot."

Personal Notes

Born in Brooklyn, New York, 1928

Graduate of Bushwick High School

Married with four children

Former apartment manager

Resides in Houston, Texas

John Bonetti didn't get his start in poker until he was 55 years old, five years after he moved to Houston to get away from New York City. "Believe it or not," he says, "I never played in New York." In Texas, John took a job as a salesman, and it was the owner of the company who first invited John along to a friendly game of poker. "I went there," he remembers, "and I had no idea what I was doing. I lost most of the time."

Then he discovered hold'em, and picked up the game right away. In 1985, he rode out with some friends to Lafayette, Louisiana to get a taste of his first tournament. "I wanted to see what a tournament was like," he says, "and I ended up winning $28,000 there"—his first in a long series of big wins.

Due to the oil crisis, the early 1980s were hard times for the Texas economy. Consequently, John decided to quit business and try his hand at poker for a living. "I found out quickly that poker paid much better." Since that first tournament in Lafayette, John has been a near constant presence on the poker circuit, and has chalked up more than $1.5 million in World Series of Poker wins alone, which puts him high up on the map of the all-time winners.

With his aggressive play John Bonetti has established a reputation as a player to be feared. "I don't back off," he says. "When I feel like I've got the winning hand, I go for it," he explains. "I'm not a mind reader or a magician; I go with what my first instinct tells me to do. The very good players go with their first instinct and don't change. When you change, that's when you go wrong."

Although aggressive at the table, John is relaxed and humble away from the game. He says he's never considered himself better than anybody; rather he has taken the attitude that if he won a tournament, then he was very lucky. John is also known for encouraging others when they hit a trough. "I know a lot of good players who have been through ups and downs; they come to me and ask, 'what's wrong with me? What am I doing wrong?' I tell them it's just the flow of the cards. Sometimes they go against you. If you play your game, it's usually going to level out."

"Many bad players will not improve because they cannot bear self-knowledge."

-David Mamet

Even for himself, John admits, the ups and downs—especially the downs—of the game can be difficult to deal with. "It's a funny game," he says of poker in general. "You can be flying high and doing everything well and then lose a $20,000 pot to a guy who had a 50-1 shot. These things happen. You've got to be able to roll with the punches."

On the sunny side, John says that being a poker professional has it's perks, especially these days. When he started playing poker in the 1980s John found that he was frowned upon by others who felt that poker was an illegitimate pursuit. "Now in the past couple of years," he observes, "poker has blossomed because of television coverage. It has gained respectability and is being treated more like a sport now—like golf."

John is surprised that he's recognized now in the places he's long frequented in and around Houston. "People are always telling me they saw me on TV. These same people have known I was in the poker profession for years, but now they're all excited about it because they can watch it on television. Poker has come out in the open and gained respectability even in a backwoods place like Texas."

Even with all his poker wins, John says his greatest win was beating cancer. In 1992 he was diagnosed with prostate and spinal cancer. "In 1993, the doctors told me it looked pretty bad. They didn't think I'd make it, but I'm still here today. So far it's been in remission."

Speaking of his battle with cancer, John says his one wish would be that he had taken up the poker profession as a much younger man. "When I was younger," he laments, "I didn't have any interest in sitting around a table and playing poker. I liked playing sports. I loved to play ball. I loved to be competitive, but I never thought of poker." That may be one reason John admires some of the young "crackerjack players," as he calls them. "Hellmuth, Lederer, Ivey, and Flack—these guys are champions. I'm happy that I can be associated with them in the same paragraph."

Major Poker Accomplishments

2004, Seventh place, WPT World Poker Open, No Limit Hold'em Championship

1996, Third place, WSOP, No Limit Hold'em Championship

1995, First place, WSOP, Deuce to Seven Draw

1993, First place, WSOP, Pot Limit Hold'em

1993, Third place, WSOP, No Limit Hold'em Championship

1990, First place, WSOP, Deuce to Seven Draw

Humberto Brenes 

"When I told my friends I was going to America to play in the World Series they said I was *loco.*"

Personal Notes

Born in San Jose, Costa Rica, 1951

Married with three children

Owner of Nueces Industriales (Industrial Nuts)

Former baccarat tournament player

Resides in San Jose, Costa Rica

Despite the fact that poker gets a bad wrap in Costa Rica, Humberto Brenes has been playing the game with a few dozen of his best friends for years. The San Jose native describes the public's perception of poker-playing in his country this way: "They think it's like it has been depicted in the movies. We're all cheating, smoking, involved with the Mafia, and killing the person who beats us."

Although Humberto was first introduced to poker as a child, he didn't start playing until he was 23. "Every time I played I was making money," he remembers, "and people told me I was good, but that I only played with suckers." Inspired by this confidence, Humberto reasoned there'd be a whole lot more suckers in Vegas. He decided to take a trip there in order to play the tourists. "But when I arrived in Vegas," he says, "I figured out pretty quickly who the tourist was: me!"

Humberto suffered some embarrassing defeats during that first poker trip to America. "I lost big," he says. "I paid out maybe $2,000 in losses in order to learn the ropes. There was no internet then, where I could practice for free."

A year later in 1988, after practicing No Limit Hold'em with his Costa Rican poker cohorts—including José Rosenkrantz—Humberto returned to Las Vegas for the World Series of Poker, where he took fourth place, playing against T.J. Cloutier and Johnny Chan. "When I told my friends I was going to America to play in the World Series," Humberto remembers, "they said I was *loco.* But when I came back after winning, the same people told me I was better than they thought."

Since 1988 Humberto has kept poker as a "serious hobby," traveling to several major poker tournaments each year. "I don't consider myself a professional player," he explains, "and I certainly don't try to make a living off it." When Humberto does lose, he doesn't cry, and when he wins he looks at the prize money as a bonus. "That way I never have this pressure to win. I don't have to deal with the stress of losing all of my money. I play with nothing to lose and everything to win."

"Talent is something that you are born with, but concentration is something that you must teach yourself."

-Humberto Brenes

During the months of January and February when his children are on holiday from school, he likes to take his family along with him when he plays week-long tournaments. "They cry when I get knocked out of a tournament," he says of his family, "and they get happy if I win." For Humberto, poker is a real family affair. "When I go off to play poker I tell my family that I'm going to kindergarten. One player will be crying, another throwing a temper tantrum, and another jumping around. A poker tournament is like one big kindergarten." While Humberto is off at "kindergarten," his wife Patricia goes shopping, and his kids head for the pool and the sauna. "I want my family to see that my poker playing is good for the life." And he sees to it that they share in the perks of his poker experiences. Humberto is a family man with family values.

Back in Costa Rica, Humberto's professional trade is nuts. He is the country's largest exporter of indigenous nuts and legumes—peanuts, pistachios, almonds, cashews, grains and even prunes. "That is my business," he says, "and my main occupational focus." It is as a successful businessman that he is known to people in Costa Rica, not as a poker celebrity. "I don't go around telling people I'm a poker champion. I don't come back and tell everyone I just won this tournament or that. More people know me in Vegas than in my own country."

When his 13-year-old son Roberto is asked what he thinks of his dad being a famous poker player in the United States, he answers: "My brain still doesn't realize that he is a famous person, but even if he weren't famous, I'd look up to him like I would a star."

Major Poker Accomplishments

2004, Second place, WPT Celebrity Invitational

2002, First place, World Poker Open, No Limit Hold'em Championship

2001, Second place (to brother Alex), Costa Rican Spring Fling, No Limit Hold'em

1993, First place, WSOP, Limit Hold'em

1993, First place, WSOP, Pot Limit Omaha

1988, Fourth place, WSOP, No Limit Hold'em Championship

Doyle Brunson

"I had never had over five hundred dollars at one time in my life, so I still remember the thrill of that game."

Personal Notes

- **Born in Longworth, Texas, 1933**
- **Holds Masters Degree in business from Hardin-Simmons University**
- **Married with four grown children**
- **Longtime professional cash poker player**
- **Spends his summers on Flathead Lake, Montana**
- **Resides in Las Vegas**

Doyle Brunson has had a long and successful career at the poker table, and after fifty years of card playing he's trying to slow down and smell the roses. "But I'm having trouble doing that," he admits, "because I crave the action and enjoyment of playing poker." He's also been contending with his own fame. Some Hollywood writers recently completed a movie script about his life, he's writing two books, and he's considering being a spokesman for an Internet poker site—never a dull moment for this Doyle.

Texas Dolly's poker career stretches way back to his days of playing high school basketball when his team went to Austin to play in the state finals. It was there in Austin, between championship basketball games that Doyle first played poker. He won $23 over three days. "That was 1950," he says, "and I have never stopped playing."

Though he enjoyed a good game of poker, at that point he hadn't yet given up on his dream to become a professional athlete. His naturally competitive nature led him to pursue an athletic scholarship to college. His choice from over 100 offers was Hardin-Simmons University in Abilene where he went on to become the second best mile-distance runner in the state collegiate ranks and Most Valuable Player in his conference. Fate intervened however, in the guise of a serious knee injury. "That ended whatever aspirations I had of becoming a pro athlete," says Doyle. "Once I accepted the fact my career in sports was over, I started playing poker to support myself."

It was at this time, as a young college student, that Doyle played the most memorable poker game of his life. "Even my back-to-back WSOP championships pale in comparison to winning $3,700 from a wealthy Texas oil man," he says. "I had never had over five hundred dollars at one time in my life, so I still remember the thrill of that game."

Doyle gradually worked his way up to playing in the bigger private games in Texas, eventually hooking up with two other poker legends, Sailor Roberts, the 1975 World Poker Champion, and "Amarillo Slim" Preston. Doyle remembers those days as a constant tap dance to avoid getting arrested for playing an illegal poker game or looking down the barrel of a gun or at the shaft of a knife. "It was a harrowing experience," recalls Doyle. "People today who play in all the big fancy (legal) cardrooms don't understand what it was like back in those days to be a poker player with all the problems we had."

"Go slow at first. Be sure you can win at the level you are currently playing before you move to bigger games."

-Doyle Brunson

Texas Dolly credits much of his success at the tables to an intense study of the game. "Back in those days, there were no computers—so I did all the strategy work manually. I dealt out a hand here. I put another hand there. I just kept doing it thousands and thousands of times, over and over." He also considers himself to be a student of the game who is now teaching others (through his books) what he learned by the sweat of his brow over the many years he has played the game.

If Doyle had anything to say to a young player just starting out it would probably be to be careful and play as much as possible and to read some good poker books (presumably some of the many that Brunson has authored would do). He also recommends that if marriage is in the future, that the player "had better get an exceptional spouse because the spouse will have to put up with a lot of unusual things. Fortunately, I found the perfect (for me) soul mate over 40 years ago," boasts Doyle.

Although Doyle made his name in cash poker games, he was also instrumental in giving tournament poker a major boost. His best friend was Benny Binion, the man who started the World Series of Poker at his Horseshoe Casino, and Doyle did everything he could to make the tournament a success. "The idea was to get people to come to Vegas, where we could have better cash games," he says. "This happened for ten years or so until the satellites started up and took the players out of the cash games."

Doyle has never been a stranger to the WSOP final tables through the years. In fact, he still holds the record (tied now with Johnny Chan and Phil Hellmuth) for the most gold bracelets at nine. His goal, of course, is to win even more. And he says that he hopes he can play poker profitably until he's ninety years old. Given that he's only a young septuagenarian, that would give him two more decades to compete at the table. In the meantime, he says he'll continue to enjoy his grown children and his extended family. "Life is good!" he says.

Major Poker Accomplishments

Winner of nine WSOP gold bracelets

1977, 1976, Back-to-back WSOP, No Limit Hold'em Championship events

Two wins at the Super Bowl of Poker in Reno

Four Queens championship in Las Vegas

Texas Hold'em championship in Dallas

Two Frontier Hotel Poker Championships in Las Vegas

Vince Burgio

"If you're not well known, I suppose you can throw the cards and cuss at people. Once you're known, you even have to shave every day."

Personal Notes

- **Born in Kansas City, Missouri**
- **Graduate of the University of Missouri**
- **Former go-go bar owner**
- **Columnist for *Cardplayer* magazine**
- **Married with four grown daughters**
- **Resides in West Hills, California**

A native of Kansas City, Missouri, Vince Burgio moved to California in 1976 to open a construction company, which turned out to be a successful endeavor. But eleven years later he discovered tournament poker. "The first week I played in a tournament I won $8,000 at the Hilton," he says. But that was peanuts compared to his next tournament. "Two weeks later at the Riviera I won $54,000." That's when Vince said to himself: "You know what, maybe I ought to give this a shot." A few months later Vince sold his construction business and has been playing tournament poker ever since.

Unlike some of his business associates, Vince and his wife didn't see it as a reckless move. They had savings and assets to speak of by then, and by nature Vince is a financially conservative person. "I've never been broke," he says. "One year I won half a million dollars, and we invested it."

Although Vince plays some cash games, it's the tournaments that he really enjoys. The value of tournament play goes way beyond the rewards of the money, he says. "There's a real element of desire. If you're just playing for the money you could probably find professions where you could devote as much time and energy and make a whole lot more money. Or as a poker player you could get into side games for half the stress and grief and make as much money."

Without playing the tournaments, Vince recognizes, poker players aren't going to get famous and get all the adulation from a huge television audience. "That's part of my motivation," he admits. "I love to get on television." After he appeared on the World Poker Tour in 2003 he says he returned to Kansas City for a wedding. "It was the first time anyone ever acknowledged that I was a professional poker player," he says. "About two-thirds of them said they saw me on TV." That was quite a turnaround according to Vince, and it gave him a certain satisfaction.

Vince also realizes that there are two sides to every coin. The down side in tournament play for him is the fact that the vast majority of time he will finish a loser—just like everyone else who plays tournament poker. "What makes me a good tournament player," he believes, "is that I am able to get banged, knocked down, get up, get knocked down again, go to bed at night and wake up the next day and say I'm going to do it all again."

"My number one tip is to decide why you are playing poker; then do what is appropriate to succeed."

-Vince Burgio

Persistence is the virtue Vince has been cultivating through the years because it's the one that keeps him on the winning track. "You've really got to want to do it," he says of winning tournament poker, "and you've got to have the intestinal fortitude to come back from getting knocked down flat on your face day after day. To be an excellent player you need to be able to come back from these heart-wrenching beats."

Vince Burgio has been called the Andy Rooney of the poker world. Not for his poker playing, but because of his quirky human interest column published for the past five years in *Cardplayer* magazine. That's one of the reasons Vince has become such a high-profile player in recent years. It's partly this high profile that keeps Vince in line at the table. "Being a columnist and having some success," he explains, "I don't want to standout as a sorehead like some other prominent players. If you're not well known, I suppose you can throw the cards and cuss at people. Once you're known, you even have to shave every day."

He says, however, that his daughters tease him for being too middle-of-the-road—in their words: "too *blah* for TV." They think their father needs to wear gold chains or to distinguish himself in some other way, but he eschews their advice, not wanting to stick out or seem obnoxious at the poker table."

His columns give Vince a chance to express his personality a bit more, and that's where he's earned his reputation as a humorous fellow. Vince's favorite column ("Open Wide") tells of his trip to the dentist's office to get a root canal. Once the dentist found out that Vince was a poker pro, he got to talking to his patient about the game, pounding Vince with question after question. "The bottom line," says Vince, "is that I tried to answer all these questions with his mitts in my numb mouth. When you go in for something like that, it's better to tell the dentist you're a crossing guard."

Major Poker Accomplishments

1999, Inducted into the Seniors Poker Hall of Fame

1999, First place, LA Poker Classic, Lowball Championship

1994, Fourth place, WSOP, No Limit Hold'em Championship

1994, First place, D.J.B. No Limit Hold'em Championship

1994, First place, WSOP, Seven Card Stud Split

Garry Bush

"If you don't go in there and feel mentally strong, it will affect your play. At the end of the day, there is still next year."

Personal Notes

- **Born in London, 1969**
- **Married with one child**
- **Appeared in the first season of *Late Night Poker***
- **Wants to open a Subway store in the Canary islands**
- **Resides in London**

Being voted European Poker Player of the Year in 2002 made Garry Bush feel something like a celebrity. He likens it to winning a European Oscar. Yet he didn't even play in the 2003 World Series of Poker. He places great weight on his mental state in playing tournament poker and felt that (at that time) he just wasn't in a good place mentally to play. "If you don't go in there and feel mentally strong," Garry declares, "it will affect your play. At the end of the day, there is still next year." This is certainly an unusual attitude for someone who had accomplished so much in Europe in the previous year; and maybe this is what makes Garry Bush stand out from the crowd.

That's not the only attitude that sets him apart from most other tournament players, however. Garry does not see the value—to a poker player, that is—to playing on television. In weighing the monetary gain to a player as opposed to the risks to a player in exposing his game to the world, he doesn't see the advantage. "In the United States, you can't even wear logos for a sponsor," he laments. "So there isn't much but fame that you get out of it. The people making the big bucks out of poker are not the players!" Yet, even with this attitude he looks back on participating in the inauguration of televised poker on "Late Night Poker" in Europe as being a memorable experience.

Lately, though, Garry finds that the excitement of playing tournament poker has faded. When he first began he says he had a passion for the game. Now he sees it as more like a chore, just a job that he has to do. He recognizes that fans of poker who just see the big wins on television may not be aware that tournament poker is a business. "Even for the people who win millions in the World Series of Poker," he points out, ". . . they may have paid more than millions in tournament entry fees over the years." This, along with the fact that sponsorship is not allowed in the U.S. has discouraged a number of players. And Garry counts himself among them.

With the skyrocketing numbers of people now playing in poker tournaments, Garry just hopes that the skilled players can last until the end of a tournament. He knows that even with skill, luck on the flop comes into play on many occasions. "It is not like any other sport where the best necessarily beat the other players," Garry realizes. " It is on the turn of a card." He recalls a couple of particularly discouraging beats that he recently experienced. In a major tournament with only four people left he was a 12-1 favorite and still lost. "You have no control over it," Garry remarks. "If you have these situations many times in the course of the year, it can mean the difference between your being a winner on the year or a loser." This is an important fact for new players to recognize, he says.

"Let it be fun. Don't take it too seriously. It's not life or death."

-Garry Bush

The disappointments and mood swings involved in poker playing made his mother none too keen on Garry's poker career. "But," he says, "she has come to accept it." Garry considers himself to be his greatest supporter, though. He is not going to rely on encouragement from anyone other than himself. And when he feels that poker has become too important to him he simply "chills out" with his two-year old child. This puts everything into perspective. When he is done "chilling" he can approach the felt again with confidence.

A lot of this confidence comes from the fact that Garry has learned all of the games of poker and has years of experience playing them. His experience began when he was a youngster playing in the billiard halls with his friends. "I learned to play by trial and error," he recalls, "watching people and situations." He considered this his poker apprenticeship, "whether he was cut out for it or not." But cut out for it he was, and within 18 months of starting to play in tournaments, he had won two big ones. As to cash games, he doesn't like them much and confines most of his cash games to the ones he plays at home with friends.

Garry considers himself to be a solid player. He feels confident in his play and waits for others to make mistakes. Then, like a bird of prey, he swoops in and capitalizes on their errors. He doesn't worry about the others at the table and will not be intimidated by anyone's reputation. "I just play my hand and my game," he states.

Preparing mentally for a tournament is important to Garry. He likes to relax in a Jacuzzi or steam room for this mental preparation. This allows him to play at his best in a tournament. His reputation as a solid player gives him an edge when he plays. He perceives himself as a player to be avoided. Though this European champion has all of the credentials of a great player he modestly rejects the title of "best" and is happy to be a good solid player, with a more than even chance of success.

Major Poker Accomplishments

2004, Second place, WSOP, Pot Limit Hold'em

2002, European Player of the Year Award

2002, 32 in-the-money finishes throughout Europe

2001, Four first place finishes in European tournaments

2000, Four first place finishes in European tournaments

"Miami" John Cernuto

"If you can't learn from your experiences, you just aren't going to win."

Personal Notes

- **Born in Jersey City, New Jersey**
- **Married with three children**
- **Former air traffic controller**
- **Lived in Miami for 27 years**
- **Graduate of Florida State University**
- **Resides in Las Vegas**

A former air traffic controller, John Cernuto says he moved from one high stress profession to another. But it's poker that he finds the more stressful of the two. "The stress of poker is on an individual daily basis, all the time," he explains. "If you're ever low on money, it's even more stressful. It's like being out in a combat zone."

Air traffic control, he says, is stressful because you've got other people's lives in your hands when you're on the job. With poker it's your own life you've got to protect. "When I was an air traffic controller, I used to thrive on stress," John says. "We were known as 'stress junkies.' We actually enjoyed it. We liked the rush." The stress of poker, he adds, is a different kind of stress. "You don't always rush with poker," he adds. "Sometimes you flush instead."

During the seventeen years he worked in the air traffic tower at Miami-Dade International Airport, John was "buried with airplanes." His job was to spit out commands. "Everything had to be accurate," he says. "Everybody has to listen to you." In 1981, however, he and 11,500 other air traffic controllers found that the Federal Aviation Commission (FAA) didn't want to listen to him. "We all went on strike," he recounts, "and we all got fired. [President] Reagan only gave us three days to cool down, and for most of us that wasn't long enough. We were like a bunch of bees out of a beehive. We were young, hostile, and very upset with the FAA." John never returned to air traffic control. By 1981 he had already become "Miami" John at the poker tables. He explains that the nickname has a little history behind it: John had won several minor tournaments, but never

"A lot of fortunes are made on what you don't play."

-John Cernuto

any of the big money ones. "I always seemed to be just out of the money," he says. In fact, his first poker nickname was "One out of the money."

During one big tournament he decided to enter as Miami John. At that time there were a number of hard-hitting poker professionals who used city names as their nicknames. "So I went with Miami John one time," he remembers. "In that tournament, from start to finish, I only lost one hand, and I came in first, winning $50,000. Since I won under that name, I stuck with it."

After being fired from his air traffic job, Miami John went straight to Las Vegas with poker in mind. Since he did well in home games he thought he'd be good in the poker rooms of Vegas. "I found out there's a lot of difference between home games and playing professionally," he says. "So I had to go through the hard knocks and learn the hard way. It took a couple of years before I realized I didn't really know what I was doing, but the demon of gambling just got me hooked."

Seven years later, in 1988, Miami John won his first major tournament in Las Vegas, pulling in $50,000 at Caesar's Palace. "It was one of those days that nothing went wrong," he remembers. From there, Miami John went on to prove himself as a successful poker player.

He attributes part of his success to his experience at air traffic control. "It's like a three-dimensional chess game," he explains. "You've got the vertical and horizontal to deal with when the planes are coming in and going out." What that taught him more than anything was how to plan ahead, a technique that not only comes in handy at the poker table but is in actuality a necessity for the great player. "Air traffic controllers always have to plan ahead," he says. "I couldn't wait until the last second to do something. I had to visualize a plane three hundred miles away. In poker, I apply that same principle. I always want to be at least two steps ahead of my opponent. *If he does this, then I am going to do that.* I pre-plan my poker moves. That's a subconscious technique that I use."

Major Poker Accomplishments

2002, First place, WSOP Limit Omaha

2000, First place, Legends of Poker, No Limit Hold'em Championship

1997, First place, WSOP, No Limit Hold'em event

1996, First place, WSOP, Seven Card Stud Hi/Lo

Johnny Chan  

"Not too many players try to bluff me. If there's any bluffing or stealing. I'm going to be the one to do it."

Personal Notes

Born in Canton, China

Immigrated to the U.S. when he was nine

Married with six children and six houses

Sits with a "lucky orange" and wears a diamond rattlesnake ring

Nicknamed the "Orient Express"

Resides in Las Vegas

Johnny Chan has been known as a living legend in the poker world ever since his back-to-back wins in the World Series of Poker's main event in 1987 and 1988. His second WSOP win was immortalized in the Hollywood movie *Rounders*, in which Johnny played himself as the world's best poker player.

The movie shows actual footage from the tournament when Johnny beat Eric Seidel in an exciting final hand. (Matt Damon's character watches this footage repeatedly on videotape, and later beats Chan in a fictitious poker game). Seidel had led the heads-up play most of the way until Johnny flopped a straight and induced Seidel to move in on him with pocket queens. Another interesting tidbit from 1988: That year Johnny lost the biggest pot in the history of the tournament before rebounding to claim the title.

The next year was just as exciting for Johnny. L.A. Lakers owner Jerry Buss was so impressed with Chan's back-to-back titles, he promised Johnny an NBA championship ring if he won three in a row. (The Lakers won back-to-back NBA championships in 1987 and 1988). Johnny came darn close. In the 1989 WSOP main event he got down to heads-up play with the young Phil Hellmuth. But this time Johnny came out on the losing end when Hellmuth busted Johnny with pocket nines. Consequently, Johnny missed being a three-in-a-row WSOP winner by just one spot, taking second that year.

Since the late 1980s Johnny has been seen as the man to beat. Respected and even feared by most players, he's known for his deliberate and extremely aggressive style. He's also one of the most liked players because of his amiable personality and approachability.

The "Orient Express", as he is known, has picked up steam even since then, collecting nine WSOP gold bracelets to tie the world's record with Phil Hellmuth and Doyle Brunson. He and Brunson are the only two living card players to have won two WSOP main events and Chan is running neck-and-neck with Phil Hellmuth to be the all-time leader in WSOP winnings.

"We're [the pros at the poker table] not playing together, but we're not playing against each other, either. It's like the Nature Channel. You don't see piranhas eating each other, do you?"

-Mike from *Rounders*

Amazingly, Johnny Chan wasn't inducted into the Poker Hall of Fame until 2002, after he won his seventh gold bracelet. He is the first Asian-American to be inducted. In 2003, he added his latest two to his WSOP collection, but was outplayed by the unknown Chris Moneymaker in the main event.

Although Johnny is a Class A tournament player, you can also find him at the high stakes tables in Las Vegas, where he is every bit as feared. Along with Brunson and Chip Reese, Johnny is the nucleus of many of the big Vegas games. Even some of the most well known high-stakes players don't like to get near him. In fact, Johnny once claimed that Amarillo Slim wouldn't dare sit down at the poker table with him. "I'd eat him alive," he declared.

As any Chan-watcher knows, this guy is one aggressive player. "I like to attack," he says. "Not too many players try to bluff me. If there's any bluffing or stealing, I'm going to be the one to do it." Nevertheless, Johnny sees himself as one of poker's coolest customers.

Johnny made his first gambling trip to Vegas when he was just 16. Taking a bankroll he earned working at his father's Chinese restaurant in Houston, he headed straight for the high-stakes blackjack tables. In two days he was broke. Several more gambling sprees followed, each of them ending in a financial disaster. After several years of studying Hotel Management at the University of Houston, Johnny gave up that path and moved to Vegas to play cards. His first year as a professional gambler was another disaster. Doyle Brunson once said of the young Chan: "He was just a hot-headed kid with some talent. Something would go bad, and he would just go off the deep end. He was too impetuous and lacked discipline."

During those first losing years, Johnny worked as a chef, a casino dealer, and a floor manager to support his gambling. He borrowed money from friends, hocked his jewelry, and ran up his credit cards. It was a rough existence for Johnny until he turned the corner. The key was learning when to quit and how to control himself. Once he did that, he became known as a formidable contender.

Major Poker Accomplishments

Winner of nine WSOP gold bracelets

1992, Seventh place, WSOP, No Limit Hold'em Championship

1989, Second place, WSOP, No Limit Hold'em Championship

1988, 1987, Back to back wins, WSOP, No Limit Hold'em Championship

T.J. Cloutier 

"If you don't learn something new every time you play poker, then you aren't doing your job."

Personal Notes

- **Born in Albany, Texas, 1939**
- **Graduate of U.C. Berkeley**
- **Played in the 1959 Rose Bowl**
- **Played pro football in the Canadian Football League**
- **Travels to tournaments with his wife, Joy**
- **Resides in Richardson, Texas**

T.J. Cloutier is one of the most recognizable faces in professional poker today, and until recently he led the pack in lifetime tournament winnings. But, he says, he wasn't always a winner when it came to poker. "The first time I played," he recounts, "I was 17 years old working as a caddy. I'd go out there on the golf course and earn $7 for the day. Every day when I came back with my pay in hand, some of the older guys would grab it in a poker game."

Around the same time he started to frequent Lucky Buck's, which used to be one of California's most famous gambling halls. Even though he was just a kid of 17, the first few times he played, he sat at the table with the owner. "I beat him in draw poker, strictly by luck," he admits. For the next four years, every time he played poker at Lucky Bucks, he lost.

By then, T.J. was going to school at the University of California at Berkeley, where he played tight end on the football squad. He made up for his shortcomings in the poker room by excelling on the gridiron. In fact, in 1959, he played in the Rose Bowl (although Berkeley lost to Iowa that year).

A talented football player, T.J. went on to play professionally for a few years. In the U.S. the pro teams were paying rookies just $7,500 per year. So T.J. headed north, where he made $18,000 per year in the Canadian Football League. These were the days before the NFL, and in Canada the ice and snow, as well as the lack of protective equipment, made football a pretty rough game. T.J. says he remembers playing on fields of ice that felt like spikes.

When he was playing for the Montreal Alouettes, he took an elbow in the face that crushed three of his teeth. "We only had one bar on our helmets in those days," he says, "And two of my teeth went through my lip. They sewed my lip up right there on the sideline, and then I had to go back in and play the rest of the game."

"Knowing your opponent is the most important thing in Big Bet Poker."

-T.J. Cloutier

After five years of playing for Montreal and the Toronto Argonauts, T.J.'s knees gave out, cutting short his football career. But he took his competitive spirit with him back to the poker table. With a bit more poker experience under his belt he returned to the U.S., first working in the oilfields near Longview, Texas, before he moved on to Shreveport, Louisiana, where he got serious about playing poker. By that time, he was playing poker every day—and he started winning more than losing.

"I used to drive over to Dallas to play pot-limit games three time a week," T.J. remembers. "The first twelve times I played there, I won. I was playing with the best players in the world." The next time T.J. arrived there to play, the owner told him that he was "dropping the latch" on him: "He wasn't going to let me play there anymore unless I let him have half my earnings." T.J. acquiesced. The owner put up half the stakes for him, and took away half his winnings. "The place eventually got shut down," T.J. adds, "because they were illegally making a profit from the poker action. When the place got shut down, it was like taking $200,000 out of my pocket each year."

From Texas, he went on to play tournaments in Las Vegas. "I went to the World Series of Poker for the first time in 1983," he remembers, "and I've had only one year since then that I haven't cashed." Although T.J. has yet to take first place in the big one, he's finished second twice, third once, and fifth once.

T.J. attributes his success at tournament poker at least partly to his photographic memory for people he's played with in the past. "If I played with you ten years ago," he says, "I might not remember your name, but I'd remember your face and how you played your hands." And that's the key to success, he adds: "I play every player differently. I know who I can bluff and who I can't. I go with my instincts, and those instincts are formed on what I've learned over the years. If you don't learn something new every time you play poker, then you aren't doing your job."

Major Poker Accomplishments

2004, First place, WSOP, Seven Card Razz

Winner of five WSOP gold bracelets

2003, Third place, WPT Legends of Poker, No Limit Hold'em Championship

2003, Sixth place, WPT World Poker Challenge, No Limit Hold'em Championship

2000, Second place, WSOP, No Limit Hold'em Championship

1998, Third place, WSOP, No Limit Hold'em Championship

1988, Fifth place, WSOP, No Limit Hold'em Championship

1985, Second place, WSOP, No Limit Hold'em Championship

David Colclough

"Winning a $100,000 event just doesn't give the same buzz anymore—but it's still pretty damn good fun."

Personal Notes

Born in Wales, 1964

Father of one daughter

Twice received detentions for playing poker at school

Former IT consultant and club owner

Resides in Stoke-on-Trent, England

Dave Colclough started playing poker 19 years ago after a roommate gave him a few lessons on how to play Seven Card Stud. Later that evening the two friends headed off to the Northampton Rubicon Casino to play a £10 tournament. "I suspected a few flaws in my strategy on that first night," says Dave. "Three months later, I had refined it enough to win my first competition."

After years of continuing to refine his strategy—and winning a few tournaments along the way—Dave started to feel that his career as a large project systems testing manager was getting a little too much in the way of poker playing. "I finally gave up my career in IT and washed my hands of the dodgy nightclub I owned with a dodgy business partner," he says. "Unremarkably, my poker results went through the roof. But I don't have any regrets. I met loads of friends and had shedloads of fun. I wouldn't swap that for nine gold bracelets."

It's tournament poker that really tickles Dave's fancy. "It's a bigger challenge. The highs and lows are greater; it's more interesting and generally more fun," he says. But through the years he's noticed that even the highs and lows don't seem quite as dramatic as they once did. "When you have been kicked in the teeth a few hundred times, it just doesn't hurt as much anymore," he says. "Unfortunately and likewise, winning a $100,000 event just doesn't give the same buzz anymore—but it's still pretty damn good fun."

Quite a lot of all that fun has something to do with the people—and Dave realizes as much as anyone that not all people are exactly the same. "About 95% of the players like me," he estimates. And the other five percent: "They tend to hate me with a vengeance."

That may be due to Dave's philosophy of dealing with other players. "I always try and be friendly to people," he says. "But I tend to treat people the same way as they treat me." One of his pet peeves in poker is seeing people belittle other players. Take Phil Hellmuth, he says. "A lot of people saw me refuse to shake his hand at a 2000 WSOP final table, but he'd been bad-mouthing me. And surprise, two days later he had written an article that I was a lucky idiot who was not worthy to win a WSOP event. My mouth can be too big and too harsh at times." Just ask Phil Hellmuth.

"The best coaches are usually in the car park."

-David Colclough

But critics can't stop Dave from making his mark in poker, not only at the poker table but also on poker sites. Dave writes a poker advice column at bet365poker.com where he shares with visitors his unique poker philosophy. In one of his columns, he stepped away from imparting advice to keep his readers informed on how he was doing with his tournament play.

Recounting his trip "down under" to play in the Australasian tournament in Melbourne, he says (with tongue in cheek), "It's been a hard life since giving up my 70 hours a week as an IT Consultant. I really miss getting up at 7:30, working late, long weekends, meaningless meetings and dead important deadlines." Even the long flight from Birmingham to Dubai to Singapore to Melbourne didn't faze him. "Ho hum, the sacrifices we have to make," he wrote. Even the early morning call from a television station to do an interview after about two hours of sleep failed to disturb Dave. And that's after the station cut him off to watch what he describes as "some Waugh twin geezer poking in the dirt."

Most of Dave's columns, however, help the online poker players to see what they are doing wrong and how they can improve their games. One of the columns points out the importance of position at the poker table. "Position is just plain common sense," Dave says. "The further you are from the big blind, the more information you have." Dave refutes the notion that being in the last position is always best. In his own inimitable style, Dave calls this "incorrect, wrong, short sighted, simplistic rubbish!" And he goes on to show why this is so, in no uncertain terms. His next column follows up on how to use position to bluff, warning the reader that "most bluffers get carried away, do it too much and lose in the long run." Whatever his advice, whatever his story, Dave Colclough can be counted on to spin it with a good humor that is hard to resist.

Major Poker Accomplishments

2004, Euro Finals of Poker, Pot Limit Omaha Championship

2004, Second place, Euro Finals of Poker, No Limit Hold'em Championship

2003, European Poker Player of the Year

2003, First place, Aviation Club Summer Tournament, Pot Limit Omaha

2003, First place, Midland Masters, No Limit Hold'em Championship

Numerous WSOP final table appearances

Diego Cordovez 

"Around 1991, I walked into a small card room in Palo Alto called the Cameo Club. I started playing and never stopped."

Personal Notes

Born in New York City, 1965

Graduated from Stanford University

Developer of internet software for poker sites

Single

Resides in Palo Alto, California

As CEO of Advanced Global Applications, LLC, Diego Cordovez knows that there are concepts and intuitions that apply to both business and poker. In fact, in an article he wrote in the May 2002 issue of *Optimize* magazine, Diego states that he would like to take his employees, clients, partners and competitors to the poker table. As he so aptly put it, "No other game so profoundly—and quickly—reveals the essence of a person's soul. Poker strips away all the façades that we wear. There is no hiding across the green felt—not from the rest of the table, and not from yourself."

These are words which poker players, both old and young, should take to heart. This software developer knows whereof he speaks. For the past two years he has run a software company that builds internet poker sites and develops software for licensing. The talent and skills he uses in business, he applies to his play at every poker table. Successful businesspeople understand these concepts, he observes, and intuitively use them.

Diego found that when he was playing poker full time, it soon became a grind. Though he enjoyed the competition, he did not enjoy the stress. "Playing full time for a living took some of the fun out of it," Diego concedes. "When I relied upon it as my sole occupation, my sole source of income [it became] an obligation. It brought out parts of my personality that I didn't want to bring out." Diego decided it was better to stop while he was still young and still connected enough with the business world to become a success in whatever business option he chose. That is why he advises aspiring players to do it while they are young and don't have too much to lose.

Believe it or not, Diego was taught to play poker by his first grade teacher. "He taught us the basics of arithmetic by playing poker," says Diego. In his school, the idea was to engage kids and make learning fun. "They tried to come up with creative and fun ways to learn math, reading and science." Diego recalls. For math, they decided it would be a lot more fun if you were playing games." Diego credits this teacher with helping him get a sense that math was fun, not a dreary subject.

"Really watch everything that is going on in a game. Concentrate all the time ... and you'll do better than more talented players who are distracted."

-Diego Cordovez

Though Diego did not really play much after that first grade experience, as an adult, he continued his poker education by reading almost every poker book. "I really think there is a lot of value in books," he says. "Not as manuals, because usually I tend to disagree with a lot of what's in there. But just to stimulate thinking about the game."

Diego is nothing if not a thinker. He thinks about the situations, strategy and plays while he looks for ways to organize his thoughts. He also sees a great value in learning all of the games, not specializing in any one game. "Now No Limit Hold'em has really become a popular game," he notes, "which is kind of ironic because it's the first game that I really learned how to play and that I achieved some success in." Still, Diego likes the variety in playing different games. He says that it keeps him fresh and staves off boredom.

After reading all the books, Diego began to play poker in earnest. "Around 1991, I walked into a small card room in Palo Alto called the Cameo Club. I started playing and never stopped." His first tournament play was at the Peppermill Club in Reno. "The second or third time I played there, I won best all-around player. That was very early on, when I was still playing pretty low limits, he recounts. "It got me to thinking that maybe I could succeed at tournaments and I should pay more attention to them. Today, Diego plays about 20 hours a week, with plenty of online play. And he is still a force to be reckoned with in tournaments. When he won the Commerce Million in 2002 the prize pool of $1.6 million was the largest to date.

When Diego was young, his parents were confident in his ability to succeed in poker, "or anything, really," Diego adds. "Even from early on they've always been very excited to see my results and they were always following how I was doing." His girlfriend is also a source of great confidence. She is also interested in poker and supports his avocation with encouragement and a sense of confidence in his abilities.

As Diego wrote in the *Optimize* magazine article, the lessons this successful businessman and poker ace brings from the card room to the board room are: "To focus on people above all else. To be prepared to play the cards we are dealt. To confront head-on the unexpected challenges that surely await us. That adaptability is the essence of success, in the casino and in the corporate office."

Major Poker Accomplishments

2003, Second in *Card Player* rankings of Mixed Games

2003, Fourth place, WSOP, S.H.O.E.

2003, Second place, WSOP, Half Stud/ Half Hold'em

2002, First place, LA Poker Classic, Limit Hold'em Championship

2000, First place, Legends of Poker, Limit Hold'em

2000, First place, WSOP, No Limit Hold'em event

Peter "the Poet" Costa

"I saw poker as my savior. It gave me a reason to go on."

Personal Notes

Born in Kiti, Cyprus, 1956

Moved to Liverpool, England at age seven

Former fish and chips shop owner

Started a "new life" in 2000

Loves to read and write poetry

Resides in Leicester, England

Three years ago Peter Costa wanted to go somewhere and die in peace. His marriage, his business—he wanted to throw it all away and start his life anew. Peter's father died when he was seven years old, leaving his mother with nine children. In order to avert the tragedy of the Turkish invasion of Cyprus, where Peter and his siblings were born, his mother moved the family to Liverpool, England.

His family started a fish and chips business. "Since I was the youngest one," he explains, "I'd go wherever I was needed. I'd just pack my bags and go." The family's restaurants were located throughout England—in Birmingham, Nottingham, Leicester, and London. "Once you get into the fish and chips business, there's no escape," he laments. "I didn't like the business at all. It wasn't a way of life as much as it was a way of just barely existing."

When Peter was just 19, he married a refugee girl from Cyprus. Their parents had suggested the marriage. "I had just spent my whole life saying 'yes' to everything," says Peter, "and when they suggested marriage I said 'yes' again." Even so, he adds, he didn't think the marriage was right; he felt forced into it.

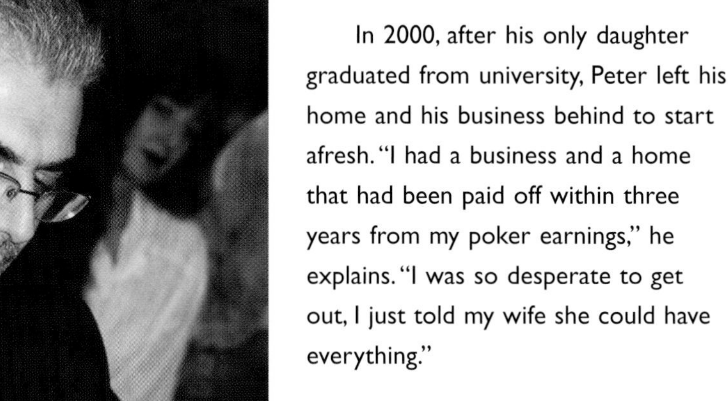

In 2000, after his only daughter graduated from university, Peter left his home and his business behind to start afresh. "I had a business and a home that had been paid off within three years from my poker earnings," he explains. "I was so desperate to get out, I just told my wife she could have everything."

Peter left with just enough money to cover one month's rent. He answered an ad looking for a lodger in a house. The owner turned out to be a woman called Jo, a student finishing her advanced degree in psychotherapy. "Here I was, a lodger who arrived with more psychological baggage than you can believe," he admits. "Jo spent a good year-and-a-half working with me, and it was because of her that I was able to get on with life."

Peter told Jo that he'd been playing poker for years, that he liked playing and that he was quite good. "She told me if poker is what you're good at then why don't you do it for a living? And I did," he says. "I saw poker as my savior really. It gave me a reason to go on. I always had a desire for challenges, and I saw this as something to go for."

"Life is like a game of poker; if you don't put any in the pot, there won't be any to take out."

- "Moms" Mabley

At first, however, Peter couldn't get inspired to play. He would bathe, shave, get in his car, turn on the engine, and then just turn it back off and go right back home. "I just couldn't face playing poker at first." A few months later, he finally started in on his full-time poker career. Ten times during that first year, says Peter, he was desperately in need of money just to cover his basic living expenses. "Every time I'd hit rock bottom," he remembers, "I came into the money. I felt like I was some miracle man."

About nine months after he left his wife, he called her to ask for some money. "She declined," he recalls, "and my stomach hit the floor." It wasn't so much the money as it was the rejection, he says. "That hurt. It really pushed me to start playing poker seriously." He turned to a friend to borrow £100 and won £500 in a tournament that Friday. Two days later Peter went to the European Championships in London and turned that £500 into £60,000, which was exactly how much he had asked his wife for. "I think that's a bit uncanny really."

Since then, Peter Costa has been one of the most successful poker players in the world. He went on to win a tournament that was aired on Britain's *Late Night Poker*. That brought him celebrity status in England and a financial backer by the name of Laulie Butters. "He made me feel ten feet tall," says Peter. "He asked me how much I needed to go to a major tournament in Los Angeles, and when I told him I needed $8,000 he gave me the money and told me not to worry if I should lose."

Peter traveled to LA's Commerce Casino and played two one-table satellites. He won both. The next day he woke early and registered for the big No Limit Hold'em event. "I got assigned table one and seat one," he remembers. "I just knew I was going to win the tournament." The guaranteed first-prize payoff was $150,000 and 460 players entered. Before the first hour of the tournament, Peter was down to 200 chips, but amazingly went on to win first place. The following week he played in a tournament in Vegas and won first place there too. The next month he returned to London and won the European Championship. Peter later went on to win Binion's Hall of Fame tournament and then the Melbourne Championship in 2003, making himself a major winner on three continents.

Major Poker Accomplishments

2003, First place, Aussie Million, No Limit Hold'em Championship

2002, First place, Hall of Fame Poker Classic, No Limit Hold'em Championship

2002, Second place, European Poker Classic, No Limit Hold'em Championship

2001, Second place, European Poker Classic, No Limit Hold'em Championship

Allen Cunningham 

"What made this experience memorable was how I was praised and awed for my work done in what I previously thought was a silly, selfish endeavor."

Personal Notes

Born in Riverside, California, 1977

Former paperboy

Formerly a civil engineering student at UCLA

Resides in Marina del Rey, California

Allen Cunningham was twelve years old when he realized just how much skill is required to play poker. One night, while playing a home game with his parents and his sister, he came to understand how "vastly superior" he was to his three opponents. "I couldn't wait until I was old enough to take on the real players in Vegas," he says.

His first experience playing for money came about four years later at summer camp. "A few of us played Five Card Draw with wild cards at a stake of about twenty bucks apiece," he remembers. "I was holding my own and having fun through most of the game when we finally decided to make the next hand our last." Threes were wild that hand and Allen was dealt three Kings. "My opponent was talking and talking about what a great hand he had, and how many threes were in it, but I called him down, assuming it must have been an act." Allen got busted. His opponent laid down five of kind. "All I learned from that experience was how much I didn't like losing at gambling," he says.

Allen started playing poker seriously when he was a 19-year-old student at UCLA. He played at little casinos on Indian reservations where he heard plenty of stories about big tournaments, huge prize money, and world-class poker champs. "It seemed just fantastic," he says. "Of course, as soon as I was old enough I jumped right in." When Allen turned 21 he played tournament after tournament, and lost most of the time. "It's funny," he says, "most people who are addicted to poker started off on a winning streak, got hooked, and then are disappointed with their results after things level out. I always lost in the beginning only to come back and try even harder before really excelling."

"The poker player learns that sometimes both science and common sense are wrong."

-David Mamet

It was in 1999 that he "really excelled." That year Allen won six major tournaments and was named "Best All-Around Player" at the Legends of Poker. He decided not to return to UCLA. His poker career was much too lucrative. Since then he has made final tables at WPT events and won two World Series bracelets.

Despite all these grand tournament games, Allen says his most memorable was a game he played with amateurs at Yale University. His friend Daniel Negreanu had been communicating with a group of students who had a weekly poker game. Daniel accepted a request from the Yalies for an appearance at their regular game. "Since they wanted Daniel to show them how a good player plays, he took me along," says Allen. "By this time I had already made a name for myself on the tournament scene."

When Allen arrived on the Yale campus with Daniel he says they were both "bombarded with questions about what it's like to play tournaments, and how you play this hand, and what was the biggest pot we won." Allen was impressed at how enthusiastic the students were, and he was glad to be able to teach them a little something about the game." We went into some underground chamber where the game was held," he remembers. "Daniel, as I had expected, played like a lunatic, and I tried to play well enough just to keep us even." Over the course of the evening, students and faculty members continuously filed in to meet the pros or just watch a bit of the game. "It was really strange that so many Ivy League types wanted to meet a couple of professional poker players," says Allen.

"After some time, the game was down to me and a very young looking freshman named Berger," Allen recalls. "A more intense crowd gathered than in many big tournament finals I'd been at. I had to decide whether to crush the freshman to show my might or to throw the game and make the kid's day." Allen didn't end up throwing it, he says, but he took it easy on the student, who finally won. "He was a hero," says Allen, "and I felt good. What made this experience memorable was how I was praised and awed for my work done in what I previously thought was a silly, selfish endeavor. I guess it lent some validation to my poker existence."

Major Poker Accomplishments

2004, First place, Five Star World Poker Classic, No Limit Hold'em

2003, Second place, WSOP, Deuce to Seven

2002, First place, WSOP, Deuce to Seven

2001, First place, WSOP, Seven Card Stud

2000, Second place, WSOP, Omaha

1999, Best all-around player, Legends of Poker (at age 22)

Finished first in six major tournaments in 1999

Bonnie Damiano

"I have no fear, manage my money well, and I have patience. Plus common sense and that woman's intuition."

Personal Notes

Born in Green Bay, Wisconsin, 1954

Graduate of the University of Wisconsin, 1978

Former corporate travel manager and professional event planner

Produced the pre-game show for the opening of Joe Robbi Stadium in Miami

Resides in Las Vegas

Bonnie Damiano enjoys her life! She has successfully combined her passion for poker with her tremendous talent for organization. An excellent poker player in her own right, Bonnie keeps herself busy away from the table producing and coordinating a number of major poker tournaments such as the Four Queens Classic and the Desert Poker Classic. She also assisted in the 2001 and 2002 World Series of Poker.

Bonnie's career as a professional event planner kept her very busy in the '80s. She was president of Meeting Planner International in Miami, Florida where she coordinated major conventions and events of such corporate giants as Nestles, Prudential and ReMax. Since Bonnie had been a poker player from way back (her earliest memory is playing with her family at the tender age of eight), it was a natural progression to move from producing corporate events to producing poker tournaments.

As a partner in Card Player Cruises, Bonnie participated in the first Party Poker Million. "What a great event that was!" Bonnie remarks. She was also the originator of the poker tournament in Aruba, first called the Caribbean Poker Classic. "Then it became connected with Ultimate Bet," says Bonnie, "and the rest is history." She continued to coordinate that event for the years 2002 and 2003 but has now directed her energies to coordinating the Caribbean Poker Classic in St. Maarten which will be an annual event for classicpoker.com in December.

As if these major events did not keep her busy enough, Bonnie takes the time to pursue her passion for poker with much success. Bonnie's "poker gene" was inherited from both of her parents who loved all types of card games. Besides playing on birthdays and holidays with the family who gathered to celebrate, they played whenever it snowed. "That was everyday in the winter," she recalls with some humor. "What else is there to do in Wisconsin in the winter?"

The challenge and the difference in strategy in tournament poker is what attracts Bonnie to these events. She says that she finds the live action full of excitement. "I have no fear, manage my money well and I have patience," she says. "Plus common sense and that woman's intuition." When she first started playing in the World Series of

Poker, however, she was virtually unknown and knew few of the players herself. An encounter with Men "the Master" Nguyen at the WSOP Stud Eight or Better tournament that year demonstrates the extent of her naïvete at the time.

"In no-limit, if the board pairs and you are not helped on the high end of the full house DO NOT MOVE ALL IN. Beware!"

-Bonnie Damiano

Bonnie sat down at the Horseshoe to play her first tournament and eventually ended up across the table from Men "the Master." Taking a look at her large stack of chips, he bluntly said, "How did you get all those chips—and who are you?" Bonnie wryly replied, "I'm Bonnie and I won them and I would like to have some of yours!"

Bonnie says that she had no clue just what a great player she was up against, but at the dinner break that evening, she got to know him better. When Men asked her where she played Stud Eight and what limit she played she told him she played at the Fremont 3-6. Men said he didn't realize they had such a big game there. Puzzled, Bonnie replied that she didn't think it was such a big game. "You don't think $300-$600 is big?" asked Men incredulously. He was more than a little surprised when Bonnie explained that it was $3-$6 stud that she played. They both had a good laugh and Bonnie was now officially a part of the world of tournament poker.

But event planning and poker tournaments take a back seat to her family life. Bonnie's three children (whom Bonnie calls the "light of her life") and her "significant other," Chip Penney, are tops on her list of important people. Chip is a professional golfer and part-time poker player, which Bonnie says, makes it easier to understand each other's ups and downs. They often discuss poker strategy and enjoy making side bets as to who can last longer in a tournament. Bonnie won't say who is ahead on that score!

Bonnie is happy to tell anyone who asks, that she enjoys her life. "I am always in a positive frame of mind. I smile and enjoy everyday and everyone," she says. "It makes me happy when I can make someone else smile." She considers her fellow poker players as part of one big happy family and would like to see her "family" get the same respect as other sports figures. Some of them join her at classicpoker.com, an online poker site that Bonnie is associated with, to promote poker on the web.

Poker still serves up excitement to Bonnie, more now than when she first started playing. Her aspirations for the game reflect this attitude. After years of observation and participation, Bonnie wants to "bring poker to corporate America and get sponsorship for players that they so rightly deserve." With her attitude and talent, it's a dream most likely to succeed.

Major Poker Accomplishments

2003, First place, Ultimate Poker Classic, Pot Limit Omaha

2002, First place, Four Queens Poker Classic, Ladies' No Limit Hold'em Championship

Has finished in the money a number of times at the WSOP

Paul Darden

"The tournaments are big, and I've got to stay focused."

Personal Notes

- **Born in New Haven, Connecticut, 1968**
- **Graduate of Cross High School, New Haven**
- **Married with four children**
- **Former music promoter**
- **"Trained" by Phil Ivey**
- **Resides in Hamden, Connecticut**

Ever since Paul Darden won the WPT's Lucky Strike tournament in 2003, he says poker has taken over his life. "I still have a music business," he says, "but I haven't done anything with it lately. With my success in poker, and now with TV and everything, it's hard to get away."

Until a few years ago, Paul was a partner in a New Haven night club. "I did a lot of rap shows, hip-hop, R & B, and a little jazz too." But for Paul, even before music there was poker. "My father had a little poker club in New Haven when I was a little kid. So I've been around that all my life, and my dad taught me to play." Paul says he started his poker playing when he was eight years old in games of Five and Seven Card Stud. "My dad was real good at poker," he says, "and I think I inherited some of his talent."

As an adult, Paul started playing poker when Connecticut's Foxwoods Casino first opened. "I did well there," he says, "and I like the casino-style games." Paul's next stop was Atlantic City, where he met Phil Ivey. "Phil asked me if I ever heard of the World Series of Poker," he remembers. "I told him no, and he said I should come out to Vegas and play." Phil also encouraged Paul to take up the game of No Limit Hold'em. "If you're going to risk some money, he told me, it ought to be on that game."

Paul says at that time he had never even heard of No Limit Hold'em. "I had no idea what it was." Once Phil explained it to Paul, he was a bit skeptical of playing a game at which he could lose everything in one quick hand. So Paul first started playing Limit Hold'em, and then went off to Las Vegas.

"I wasn't doing very well on the first trip to Vegas," Paul recalls. "Phil told me again that I ought to play no-limit, but I told him I couldn't afford it; I didn't have the money, so he loaned it to me! He told me I had to take the $10,000 shot at a million." Paul says that without Phil's encouragement and help, he never would have played. "I entered the big tournament and survived the first day," he says, recalling the relief he felt then.

Since then Paul has become great friends with Phil Ivey. "He gave me all the pointers and told me all about No Limit Hold'em. So he trained me. He's my coach."

"Air power is like poker. A second-best hand is like none at all—it will cost you dough and win you nothing."

-George Kenney

From that point on, Paul has been riding the poker circuit all over America, often with his wife Vicky, who is happy to have the chance to travel to out of the way places like Aruba. Because the tournaments are getting so big now, Paul says he's all but ditched playing side games. "The tournaments are big," he says, "and I've got to stay focused. Sometimes it's hard to juggle both types of games."

The only downside to Paul's poker playing, he says, was that his business at the night club was suffering. In the end, Paul decided that it would be best if he would drop his music business in order to concentrate on poker. "I couldn't do them both," he says, "and since I was successful at poker, my friends all said, 'why not?'"

Paul's success at the poker tables may have overshadowed his business successes but not his family life. Paul says his goal in life is to be a good parent to his four children, ranging in ages from toddler to teen. He enjoys his "other family" of poker professionals as well. He likens them to one big (usually happy) family. "Most are very nice people," says Paul. "They have shown me a lot of love."

This calm and self-possessed player admits that it is hard to keep his composure when he loses, but he manages to hide his disappointment well. Paul considers poker a challenge and wants to excel in it. He enjoys the strategy of the game, something you can detect in his play. "My strength is to try to play my opponent's hand, not mine," Paul declares, "because I have my cards; my cards are easy to play. I try to put myself in their hand and play at me." This enviable skill has served him well in tournament play taking him to many final tables when others are relegated to the rail.

Major Poker Accomplishments

2002, First place, World Poker Classic, No Limit Hold'em Championship

2002, First place, WPT Gold Rush, No Limit Hold'em Championship

2001, First place, WSOP, Seven Card Stud

"Freddy" Deeb  

"When I'm playing poker and I'm fresh, I end up making money. I don't care who's in the game."

Personal Notes

- **Born in Beirut, Lebanon, 1955**
- **Married with four children**
- **Immigrated to the United States at age 19**
- **Studied to be a mechanical engineer**
- **Has always been a professional poker player**
- **Resides in Las Vegas**

"I still haven't told my parents that I play poker for a living," says 49-year-old Freddy Deeb. "I tell them that I am in investments—and it's not a lie. I invest in poker." Freddy prides himself on never having had a career outside of the world of professional poker. But until recently he was cagey about telling people exactly what he did for a living.

Before poker came to prime time television, Freddy was living in Long Beach, California. "If I was socializing at a bar there and someone happened to ask me what I did for a living, I would tell them I was an investor. I wouldn't tell them I play poker. What am I going to tell them? That I play for $10,000 or $50,000 a day, or that I sometimes lose $20,000 in a poker game? There's no way they were going to believe me."

Since poker has become a televised "sport," Freddy sees a change in how people react to him. "Now they might have to believe me," he says. "TV makes poker look like prestigious fun nowadays. It's a respectable business to be in."

Freddy got into poker-playing quite by chance—and an act of war. When he was 19 years old he left his home in Beirut to attend university in the United States. When he arrived in Los Angeles, where he thought he'd be going to school, he found that he didn't like the city. "It was too big for me," he says. After taking a bus trip to visit a Lebanese friend at Utah State University, he decided to stay in the small town of Logan, nestled in a quiet valley between two mountains.

Freddy had been studying mechanical engineering in Utah for three years when the Lebanese Civil War broke out. For a year and a half Freddy could not get in touch with his parents back in Beirut. "Each year my parents would send me enough money to pay for my tuition and living expenses for the whole year. But when the war broke out we had no phones, no mail—no means of communication."

"Play when you're fresh; play in the right games and lose the minimum when you lose."

- "Freddy" Deeb

Unable to continue in college and not able to accept legal employment in the U.S., Freddy started to go gambling in Wendover on the Utah-Nevada border. "That's the only way I could legally make money," he says. "I didn't have a lot to blow, but I did well and started to earn a pretty good living playing poker." Although he had only 12 credits to finish at Utah State, he never returned to school.

He soon moved on to the poker rooms in Reno and Las Vegas. When, in 1986, California started allowing poker games in casinos, Freddy moved to Los Angeles to earn a living. He started playing the big tournaments in the 1980s, but remained mainly a cash player. "I play the big ones—the $10,000 buy-ins," he explains, "but if there are side games going on, I'd rather play there. That's where the money is. If you're a good tournament player then you can make money in the long run, but it's a longshot and not something I can depend on."

Freddy says the key to his poker success is what he calls "doing the right things": play when you're fresh—not tired, play in the right games, and lose the minimum when you lose. "If you do that," he says of cash games, "you'll always make money, even if you're not the best." By the same token, he adds, one can be the best poker player and do none of the above and go broke.

"I've been in that situation a few times," Freddy admits. "I've made a lot of money in poker, but couldn't keep it because I played in casino games like baccarat and craps. But when I'm playing poker and I'm fresh, I end up making money. I don't care who's in the game." Freddy likens this to business: "If you're up all night drinking, you can't go into the office the next morning expecting to perform well. If you're not on top of your business, you're not going to succeed. In poker, if you're not on top of your game, you'll fail."

Major Poker Accomplishments

2004, First place, Festa al Lago, No Limit Hold'em

2004, Second place, Poker at the Plaza No Limit Hold'em Championship

2003, 13th place, WSOP, No Limit Hold'em Championship

2003, First place, LA Poker Classic, No Limit Hold'em event

2002, Third place, WPT Five Diamond World Poker Classic, No Limit Hold'em Championship

1996, First place, WSOP, Deuce to Seven Draw

Martin de Knijff

"To win the World Poker Tour Championship and the biggest tournament ever in poker . . . it is just overwhelming."

Personal Notes

- **Born in Gothenburg, Sweden, 1972**
- **Professional bridge player**
- **Father of one son, Robin**
- **Plays golf to relax**
- **Professional Sports Bettor**
- **Resides in Stockholm, Sweden**

When Martin de Knijff won the largest prize ever paid to a single individual place finisher in a televised poker tournament or North American sporting event, his first thought was to call his seven-year-old son to tell him the good news. "This is a dream come true," Martin exclaimed. "To win the World Poker Tour Championship and the biggest tournament ever in poker . . . it is just overwhelming!"

Long before he won the largest prize in the history of poker (at that time), Martin remembers playing for much smaller stakes. "I remember playing poker with my grandma as a seven-year-old boy. I managed to beat her to earn my Saturday candy." From playing for candy to winning millions, Martin's life has revolved around sports and card-playing.

When Martin was only 21 years old he became a Life Master in bridge. He recalls playing bridge at a card club in Stockholm when he moved there in 1992 and being introduced to the "American" poker games by some of the players there. "Most players at the club were at a very high level—Chris Bjorn and Jan Lundberg, to name a couple—which of course speeded up the learning process." He supplemented his hands-on education by reading poker books, such as Doyle Brunson's *Super System*, and his professional poker career took off.

Martin has been a sports bettor ever since he graduated from high school and he sees a number of similarities between his professional betting and his poker career. "You have to study hard, keep focus and concentration at a very high level," Martin emphasizes. "Stamina is paramount; otherwise you are bound to make mistakes. In that way poker is very much like my profession." He adds that it is important to be in shape when you are playing poker, especially in the multi-day tournaments.

Another facet of poker that Martin views as very

important is a player's interaction with the other players. "I am good at reading people and making laydowns," says Martin, who is a perceived by others as a solid player. Maybe that is because Martin's motto is "Respect but don't fear any of your opponents." He adds that "being a positive and open person works with all different people."

"Work hard. There is no shortcut to success!"

-Martin de Knijff

Martin became interested in tournament poker because it is a very dynamic form of poker. "Before making a decision, you have so many things to consider which do not apply in cash games," he cautions. "The chance of winning tons of money with a limited bankroll is of course a thrill." Not that the money is the most important thing for Martin. "When I play I don't think about the money. I just want to win the whole thing." But he adds, "Apart from that, money comes before fame!"

After his win at the WPT Bellagio event, there are a lot of poker players who would like to know his secret to success. He has only one bit of advice for them about how he plays long tournaments: "I like to play a lot of hands when I play No Limit Hold'em, especially in 3-5 day tournaments which give you a lot of play." And he adds that superstitions have no part in his game!

Though he is not superstitious, Martin is not averse to a little good luck. In a *Cardplayer* magazine interview after his big win, Martin related how his son, Robin, gave him three swift kicks in the rear so that his dad would have good luck the Swedish way. "That's how it works," laughed Martin.

When Martin is not working hard at the poker table, he enjoys a good round of golf. He loves the sport, he says, "It's so much fun and challenging. It also helps you to relax from everything stressful." He plays golf in his native Sweden in a club with about 30 other fellows, who hold a tournament at the end of every summer. It's a great sports and social event that has been going on for about 10 years, he says. After a day of golf they relax doing what else but playing cards.

Though Martin has been a great success in everything that he has undertaken, the most important thing to him is being with his son as he grows up. A devoted father and a warm man at peace with himself and the world, Martin de Knijiff has it all!

Major Poker Accomplishments

2004, First place, WPT Five Star World Poker Classic, No Limit Hold'em Championship

2004, Second place, WSOP, No Limit Hold'em event

2003 and 1995, First place, Swedish No Limit Hold'em Championship

2001, Third place, World Poker Open, Pot Limit Hold'em

Asher Derei

"Some are afraid to play against me because they're afraid they might make a mistake."

Personal Notes

- **Born in Jerusalem, Israel**
- **Married with two children**
- **Former restaurant owner**
- **Served in the Israeli army during three wars**
- **Moved to England in 1998**
- **Resides in Sheffield, England**

Asher Derei started his poker-playing career in the Israeli army. "It was a good way to pass the time during the war," he says. From the age of 18 to 21 he served full-time and then one month each year after that in obligatory part-time service. "When there was a war," he says, "I also had to serve." Asher has seen action in three wars, and each war gave him the opportunity to practice his poker. "I was making ten times as much playing poker than from the salary the army was paying me."

Apart from the army, Asher says he had a difficult time finding a game anywhere else in all of Israel. First, because casino games are illegal throughout the country. Second, because poker is stigmatized in Israel as "a dirty thing," says Asher. "It's very difficult for me to tell my family in Israel that I am a professional poker player. Not only is poker seen as a backroom activity there, it's regarded as a dishonorable activity." In other countries—in Italy and Spain, for example—he says he's found this also to be true.

But Asher says he thinks Israelis view poker in the worst light. "If someone were to ask me what I did for a living, and I told him I was a poker player," explains Asher, "I might as well have said I was a drug addict." Another misconception, he says, is that if you are successful at poker, then you must be cheating. "They don't view it as a game of skill," he says.

Asher first played poker outside of Israel in 1973. On a trip to London his friends took him into the Victoria Casino. "I didn't go there specifically to play poker, but I sat down at the table there and started losing pretty big that first day because I was playing games I never knew. We never played most of those poker games in Israel."

It wasn't until 1996, however, that Asher got the bug for big-time tournament play. He began leaving his restaurant in Jerusalem for weeks at a time to travel to the poker hotspots of Europe—Paris, Vienna, and Amsterdam. "I won titles from most of the different venues," he said. Shortly thereafter, he began flying to the U.S. to play in the tournaments there. Two years later, after a round of successes, Asher sold his restaurant and moved his family to Sheffield England, his wife's hometown, in order to have a home base that was closer to the European tournament venues.

"I must complain the poker cards are ill-shuffled till I have a good hand."

-Jonathan Swift

Comparing England to Israel's attitude toward poker, he says, "In England, my friends and family just keep asking when they'll next get to see me on television." Although poker playing isn't recognized as a profession in England—poker players don't pay tax on their winnings—in Asher's observation, it seems acceptable to be a professional poker player there just as it is in the U.S.

To be sure, Asher does consider himself a professional player. "I enjoy playing poker," he explains, "but that isn't my primary motivation for playing. This is a lucrative time to be a poker player, and it's a business for me. Just like any other business, it's not always fun. In fact, sometimes it hurts really bad. If you don't have a lot of money, you need to win. It can be a painful process. There are good months and there are bad months."

Despite the bad months he may experience, Asher says he is a very "prudent" player, not one to risk going broke. "I don't have a gambling habit," he says. "I'm probably one of the few poker players who doesn't have one." First, he doesn't risk his own money when he plays. He's playing for others when he enters the big tournaments. "Even when I play live cash games I never play big. I have a responsibility to my family. I am one who is conservative in lifestyle. I'm not a flashy player. I don't feel the need to impress anyone. In general, I am not investing so much that I could lose it all. That's the bottom line."

Asher attributes his poker successes partly to his unique personality. "I act like I know everything," he explains. "I like to give advice and tell others what they're doing wrong. That often intimidates people. Some are afraid to play against me because they're afraid they might make a mistake."

Major Poker Accomplishments

2003, First place, Showdown at the Sands, Seven Card Stud Hi/Lo

2003, First place, World Poker Open, Seven Card Stud Hi/Lo Split

2001, First place, U.S. Poker Championship, No Limit Hold'em

2000, First place, Aviation Club Summer Tournament, Pot Limit Hold'em

2000, First place, Euro Finals of Poker, Pot Limit Omaha

Annie Duke

"I make sure [the chauvinists] know it when they lose a pot to me. For example, I will discuss the hand afterwards just to get them mad."

Personal Notes

Born in Concord, New Hampshire

Mother of four children

Graduate of Columbia University

Former doctoral candidate in Cognitive Psychology

Sister of poker pro Howard Lederer

Resides in Portland, Oregon

Annie Duke learned poker from her brother. She makes no effort to hide the fact, and she's proud that her brother is poker champ Howard Lederer. "He started me off with a list of playable hands in limit hold'em by writing them on a napkin in the coffee shop at Binion's Horseshoe." Four years later Howard began to tutor his sister in earnest. That's when Annie dropped out of graduate school as a doctoral candidate in Cognitive Psychology at the University of Pennsylvania to embark on a career in poker. "Howard's teaching and experience made me a winner right from the start," she says.

When Annie was a Ph.D. candidate she needed a good grasp of probabilities and general statistics in order to do her research. "I carried that knowledge with me into my poker career, and that has truly helped," she says. Most helpful to her poker career, however, has been raising her four children. "It has taught me to be emotionally even," she explains. "It has taught me that there are more important things in life than whether I won or lost on a given night. This has made me a tremendously better player."

Since having children Annie says that she no longer gets the terrible emotional swings from playing poker—except, that is, when she's pregnant. That's another story. "When I was pregnant with my last child I played poker when I was tired and hormonal," she says. "I lost my good judgment for about two months—playing sessions that were too long, playing when I was tired, playing when I was emotionally upset. I didn't go all the way broke, but I decimated my bankroll."

Annie started out playing cash games, but when her brother saw just how good she was doing at the side tables, he encouraged her to come play in the $1500 Limit Hold'em event at the World Series of Poker in 1994. When she came in 13th, Howard suggested that she play in another. The second event was a $2500 Limit Hold'em tournament. This time she finished third.

"Baseball is like a poker game. Nobody wants to quit when he's losing; nobody wants you to quit when you're ahead."

-Jackie Robinson

Her most memorable moment at the poker tables, however, was in the big event at the WSOP. Annie won a super satellite, earning her a seat in the main event. Coincidentally, she was assigned to the same starting table as Howard. "Halfway into the day," she remembers, "Howard was struggling with only about $6,000 in front of him. I looked at my hand and saw pocket Aces. I made it $800, and Howard moved in on me! I called, and he had A-K, and was out the door."

This particular game was so memorable to Annie not because she took any pleasure in busting her brother, but because she felt so bad for him. "It was heartbreaking for me," she says. "Howard had been playing this event since 1983, and I felt terrible knocking him out. I actually burst into tears right then!"

Annie doesn't typically bawl at the table when knocking other men out of tournaments. Often, she admits, she takes quite a lot of pleasure in beating men, especially those whom she considers chauvinistic: "I make sure they know it when they lose a pot to me. For example, I will discuss the hand afterwards just to get them mad."

Annie often gets asked what it's like to be a mother of four young children while juggling a poker career. She answers by pointing out that any career is difficult when you've got four children to raise, but she believes the flexibility that poker provides her is the best in the long run. "When I'm home, I can spend the maximum amount of time with my children," she says. "I believe that it's easier to successfully accomplish the balancing act with poker as a career because it's not 9 to 5, and you have no boss to answer to. Overall I couldn't imagine doing anything I could possibly enjoy more."

Major Poker Accomplishments

2004, First place, Five Star World Poker Classic, Limit Hold'em

2004, First place, WSOP, Omaha Hi/Lo Split

2003, Second place, WSOP, Limit Hold'em Shootout

2000, Tenth place, WSOP, No Limit Hold'em Championship (while nine months pregnant)

More in-the-money finishes and final table finishes of any woman in the history of the WSOP

Leading money winner for women in WSOP

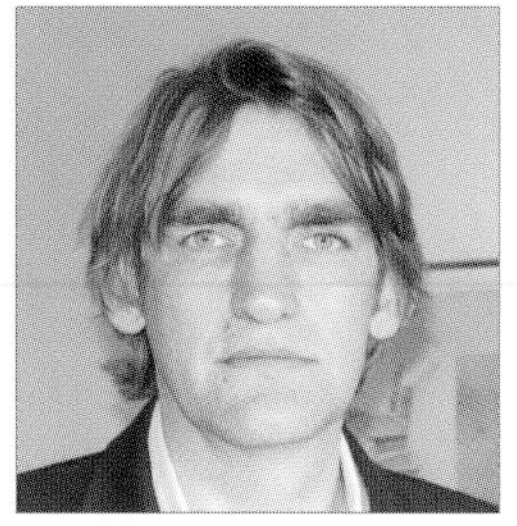

John Duthie

"In life, when your back is right up against the wall, usually something happens to help you; to pick you up and turn it all around."

Personal Notes

Born in Yorkshire, England, 1958

Television director in England

Married with two children

Working on a European Tour similar to the WPT

Resides in London, England

If John Duthie has his way, Europe will soon have a poker tour to rival the ever-popular World Poker Tour. And he has the credentials to do it. John is a television director and is eager to put his talent to use in conjunction with his affinity for poker. "With my interest in poker, I wanted to combine it with directing," John explains. "I think the WPT encouraged me to do the same thing in Europe."

If John makes the leap from directing television drama to directing the action that takes place during an international poker tournament, he will be drawing on his roots in television. It was not until he was 32 years old that John decided he wanted to direct. That's when John started pounding the pavement for work. "I started knocking on doors and got a job as a runner, making tea for people at age 32!" John gave himself five years to achieve his goal. He did it in six.

John worked his way up to becoming an assistant director, then made his own short film with friends. He used this experience as his calling card and went to work on a British soap opera for about six months. Now he considers it a great privilege to be able to direct television drama. "You have to work very hard," John says with a smile, and adds, "you also have to be quite lucky."

Directing is not the only accomplishment that John is proud of. John has two sons and considers parenting them to be an honor and great accomplishment. He intends to show his sons everything he knows about the game of poker, but he won't encourage them to play unless they have a desire to do that on their own.

When asked how he has time for poker, he remarks

that he doesn't play as much when he is working. "When I'm not working, I play probably every day."

> **"Be true to yourself. Trust your feelings and listen to them."**
>
> **-John Duthie**

John doesn't see poker as a truly enjoyable pastime and complains that at times it can be very dull and sedentary, as well as bad for your health. He believes that all poker players feel jaded at one time or another. Playing solidly for 12 hours a day can be tiresome, he says. That's why John is anxious to begin filming the game rather than playing it. "It's going to be much more fascinating," John says eagerly.

Like a lot of other poker devotees, John sees a lot of psychology at work when he is playing the game. He adds a little mystery to his theory by saying "I think there is something spinning around; and sometimes you're in the light. When you're in the light, it doesn't matter what you're doing, what cards that you have, you're the power!" An interesting, if not puzzling, thought.

John's wife does not share his affinity for poker, however. "She hates poker," he says. She doesn't see the point in it. She sees it as a mistress." But John avoids any real conflict about the situation by limiting his poker travel. Even John sees the downside to playing poker for a living. "The real obstacle is cash flow," John laments. "You have to be specific about how much money you put aside. You just have to play in smaller tournaments, build up a bankroll, and gradually work your way up." Since John has other sources of income, he doesn't worry about that too much. But he does see it as a great difficulty for the professional player.

His advice to poker rookies is to play money at a very low limit. He suggests to them that playing online can get them the experience they need for the big tournaments without a lot of expense. Then, he says, "find a club that has very low limits. Be specific about how you play. Watch the more experienced players. And just learn from them." It is advice that John took to heart as he came up in the poker world. When he was introduced to poker, he says he called up the Gambler's Bookshop in Las Vegas, ordered some books and after learning what he could, began to play, losing at first, and working his way slowly up to coming out on the positive side. Though he will not turn down a good cash game, John finds playing tournament poker more to his liking. Still, look for John to be on the other side of the camera very soon!

Major Poker Accomplishments

2004, First Place, Vienna Spring Festival, No Limit Hold'em event

2003, Second place, European Heads-up No Limit Hold'em Championship

2002, Second place, European Poker Classics, Pot Limit Omaha

2000, First place, First and only Poker Million, Isle of Man

Antonio Esfandiari

"I never touch the deck, and even if I did, I wouldn't bother to cheat. It's much easier for me to beat people straight out."

Personal Notes

- **Born in Tehran, Iran, 1978**
- **Moved to U.S.A. when he was 9**
- **Grew up in San Jose, California**
- **Professional magician**
- **Aspires to open his own magic-theme restaurant**
- **Resides in San Francisco, California**

People are always asking Antonio Esfandiari that same dumb question: since you are a professional magician and you do card tricks, does that mean you cheat at poker? "No," answers Antonio, one of the youngest professionals on the poker tournament circuit these days. "I never touch the deck, and even if I did, I wouldn't bother to cheat. It's much easier for me to beat people straight out."

Antonio was introduced to magic by a bartender at a restaurant where he was working during the summer after his high school graduation. "The guy had a deck of cards in his hands," Antonio explains. "He asked me what my favorite card was. After I named the card, he went through his deck, and the only one that was turned over was the card I had named. Not only that, the card had a different back than all the rest. I was completely mind-boggled."

Antonio was so impressed that he ran out to the nearest magic store and bought a trick deck in order to learn how to work that trick. Once he saw the reaction that he got from others when he worked the trick, he says he was in heaven: "I was never really a popular kid in high school but I always wanted to be. As soon as I experienced just a little piece of having people interested in what I was doing, I was hooked like I had a cocaine addiction."

For the next two years Antonio spent 12 hours a day practicing coin tricks, cards tricks, and other sleight of hand magic. During that time he worked as a waiter in San Jose, California.

"I started doing magic tricks for the customers," he recalls, "but the manager told me I couldn't do that because it was a fancy restaurant—even though the people loved it." The next time the owner came into the restaurant Antonio pick-pocketed his wristwatch without his knowing it. After showing the owner what he had done, Antonio explained that he was forbidden to do his magic tricks at the restaurant. Impressed by the pickpocket trick, the owner told him he could perform anytime he wanted.

"You want all the chips; and the only way to get them is by getting in there and dancing."

-Antonio Esfandiari

Eventually Antonio performed as a full-time professional magician, working parties. That's also when he started to play poker. "One day my roommate said he was going out to play in a poker tournament," says Antonio, who decided to go along with him. "I was not yet 21 at the time, but I just walked in, played in the tournament, and lost that first time."

But Antonio decided to study up. He read a few books on poker and then returned to the casino for his second tournament. This time he won. Soon after that he started playing cash games and ran $900 up to $20,000 in three months. A few months later he took all that cash to the World Series of Poker in Las Vegas and went bust. But that didn't worry Antonio too much. He got a little cash together after that big loss and has worked that up to what he has today.

Antonio didn't start traveling the poker circuit until the advent of the World Poker Tour. "When I made the final table on TV, I had plans of cooling it with poker to go to culinary school. I had enough money where I could just relax." Antonio had plans of one day opening up his own magic-theme restaurant. But after he appeared on television, knocking out poker ace Phil Hellmuth, he noticed that people started to recognize him. "I said, 'hey, this is cool! I got to get back on TV.'"

Antonio did just that. In February of 2004, he went on to the televised final table at WPT's Commerce Casino's tournament and won over $1.3 million! A few days later he also made it to WPT's celebrity invitational final tournament, making him a veritable television star—probably the youngest player thus far to win a televised tournament.

Major Poker Accomplishments

2004, First place, WSOP, Pot Limit Hold'em

2004, Sixth place, WPT Celebrity Invitational

2004, First place, WPT LA Poker Classic, No Limit Hold'em Championship

2002, Third place, WPT Gold Rush, No Limit Hold'em Championship

Chris Ferguson

"I am always looking for holes in my own game, so that I can repair them and become a stronger player."

Personal Notes

- **Born in Los Angeles, California, 1963**
- **Has a Ph.D. in Computer Science from UCLA, 1999**
- **Runs a software development company**
- **His trademark long hair and beard have earned him the nickname of "Jesus."**
- **Taught ballroom dancing at one time**
- **Resides in Pacific Palisades, California**

The look and demeanor of Chris Ferguson may have earned him the nickname, "Jesus," but his poker prowess comes not from the divine but from the analytic mind of a computer scientist. Chris's father taught Game Theory at UCLA, and consequently he taught Chris and his brother all kinds of different games. The family would spend time together analyzing and playing games. Because of this, Chris feels that poker became second nature to him.

Perhaps it was because of this analytic game-playing attitude that Chris remembers playing the "BIG HAND" when he was younger. It happened when he was only in the fourth grade while Chris was playing with friends. He lost 35 cents in what he saw at that time as a huge loss. But it seems to Chris that he was always a poker player. "I can't remember learning to play poker; it just seems to me that I've always known how to play."

It wasn't until 1994 that Chris decided that he wanted to learn to play poker at the expert level. So he decided that he had to play against the strongest opponents possible. Until then Chris was playing in low limit cash games, but he found that at that level, the players didn't take the game very seriously. So Chris turned to the tournament poker tables and found what he wanted. "What I discovered," says Chris, "was that in poker tournaments, even $200 and $300 buy-ins, one could play against some great poker players with little risk." He saw that even his weaker opponents took the game more seriously, and that's just what he needed.

Chris put his analytical mind to work. "Intelligence and the ability to reason well are the most important qualities that all poker players share," he says. This reasoning comes into play when the player is faced with deciding which alternative to take in a hand—raise, call or fold. "Sometimes it is a close decision," admits Chris.

"If you're not sure whether to fold or call, fold. If you're not sure whether to call or raise, raise."

-Chris Ferguson

It's at these times that Chris takes into account his opponents' tendencies. "There are two types of information that opponents give you," learned Chris. "One is tells, which are conscious or subconscious actions that a person takes that give an indication of the strength of [his] hand. The other is the way they play hands, and their way of thinking about hands. For me the second is the most important." Chris likes to get inside his opponent's head. He feels that this will give him a huge edge over the other players. Chris's advice would be to "pay strict attention" at the table so as not to miss any opportunities. He likes to make plays that put his opponents in situations that are foreign to them. "I try to play the style that gives my opponents the hardest time."

Chris realizes that time away from the poker table is also valuable so he spends a lot of time on his computer concentrating on poker by analyzing hands or looking at different situations that may come up. "I am always looking for holes in my own game," states Chris, "so that I can repair them and become a stronger player."

Chris also realizes that poker, though even more exciting now that tournaments are being televised and the prize pools are huge, can be demanding and exhausting, so he tries to take his mind off the game by pursuing another pastime. "I love to dance," says Chris. "A few years ago I used to go dancing at least five times a week. Now I just go once a week if I am lucky." Chris even taught ballroom and swing dance at one time.

When he is at the table, Chris Ferguson is a target. Though some may fear him, he sees others as wanting to prove themselves by beating him. However, notes Chris, "Most people don't seem to care who their opponents are once the poker game begins." He advises the aspiring players to have fun but to remember that there is nothing more fun than winning. He tells them that to have fun you have to take the game seriously. And who can argue with a man who has had so much success?

Major Poker Accomplishments

2003, First place, WSOP, Half Hold'em/Half Stud

2003, First place WSOP, Omaha Hi/Lo

2001, First place, WSOP, Omaha Hi/Lo

2000, First place, WSOP, No Limit Hold'em Championship

2000, First place, WSOP, Seven Card Stud

32 cashes, 20 final tables and 5 wins at the WSOP

Bruno "King" Fitoussi

"I always keep in mind that poker is just a game; it's not real life."

Personal Notes

Born in Paris, France

Married with two children

President of VIP-Gaming

Graduate in Architecture from the National School in Paris

Founder of the Aviation Club in Paris

Resides in Sceaux, France

Before 1993, Bruno Fitoussi traveled the world playing poker. He won some minor tournaments and raked in some cash in side games. But that year, when his wife Isabelle told him she was pregnant, he decided to stay in Paris. His idea was to open the city's first ever poker club. That idea turned into the Aviation Club of France, just steps from the Arc de Triomphe, on the famous Champs Elysees; it later became the first venue outside North America for the World Poker Tour.

In 1999, Bruno decided to quit his official position at the Aviation Club in order to pursue another poker-related business. He started VIP-Gaming, a consulting company for the gaming business. "My activity as the president of my company gives me the marvelous opportunity to travel again, and to play in some poker events once in a while," says Bruno.

Before 2000, Bruno didn't have the opportunity to play in the big tournaments, aside from the 1998 World Series of Poker. "I was working hard and also trying to keep some space for my personal and family life," he explains.

In 2002, Bruno won his first major tournament, which remains the highlight of his tournament career thus far. It was the inaugural No Limit Hold'em World Heads Up Championship held in Vienna, Austria. What made it most memorable for him was that he squared off in the final against the legendary Amarillo Slim Preston—and whooped him, Texas style. "This tournament was a kind of step in my poker career as I gained more confidence with my style of play."

The next year Bruno went on to cash in two major Las Vegas tournaments, including finishing fifteenth in the World Series of Poker.

Nevertheless, says Bruno, poker is for him today—unlike before 1993—a hobby that he delights in rather than a full-time business endeavor. "I have to keep in mind that I can't play all the time," he says. "And I always keep in mind that poker is just a game; it's not real life."

Yet Bruno still considers this "hobby" his passion and says he has no time left for other recreational pursuits. When asked what makes him interested in tournament poker he quickly replies, "Competition and big money!"

Bruno's family understands his passion, maybe because he tries to always keep space for his family and his personal life, no matter which big tournament is calling to him. "When I was a professional poker player, my wife knew the obligations and responsibilities of my business," states Bruno, "and it was never a problem."

"Always be nice with the poker employees (dealers, floorpersons, and others)."

-Bruno Fitoussi

Maybe it is Bruno's passion for poker that keeps it exciting for him. "I feel like I never stop trying to improve my poker abilities since I started playing poker," Bruno declares, "and it's a goal for me to play better and better." Bruno does not only concentrate on himself, however. Bruno agrees with what any good player will tell you, "Psychology is the most important part of poker and it helps to deal with people." And he also sees the importance of having a good sense of humor at the table.

Bruno Fitoussi has come a long way from playing Five Card Draw with friends for matches worth two cents each to sitting across the felt from the flamboyant Poker Hall of Famer, Amarillo Slim. Did Bruno feel intimidated when it came to playing against Slim? Not on your life! Bruno considers himself to be great on offense when push comes to shove. He does not have any superstitions or carry any lucky charms; he simply plays his game.

Bruno's poker career has had its setbacks though, particularly when he built up a large bankroll and then went broke for the first (and he hopes last) time. Bruno has worked hard to assure that doesn't happen again. Yet he echoes what a lot of other players consider most important in tournament play. According to Bruno, "fame is nice; fortune is better!"

Major Poker Accomplishments

2003, 8th place, WPT Five Star World Poker Classic, No Limit Hold'em Championship

2003, 15th place, WSOP No Limit Hold'em Championship

2001, First place, Inaugural World Heads Up No Limit Hold'em Championship

Layne Flack 

"I don't think you play poker by reading other people. I think you play poker by reading how others are reading you."

Personal Notes

- **Born in Rapid City, South Dakota, 1969**
- **Former poker dealer**
- **Ran poker games in Montana**
- **Doesn't like being interviewed**
- **Known for his wry smile and "malicious laugh"**
- **Resides in Las Vegas**

Aside from playing pinochle with his grandparents as a kid, Layne Flack had no experience with card playing when he took his first job as a casino worker in Billings, Montana at the age of 18. His youth was spent between the flatlands of South Dakota and the rugged terrain of Montana.

After six months at the Billings casino, Layne was promoted to night manager. That's also when he started playing poker himself. These early games were $1-$3 Five Card Stud, and he loved it. A year later he began a short-lived college career studying business. During the summers he started dealing—cards, that is. When he wasn't dealing, he was playing. He got so busy making money from poker that he eventually decided to call it quits with college classes.

"That's when I started to run my own games," he says. "All throughout Montana: Bozeman, Butte, Missoula, and Billings. Up there I just went up to the little casinos and told them I'd pay $1,500 a month to lease out a room where I could put up two tables."

At one of his Montana games he met poker pro Huck Seed, himself a native of Montana. Impressed with Layne's game, he says Huck convinced him to go to Vegas. "Six weeks later," adds Layne, "I was playing in the Hall of Fame tournament and won the second event I played in"—a $1,500 buy-in No Limit Hold'em. "The first time I ever played in Vegas, I won!" That first Vegas win inspired Layne to stay on the poker circuit. He was also inspired by poker great Johnny Chan, who he says took him under his wing. "He let me sit behind him while he was playing," Layne explains, "and I learned a lot."

From there Layne went on to be very competitive. In 2002, he earned the nickname "Back-to-back" Flack when he took two gold bracelets in back-to-back World Series events. Those two wins catapulted him to the big leagues. "But I got really well known a year later when I beat Jerry Buss," he adds.

> **"Whether he likes it or not, a man's character is stripped bare at the poker table; if the other players read him better than he does, he has only himself to blame."**
>
> **-Anthony Holden from *Big Deal***

The owner of the L.A. Lakers lost to Flack at the 2003 Celebrity Invitational at the Commerce Casino in Los Angeles. "I walked in the door the other day at the Commerce," he says, "and Jerry said to me, 'there's the one I made famous.' That episode probably got played five times more than any other because it was the celebrity invitational." Buss, Layne adds, now lets him sit with him up in the owner's box at Lakers games where both poker and basketball are the hot topics.

Layne is known for being a "madman"—an aggressive player who is often hard to read. And that's important to the up and coming star. "I wear a smirk that I think makes me hard to read. Players will sit there and look at me and all they see is my grin. They have no idea what I'm holding, or if I'm ready to bluff." Layne says he's hard to read even away from the poker table: "People must try too hard. I'll be walking out of the casino and people will say, 'hey, it looks like you had a good day.' And I'll say, 'no, not at all.'"

When asked what makes him a good poker player, Layne scoffs at the question. "I've been trying to figure out what makes a good player, but no one really knows why they're good. It's probably just your chemical makeup." He does, however, admit to having a way with reading other people. "When I read someone, I go way more in depth than what their cards are. I read every situation. I look at what they might do and what kind of person they are. If this person is a shady person, he's more apt to be stealing a pot, and if he's friendly with me at the table, he's less likely to bluff me."

More importantly, however, he says, "I don't think you play poker by reading other people. I think you play poker by reading how other people are reading you. With my outgoing personality, I get a lot of information."

Major Poker Accomplishments

2003, First place, WSOP, Omaha Hi/Lo Split

2003, First place, WSOP, Limit Hold'em Shootout

2002, First place, WPT Celebrity Invitational

2002, First place, WSOP, No Limit Hold'em back-to-back titles

2000, First place, Legends of Poker, No Limit Hold'em Championship

1999, First place, WSOP, Pot Limit Hold'em

Ken "Skyhawk" Flaton

"A lot of things have changed in the poker world over the past three decades. It's all run much better now."

Personal Notes

- **Born in North Bergen, New Jersey**
- **Married with one son**
- **Former accountant**
- **Former professional blackjack player**
- **Met his future wife at Caesar's Palace**
- **Resides in Henderson, Nevada**

Ken Flaton was an accountant in New Jersey when he had the bright idea that he could make it as a professional blackjack player in Las Vegas. Despite the difficulty of the task, Ken felt up to the challenge. "It's a difficult game to beat," he says, "but if you count the cards then you'll know when you have the advantage. You have to be disciplined, but it can be done. Lots of people have made a lot of money at blackjack."

As it turns out Ken wasn't one of the few who made his fortune at the blackjack table, but he didn't lose either. "I was making a couple hundred dollars a week at this back in the '70s," he says. "Nothing big." That fact, however, didn't stop the Las Vegas casinos from banning Ken from their blackjack tables, a move he never expected would be made against him. In the end it cut his blackjack career very short.

"I was never actually told I was kicked out of a casino," he explains, but during the World Series of Poker at the Golden Nugget one year Ken went to sit down at the blackjack table just to kill some time between poker events. "I placed a $100 bill down, and before the dealer could change it, the pit boss came over to tell me I was not welcome to play blackjack," he remembers. "It's not like I'm a notorious counter. It's not like I made thousands of dollars. It's not that I ever cheated. I didn't know the pit boss, and I doubt he knew me, but I was amazed at how fast it all happened. He must have got a call from upstairs." Ken found that he was only banned from the blackjack table; he was told he could play any of the other casino games.

Ken had a similar experience in the old Maxim hotel casino. "I guess they were watching me closely," he recounts. "I had a pretty big day one time, but I was trying to camouflage my seriousness about it all. I was drinking a little. Everything I did was right." After a big win at the blackjack table, Ken wandered over to the craps table just to make it look like he was a random gambler, but as soon as he stepped up to the blackjack table again, he was told he was banned from any further play.

"Come to the table with nothing less than your A-game. Competition nowadays is just too good and numerous for anything less to succeed."

-Ken Flaton

In 1972, during his blackjack years, Ken met up with a friend from back in New Jersey. He had known him from home poker games years before. "He came out to Vegas to play poker," Ken remembers. "He said he thought I was good enough at poker to make a living off it out here in Vegas." That was a thought that had never before crossed Ken's mind. He hadn't given a thought to playing poker in Vegas. In fact, he had never once even as much as set foot in a Vegas poker room. The comment from his friend, however, was enough inspiration.

The next week he started his poker playing career in the card room at Caesars Palace. "I started out playing real small," he says. "Then I moved up to play $5-$10 blinds, and slowly increased the size of my game." His friend had been right. Ken found that he was indeed good enough to make a living at poker.

At the time Ken first started playing poker he says that the Dunes was run by the Mob. "I am a man of principle," he says. "But sometimes I'm not too smart." Ken felt as if he was being cheated in the poker room at the Dunes. "I knew I was," he says. "It happened a few times. The dealer was working with the guy running the room, and I caught the dealer cheating but the room manager refused to acknowledge my complaint." For years thereafter, Ken personally boycotted the Dunes. "Out of stubbornness I wouldn't even set foot in there, even though it was part of my livelihood." Years later, a friend convinced Ken that things had changed at the Dunes, and that he was only hurting himself by staying away. With some trepidation, "I finally went back."

Ken says that players had to watch out for themselves a lot more then than they have to do now. "A lot of things have changed in the poker world over the past three decades," he observes. "It's all run much better now."

In the end, after playing poker for just a few years, he found that this career suited him much better than his blackjack career. "I went broke three different times when I was playing blackjack," says Ken. "But as a poker player, I started out small and managed my money properly and thirty years later I'm still at the tables."

Major Poker Accomplishments

2004, Second place, LA Poker Classic, H.O.E.

2004, Second place, LA Poker Classic, Seven Card Stud

2003, First place, Five Diamond World Poker Classic, Seven Card Stud, 8 O/B

2000, Second place, WSOP, Seven Card Stud

1996, First place, US Poker No Limit Hold'em Championship

Ted Forrest

"I felt if I could just get up to $1,200, I'd never go broke from there."

Personal Notes

- **Born in Syracuse, New York, 1964**
- **Professional poker player**
- **Worked at the Grand Canyon**
- **Dropped out of college to play poker professionally**
- **Resides in Las Vegas**

Ted Forrest was a 20-year-old working at the Altabar Hotel near the Grand Canyon when he first decided to make a trip to Las Vegas. He was winning two to three hundred dollars off the low-limit poker games he played with his hotel co-workers. This was a staggering sum compared to the four-dollar-an-hour pittance he made as a desk clerk. "There was this one guy in our game, and he was a horrible player," Ted remembers. "He went to Las Vegas and said he made a couple hundred dollars playing stud. I said to myself, if this guy can win in Vegas, then I'm pretty sure I can too."

Thus began Ted's weekly trips to the poker room at Caesar's Palace, where he got his feet wet playing low-limit games. "I was so enchanted with poker at the time that I didn't even bother to get a hotel room," Ted recalls. "I would just play all day and all night for two straight days, and then drive back to the Grand Canyon to work a shift at the hotel without ever having got a wink of sleep."

It wasn't always easy, he admits. One weekend he was so tired on his return trip to Arizona that he pulled off the road in the middle of the desert to take a three-hour nap. When he woke up, he left the car to answer nature's call, but locked his keys in the car. "I had to throw a rock through my passenger window just to get back in."

Once Ted realized that he could make a lot more money in Las Vegas, he left the Grand Canyon and moved to Vegas, but when he arrived he had no more than a hundred dollars in his wallet. After a day of poker playing, he was down to thirty dollars—close to broke. "I was thinking, 'oh, no, maybe this isn't for me.'" Ted was too embarrassed to ask his family for money, and didn't yet know a soul in

Las Vegas he could ask for help. "I was ready to go back to school and choose a different career," he says, "when I won $150 in a $1-$2 hold'em game."

Ted lived out of his car with the goal of getting his bankroll up to a modest $1,200. "I felt if I could just get up to $1,200, I'd never go broke from there." He reached his goal in a matter of weeks and has built up his bankroll ever since.

"The game exemplifies the worst aspects of capitalism that have made our country so great."

-Walter Matthau

His mother was pretty skeptical of his chosen career path, he says, when they found out that he was trying to make a living as a professional poker player in Las Vegas. They couldn't believe that anyone could make a decent living at the tables. But when Ted returned to New York two years later with a brand new car and enough money to pay his way through college, his mother at least thought Ted could do worse. "I think she was pretty proud of me at this point," he says.

Ted decided to attend Lemoine College, where his late father had once worked as an English professor. "I ended up dropping out just nine credits short of graduation," he explains, "and it's probably one of the better choices I've made in my life. If I'd graduated from college, I might have taken some job making $36,000 a year. I'm happy with the alternative route I've taken."

Ted's departure from Lemoine meant a return to the card tables of Vegas, and there he's stayed except for his travels on the tournament circuit. In 1992, his first year of playing tournaments, Ted went on a hot streak at the Commerce Casino in Los Angeles. "I won best all-around player, making 11 final tables out of the 21 tournaments I played in. It was an unreal lucky streak."

Ted has continued playing tournaments, but he's never given up side action. He can still be seen in the high stakes cash games where he is revered for being a guy who can play almost any hand against his opponent. In fact, for a few years Ted left the tournament circuit, playing only in the World Series of Poker, which he said was "too juicy" to miss. Now that the World Poker Tour has popularized the No Limit Hold'em tournaments, Ted has taken to the tournament trail once again. In fact, Ted added two more gold bracelets to his collection in the 2004 World Series of Poker, in the Seven Card Stud and No Limit Hold'em events, bringing his total gold bracelet count to five. Experience tells us that Ted is not done yet!

Major Poker Accomplishments

2004, First place, WSOP, Seven Card Stud

2004, First place, WSOP, No Limit Hold'em event

2003, Fifth place, WPT Five Star World Poker Classic, No Limit Hold'em Championship

1993, First place, WSOP, Seven Card Stud

1993, First place, WSOP, Seven Card Razz

1993, First place, WSOP, Omaha 8/OB

Kirill Gerasimov

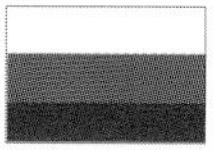

"I came to casino, sat down, and I played—one time, two times. I did good."

Personal Notes

Born in Moscow, Russia, 1971

Married with one child

Works in the insurance industry in Moscow

Considers himself a "natural"

Resides in Moscow, Russia

One of the youngest—and newest—players on the world poker circuit hails from Russia. Kirill Gerasimov considers himself a "natural" at the game. When he is not traveling to poker venues around the world, Kirill works in the office of a small insurance company in his native Moscow, and lives in an even smaller apartment with his wife and their first child. It is from here that the young Russian, who now considers himself a professional poker player, travels to points all over the globe to play poker.

It was in 2001 that this sanguine and confident Russian first sat down at a poker table. "I came to casino, sat down, and I played—one time, two times. I did good." These were cash games, and Kirill was winning as much as he was learning. "My friends kept looking at me and saying: 'Kirill is good.'" That was when Kirill decided that he ought to play in tournament poker. He found that he was as good in tournament play as he was in cash games.

In the winter of 2001 Kirill placed in two European tournaments. His first major tournament win, however, was in the 2002 World Heads-Up Poker Championship at the Concord Card Casino in Vienna. Facing a veritable "who's who" of international players such as Asher Derei, Barney Boatman, Bruno Fitoussi and "Devilfish" Ulliott, the Russian ace came out on top.

Bolstered by this prestigious win and backed financially by Paradise Poker, which put up the money for his expenses, he entered the World Poker Tour's main event at the Bellagio in 2003. Two days later the young Russian was sitting under the bright lights and cameras at the final table, at which he finished second, taking home over $500,000 in prize money. Kirill was on his way to poker ace status.

No one was counting out Kirill Gerasimov when he faced Alan Goehring in that championship. Even though Goehring had a commanding chip lead, this Heads-Up champ was not going to go down easily. Observers called the play between these two poker stars "astounding." At one point Kirill took over the chip lead by making a daring bet with absolutely nothing in his hand. But as fate would have it, the lead swung back around to Goehring and in one of the most exciting final hands of the WPT first season, Kirill was defeated. Fans call him fearless, talented and a "damn good poker player." Detractors say that he is just lucky. But no one can deny that his performance in the past few years puts him in good stead with his peers.

"Aces are larger than life and greater than mountains."

-Mike Caro

With another major win under his belt, Kirill was inspired to continue on the tournament poker circuit, but he says that the flight from Moscow to the United States is a long ordeal. "I don't want to come to America more than three times a year," he says. "I don't want to stay away from my family for too many months each year."

Between 2001 and 2004, Kirill has captured eight first place trophies in Europe and done very well in the states. With his half-million dollar second-place finish in the 2003 WPT Championship and a final table placement at one of the 2004 World Series of Poker events, Kirill can stand with the best of them. When he won the Rookie of the Year award at the 2002 European Poker Awards it was only a harbinger of good things to come.

The Russian feels that his chances of winning are boosted by his ability to read people. "When I play at Paradise [Poker] this element is obviously less of a factor," he states. "I'm forced to work on other parts of my game." This is important, Kirill thinks, because "Paradise has helped me to develop what I believe to be a strong all-around game."

Once I won the Vienna tournament, I knew I had a future as a poker player," he says. He hasn't looked back since.

Major Poker Accomplishments

2004, Second place, WSOP, No Limit Hold'em Shootout

2004, Fifth place, WSOP, Pot Limit Omaha

2003, Second place, WPT No Limit Hold'em Championship

2003, First place, Austrian Masters, No Limit Hold'em Championship

2002, First place, World Heads Up Poker No Limit Hold'em Championship

2002, First place, Master Classics of Poker, Limit Hold'em

Phil Gordon 

"My theory is that if you're going to be a professional, act like a professional. That's always a very easy way to differentiate me from 'the other Phil.'"

Personal Notes

- **Born in El Paso, Texas, 1970**
- **Graduate of the Georgia Institute of Technology**
- **Former software engineer**
- **Author of *Poker: The Real Deal***
- **Host of Bravo/ NBC's "Celebrity Poker Showdown"**
- **Resides in Las Vegas, Nevada**

Phil Gordon may be the only top-notch pro poker player to ever dress in drag in order to enter a "women-only" tournament. But Phil discovered that he plays better as a man. Whereas he finished a ragged 46th in the women's tourney at San Jose's Shooting Star at Bay 101, he took first place in the main event, dressed as regular old Phil Gordon.

If one needs any explanation as to why Phil would dawn a wig and makeup in order to play with the girls, it could be because he was taught to play poker by a woman—his Aunt Lib. "My sister and I would visit her house in Columbia, South Carolina every summer for literally months on end," he remembers. "Almost every night, we'd gather around the kitchen table to play penny-ante five-card draw."

Once Phil got started in on the tournament scene, it dulled his appetite for cash games. "I don't even remember entering my first tournament," he says, "but I know that the live games don't interest me nearly as much as tournaments. The extra strategy element of tournament play is very exciting for me." For Phil, that strategy includes patience, fearlessness and an incredible will to win.

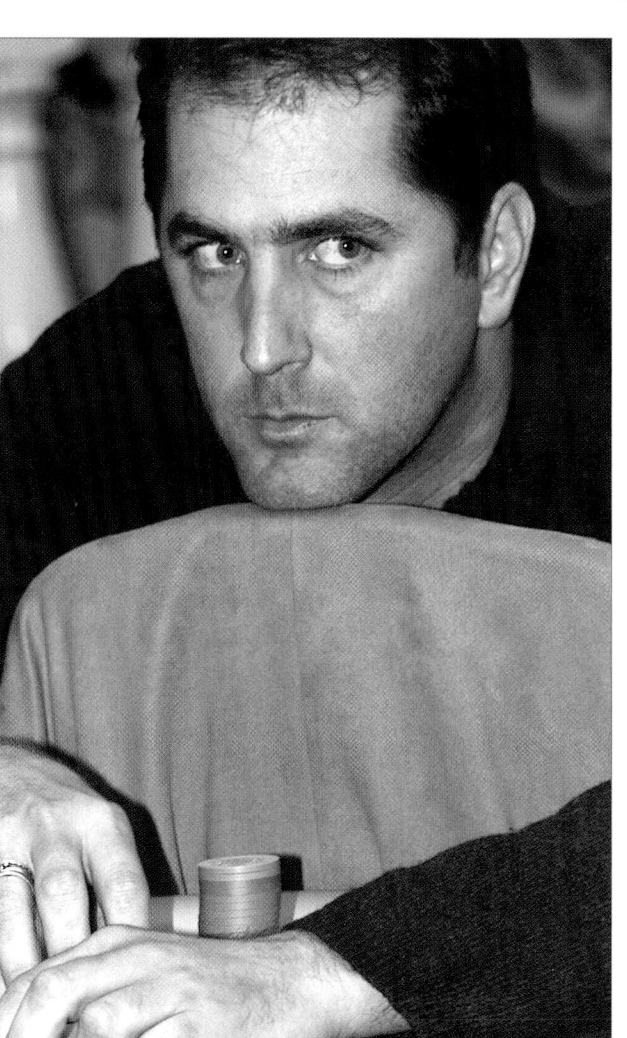

Now that he's a professional, he's just as conscious of his table image as he is of playing well. "Having people respect me for my demeanor at the table is very important," he says. "My theory is that if you're going to be a professional, act like a professional. That's always a very easy way to differentiate me from 'the other Phil.'"

Phil Gordon offers an example in relating what he considers his "most memorable" tournament game ever. In the 2001 World Series of Poker, there were thirteen players left standing. Phil was chip leader with a $650,000 stack at the time. "Phil Hellmuth was at my table and just steam rolling the game," he remembers. "The blinds were $3000-$6000 with a $500 ante, and Mike Mastasow was under the gun and raised it to $20,000. Two players in the middle folded, and I found K-K. I re-raised to $100,000 and was mentally committed to calling if Mike moved all-in. Unfortunately, Phil Hellmuth changed that plan. From the small blind he raised all-in $600,000. Mike, looking completely crestfallen, showed Q-Q to the crowd and mucked after about thirty seconds of whining. It came back to me. The pressure was enormous. I took about two minutes, and finally mucked my K-K. Hellmuth said, 'What'd you have, Phil, A-Q?' I was calm and said, no, I had kings. Hellmuth flipped up A-A. The enormous crowd ooh'ed and aah'ed. 'You didn't have kings—no way.'

"Avoid domination."

-Phil Gordon

I reached into the muck and pulled out my two cards and flipped up the kings for everyone to see. The crowd went completely crazy. Phil went on tilt: 'I can't believe my luck! I had aces against a pair of queens and kings, and I only won $120,000! I'm so unlucky!' The cheering from the crowd lasted at least a minute." That was "by far the best laydown" Phil Gordon ever made, he says. "And it sent a message to Mr. Hellmuth: I was a player and a contender."

Since that time, Phil has seen bigger wins and has achieved ever greater 'fame' especially since he started hosting television's "Celebrity Poker Showdown." He's also been able to get out and do some traveling even while not at the poker tables. "I've been to over fifty countries on six continents in the last six years." And that's only half of the fun for Phil Gordon. The recent growth of pro poker has been just as exciting for him. "The number of entrants is huge. The prize purses are enormous, and the fans of the game make playing well more rewarding."

Major Poker Accomplishments

2004, First place, WPT Bay 101 Shooting Star, No Limit Hold'em Championship

Eight in-the-money finishes at WSOP 2000-2003

2003, First place, WPT Ultimate Bet Championship, No Limit Hold'em, Pro Division

2002, Third place, WSOP, Omaha Hi/Lo Split

2002, Sixth place, WSOP, Pot Limit Hold'em

2001, Fourth place, WSOP, No Limit Hold'em Championship

Barry Greenstein

"The people all over the world who give their time and effort are the real heroes."

Personal Notes

- **Born in Chicago, Illinois**
- **Attended the University of Illinois to work on his Ph.D. in mathematics**
- **Father of two children**
- **Developed Q&A software for Symantec**
- **Working on a book about making money at poker**

Although viewers of televised poker may think that Barry Greenstein is a relative newcomer to poker circles, nothing is further from the truth. Though Barry limits his tournament play in favor of cash games, he made quite a splash on the tournament circuit in the last couple of years.

Early in 2004 Barry outlasted over 360 opponents at the Jack Binion World Poker Open in Tunica, Mississippi to win a whopping $1.2 million. It was his first win and first appearance at a World Poker Tour final table. But it wasn't his last. Barry followed up that win just a couple of months later with another appearance on the World Poker Tour at the Party Poker Million III cruise where he came in fifth. Earlier, in 2003 Barry won the $1 million prize at Larry Flynt's Hustler Casino one-table Stud event. To say that Barry is on a roll is an understatement.

All of Barry's winnings mean nothing to him dollarwise. Why? Because Barry donates every penny of his tournament winnings to a variety of charities, some through his own foundation, but particularly to his favorite charity, Children, Inc., which provides food, clothing, and education to children of poverty throughout the United States and the world. He passionately believes in their motto: "You can change the world, one child at a time."

Barry first became involved in charity work by donating to a particular family in the heart of Appalachian Kentucky. He involved his own two children in his project so that they could experience the rich feeling of giving to others. This affinity for helping children grew into his pledge to donate his tournament poker revenue to charities, some that are not even deductible to him. According to Barry he doesn't consider himself to be a hero. "The

"The commonest mistake in history is underestimating your opponent; happens at the poker table all the time."

-General David Shoup

people who give their time and effort all over the world are the real heroes," he says. For him, the contributions that he makes are the "best things I have ever done in my life."

Barry comes by his card-playing ability honestly. His father was a poker player who taught Barry how to play when he was very young. And the family enjoyed many a good card game when he was growing up. By the time he was a teenager Barry was making about $50 a night at home games and he could see playing professional poker as a reality.

But in 1984, Barry made the move to Silicon Valley in California where he became involved in what was to become a nationally known software development company—Symantec. Barry had been interested in software development since he had developed his own computer software at the age of 15. His college degree was in computer science as well. And he became an invaluable asset to the company.

Poker was still in his blood when he was working at Symantec and when his wife became ill, he decided to leave the company and resume his poker career to give himself the flexibility he would need to take care of his wife and family.

When he and his wife divorced, Barry received custody of his two children and began to instill in them the notion that any sacrifice they made for his poker career was done for a higher purpose—for the needy children throughout the world. He taught them to look beyond their own lives to share what they have with those who desperately need it.

Though there are a number of poker pros who donate some of their winnings to charity, Barry is the only one who has pledged every penny of what he wins to some worthy group. As unassuming as he is about his purpose, Barry still realizes an opportunity when he is offered one. He sees his involvement in poker along with the resultant publicity as a golden opportunity to give his causes the coverage they deserve. If he can bring a few more dollars to his favorite charities, it will all be worth it!

Major Poker Accomplishments

2004, First place, WSOP, Deuce to Seven Draw

2004, First place, Five Star World Poker Classic, No Limit Hold'em event

2004, First place, WPT World Poker Open, No Limit Hold'em Championship

2003, First place, California State Poker Championship, No Limit Hold'em event

2003, Best All-Around Player, California State Poker Championship

Hassan Habib  

"I love playing poker. It is a great rush to win tournaments."

Personal Notes

Born in Karachi, Pakistan, 1962

Came to the United States in 1980

Attended the University of Redlands

Formerly owned a chain of video stores

Tennis champion in Pakistan at the age of 14

Resides in Downey, California

Hassan Habib has a theory about maintaining stamina in a multi day tournament. "I tell myself that to relax is the most important thing. . . tomorrow is another day. I can't get caught up in thinking that it's a big tournament. If I worry too much on what is happening tomorrow, then I won't get a good night's sleep."

Hassan must have used that method in 2000 when he made the final table at three of the biggest tournaments in the world. Hassan's poker prowess landed him at the final table at the World Series of Poker, the Tournament of Champions and the World Poker Open. The final table at the WSOP included such legends as Chris Ferguson and T.J. Cloutier when Hassan took home fourth place and a hefty cash prize, but no gold bracelet.

The coveted gold bracelet did not escape him in 2004, however. Hassan outlasted 212 other entrants in the Seven Card Stud Hi/Lo 8/OB event to realize his dream of wearing the gold on his wrist. When he was interviewed after the game Hassan said, "They are going to forget about the money. Next year, no one is going to remember the money that I won here. But they surely will remember the gold bracelet."

Fearless player that he is, this may not be the last gold bracelet he wins. Though for a while Hassan put aside tournament play in favor of cash games, he is once again on the tournament circuit. "I love playing poker," he states. "It is a great rush to win tournaments."

Hassan's tournament poker pursuits did not begin until the late '90s when his friends urged him to play in a big tournament. The first time was in a small town on the way to Las Vegas. The tournament consisted of only 80 entrants—and he won! He went back there the next week and he won again! But, says Hassan with not a little irony, "I didn't win another tournament for two years."

Until 1996, Hassan divided his time between poker and his video store business. After he sold his stores he devoted himself fulltime to poker. Now he feels that he can hold his own in any type of poker game. With his laid back attitude, he can now relax and focus a lot easier.

Hassan likes to make a lot of raises and play a lot of hands. "People like to pay me off," he remarks, "and I use it to my advantage." Yet Hassan realizes that playing poker is "the toughest way to make an easy living." He realizes that a player has to endure a lot when poker is his main source of income; and more importantly, that it does not pay off most of the time. He doesn't even want to think about losing streaks. "They're no fun," Hassan notes with a grim look. "I'm too stubborn to retire. If you're not stubborn and determined, you won't make it in this profession."

He admits, though, that his game has changed considerably of late. He is playing more conservatively by not raising as much as he used to. "Before, I had to raise at least three times a round," he concedes. "But now, two or three rounds go by and I don't play a hand."

Hassan does have other interests besides poker and his family is one of the most important. He is very close to his family in Pakistan and talks to them by telephone almost every day. He visits them every other year and they travel to the United States whenever possible. He is most proud of his father who buys guar gum from farmers to make a product that is found in yogurt and salsa. He says that his father supplies this product for about 50% of the yogurt sold in the United States.

Hassan sloughs off the worries of the poker world by relaxing at home with his cat. Eventually, he would like to have a house in Cabo San Lucas where he could go to relax between tournaments. With his record—it won't be long!

"It is important to put your opponent on a hand. But as the hand progresses, you need to have an open mind. You need to be able to put him on a different hand."

-Hassan Habib

Major Poker Accomplishments

2004, First place, WSOP, Seven Card Stud Hi/Lo Split

2004, First place, LA Poker Classic, Omaha High/Lo 8/OB

2004, Second place, WPT Five Star World Poker Classic, No Limit Hold'em Championship

2000, Fourth place, WSOP, No Limit Hold'em Championship

Gus Hansen

"Not to say that I am a great player or anything, but somebody has to win."

Personal Notes

- **Born in Copenhagen, Denmark, 1973**
- **Formerly an exchange student in Santa Cruz, California**
- **Former backgammon player**
- **Known as the "Great Dane"**
- **Considered a poker tour "sex symbol"**
- **Resides in Copenhagen, Denmark**

Denmark-native Gus Hansen may be a relatively icy newcomer to the field of professional poker, but he's no stranger to competition. Before beginning to make his mark in a big way on the poker circuit, Gus excelled at ten different games, most notably tennis, ping pong and backgammon. Just a few years ago he was known among the Scandinavian backgammon community as *Mama Lustra Spillertruppen #9601.*

After winning two World Poker Tour events (the World Poker Classic at the Bellagio and the L.A. Poker Classic at Commerce Casino) during the first season and winning another already in the second season (Poker Stars Caribbean Adventure), Gus has become known as the "Great Dane" among poker professionals.

His moniker is appropriate not only because he's great and he's a Dane, but Gus is also somewhat of an attack dog at the table, having rapidly earned himself a reputation of being one of the most aggressive players in tournament history. He consistently gives seasoned veterans acute indigestion by playing wooden hands with seemingly reckless abandon. Although Gus is known for re-raising before the flop with nothing in the hole, he's not exactly foolish. That may have something to do with the fact that he was once a backgammon star. He has an understanding of what backgammon players call 'equity.' In poker it's sometimes referred to as 'expectation.' Such is a concept that is fundamental to all games that are a combination of skill and chance. It boils down to an understanding of the value of position—in a particular situation, with a particular hand, versus particular opponents.

According to Gus, few poker players have an understanding of the concept of equity. It's for that reason that he believes backgammon players have an edge when they come to the poker table. Backgammon players, he says, approach poker with more objectivity than others.

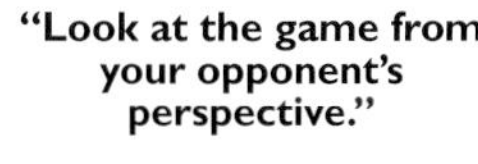

"Look at the game from your opponent's perspective."

-Gus Hansen

Commentators have pointed out that one of Gus Hansen's particular strengths rests in his uncanny ability to play his opponent's hands, rather than simply playing his own. In other words, Gus looks at the game not only from his own perspective, but from the perspectives of each of the other players.

Gus's three World Poker Tour wins have earned him an honor that is more valuable and certainly longer lasting than any poker win. He has been immortalized in the World Poker Tour's Walk of Fame at the Commerce Casino. He is one of three honorees who have made their place in the poker world by playing the game at its highest level, contributing to the evolution of the game, or celebrating poker in film, television or literature. His handprint is set forever in concrete along with a depiction of one of his most famous poker hands.

As guests approach the entrance to Commerce Casino, they will forever see the name of Gus Hansen alongside the other two initial inductees, Doyle Brunson, who is perhaps the most respected living poker player of today, and Hollywood great, James Garner who immortalized the cool-handed gambler and poker player, Brett Maverick back in the late 50s.

Early in his career—not so long ago really—Gus's style of play commonly misled opponents to think he was simply a lucky bugger. "I love that they think I'm lucky," he has said. "I don't mind at all. I mean…let them just think I'm lucky. I think it helps me if people think I'm a little bit crazy because there's definitely rationale behind a lot of things I do. They might seem wacky, but I'm not totally crazy, just a little bit."

After chalking up big tournament wins left and right, however, it's going to be increasingly difficult for people to continue to believe the Great Dane is simply dancing to the music of chance. Will that stop Gus Hansen from playing 7-2 off suit, and playing it aggressively? The answer is likely 'no.'

Gus sums it up best in his own words, "Not to say that I am a great player or anything, but somebody has to win."

Major Poker Accomplishments

2004, First place, WPT Pokerstars Cruise, No Limit Hold'em Championship

2003, Sixth place, WPT Battle of Champions

2003, Third place, WPT Five Diamond World Poker Classic, No Limit Hold'em Championship

2003, First place, WPT LA Poker Classic, No Limit Hold'em Championship

2002, First place, WPT Five Diamond World Poker Classic, No Limit Hold'em Championship

Thor Hansen

"I know what to do, who to play, what to play, and when to quit."

Personal Notes

Born in Oslo, Norway, 1947

Married with no children

Worked as a "human calculator"

Former professional pool player

Plays poker regularly with Larry Flynt and Jerry Buss

Resides in Los Angeles, California

Named after the Norse God of Thunder, Thor Hansen strikes like a bolt of lightning at the poker table. Without the magic hammer and iron gloves of his namesake, Thor survives purely on his skill and confidence. "All I know is that I'm a winner," says the Norwegian born poker veteran. "I know what to do, who to play, what to play, and when to quit."

Having a mathematical mind doesn't hurt either. When he was just eight years old he worked as a "human calculator," adding up sale items at his family's grocery store in a small town in Norway. "I was good at numbers," says Thor as a sort of understatement. "That might be why I did so well at poker when I was a kid." In the back room of the grocery store Thor watched as his brother and father played poker against other locals. "Every time they took a break from playing," he recalls, "I would sit in the hand and play a little. They figured out I was good at it because when they returned they always found that I was sitting there with more money than when they left."

Thor left school at age 13 to take up work at a hotel, but, he says, he always made more money through playing poker and pool. In his early 20's he played pool for a living. "In 1973, I played on Norwegian television against a three-time world champion from the United States. When I beat him, he complained about the rules we were playing by, so then we played by *his* rules, and I beat him again." Although Thor became quite famous as a pool player throughout Norway, he never played again. Realizing there was little money to be made in billiards, he concentrated on poker.

For years he played backroom cash games, but in 1988 he decided to enter the Scandinavian Championship of Poker. Since poker (and gambling) was then illegal in all five Scandinavian nations (Iceland, Denmark, Finland, Sweden, and Norway), the tournament was held in the beautiful seaside city of Dubrovnik—now in Croatia, but then a part of Yugoslavia.

Thor took first place honors in that first tournament and was "discovered" by a poker promoter, who ran the World Series of Poker and other tournaments at the time. He invited Thor to Las Vegas, and since he held the Scandinavian title, he earned a seat at the World Series of Poker. "That's how I got started," says Thor.

After a few more tournament wins, Thor eventually married a Norwegian-born American after moving to Los Angeles. It was there where he met controversial sex-magazine publisher Larry Flynt. "The same friends who invited me to come to America, also invited me to Larry Flynt's house to play high stakes poker," says Thor. "The first time I played there, I also played with Jerry Buss, the owner of the L.A. Lakers. This was the first time that Larry Flynt had played in 15 years."

Since that first game, Thor has become good friends with Flynt who sometimes backs him in high stakes cash games. After playing regularly in Flynt's home game for several years, Thor accepted Flynt's invitation to work as a poker host at Hustler Casino. Thor is still a regular at Hustler's poker tables, and says it's his favorite venue, partly because it's in his own backyard.

After years of playing cash games, Thor says he's returning to tournament play: "The tournaments have grown so large, I can't afford not to play." He also can't afford to lose any more money away from the poker table. "I've gone broke many times," he admits. "I can go to the racetrack and lose $100,000 in a night if I have it," he says. "I'm getting a little better at the horse races now because I'm a little older and wiser. I've been broke so many times, but I'm better. I still gamble away a couple hundred thousand every year."

That doesn't seem to worry him much. "I can always recover by playing poker," he says. "I might be bad at many things when it comes to gambling, but when it comes to poker, I'm good."

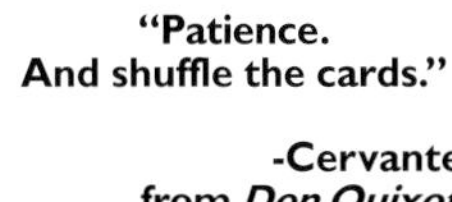

Major Poker Accomplishments

2004, First place, LA Poker Classic, Limit Hold'em

2002, First place, WSOP, Ace to Five Draw Lowball

2001, First place, LA Poker Classic, Limit Hold'em

2000, Second place, WSOP, Limit Omaha

1998, First place, Grand Prix de Paris, No Limit Hold'em

Jennifer Harman 

"For me, poker is about learning, and there is still so much to learn."

Personal Notes

- **Born in Reno, Nevada**
- **Graduate of the University of Reno**
- **Plays regularly in the biggest side action games in the world**
- **Professional poker player**
- **Resides in Reno, Nevada**

When Jennifer Harman Traniello watched her parents play cards in their home poker games when she was a girl, she says her eyes were as big as baseballs. "All I could think about," she remembers, "was how much I wanted to play too." Her parents didn't let her play, but they did let her stay up all night and watch.

Watching may be one key to Jennifer's success at the table. In 2000 she won her first gold bracelet at the World Series of Poker. Oddly, she took that first place win in a poker event that she'd never played before in her life: Deuce to Seven No-Limit. "I had watched this game many times and was intrigued by it. I decided to play it for the first time in this tournament. I got a few lessons from a poker pro before the tournament started and dove right in." Five o'clock the next morning Jennifer was wearing her first gold bracelet.

The win was not surprising to her friend and colleague, Daniel Negreanu who considers her "without a doubt the best female poker player on the planet," He is careful to add though that calling her the best female player is just not enough. "She is also one of the best all-around players in the world–period!" Hardly faint praise!

Yet Jennifer considers herself a die-hard side game player. "I've been a live action player all my life," she says. "Tournaments are different than live action. It's like playing a totally different poker game. I want to learn everything there is to learn about it."

She admits that the World Poker Tour has sharpened her interest in tournaments. "They've brought poker into the mainstream. So many people play poker, even if it's only on their kitchen table; so being able to watch it on television is fun and exciting." Of course, not quite as fun and exciting for Jennifer as *playing* poker—her life and profession. "For me, poker is about learning, and there is still so much to learn."

"Be patient, watch, listen and learn."

-Jennifer Harman

Learning something new every day is one of the reasons that Jennifer thinks she will never grow tired of playing poker. "I enjoy the challenge of playing with the best. It's a constant learning experience," she admits. "I make mistakes, but as long as I learn something from those mistakes, they can actually be good for me."

Jennifer landed at the final table of the World Poker Tour's Aruba tournament in 2002 and although she didn't win the tournament, she was one of the last two pros to be eliminated. Her play was, as usual, fiercely competitive. This same competitive edge recently won her the largest non-tournament cash game pot at a major casino—$1.7 million dollars!

Much is made of the fact that Jennifer is only 5'2" tall and is slight in build—a presence that is hardly intimidating—until you play against her. And she is not afraid to use this fact to her advantage. Jennifer Harman is not easy prey and is more likely to be on the attack than to be the one being targeted. Neither does she care what these men think of her. "I couldn't care less if my opponents don't respect my play. In fact, that could only help me in the long run."

Poker fans are sure to see a lot more of Jennifer Harman in televised tournament poker, but don't expect her to give up her high-stakes poker games yet. "If I ever got to a point where I didn't like playing anymore, I don't think I would play. I don't think that'll ever happen, though."

Major Poker Accomplishments

2003, Second place, WPT Ultimate Bet Championship, No Limit Hold'em, Pro Division

2002, First place, WSOP, Limit Hold'em

2000, First place, WSOP, Deuce to Seven Draw

Dan Harrington 

"You don't win 100% of the time. You do something adequate. You stay in the game, and you keep playing. You're going to win eventually."

Personal Notes

Born in Cambridge, Massachusetts, 1945

Graduate of Suffolk University, Boston

Former attorney, 1971-1980

1971 Massachusetts State Chess Champion

1980 Champion of the World Cup of Backgammon

Resides in Santa Monica, California

Dan Harrington has been described as "a big, ruddy Irishman with a no-nonsense Boston accent, confident of character, with a sharp intellect, deft strategy and relentless execution." At age 26 Dan became the Massachusetts State Chess Champion. At age 35 he won the World Cup in Backgammon. Once he hit age 50 he tackled the main event at the World Series of Poker to become the world heavyweight champion of tournament poker. Consequently, in the world of gaming, Dan is regarded as a triple crown winner.

He's also an astute businessman. In his early years, after graduating from Boston's Suffolk College—in between his chess and backgammon championships—Dan worked as a Massachusetts bankruptcy attorney. Later he became part of the small "Mission Impossible" team that relied on MIT-derived mathematical formulas to generate calculations on odds at winning roulette. The team played the game with a forty percent edge on each spin, that is, until they were caught by Atlantic City's Sands Casino.

When Dan first started playing poker, he remembers playing with a couple of other Harvard students: Bill Gates and Paul Allen. Those fellows went their way and Dan went his, eventually moving to California and learning the more serious games such as Texas Hold'em. But his business concerns never took a backseat to his poker play.

At present, his primary business interest is a company called Anchor Loan, which he runs with former poker pros Jeff Lipman and Steve Pollock. "I only hire former poker pros," he jests (though it's true), "and out of the 2500 loans that we've handled, no investors have ever lost any money."

Dan draws a lot of parallels between poker and the business world. As one who has also played the stock market and invested in real estate, he understands that they are all "percentage games"—"You don't win 100% of the time. You do something adequate. You stay in the game, and you keep playing. You're going to win eventually."

In recent years the former world poker champion has spent more time in the business world than at the poker tables. But in 2003, the advent of the World Poker Tour got him interested in playing tournaments again. That resulted in a third place win—and big money—in the 2003 World Series of Poker.

"Don't focus on the surrounding circumstances. Focus on the problems that you face when you're sitting at the table."

-Dan Harrington

But is it really the big money that motivates Dan? You bet it is! When he got down to heads up play against Howard Goldfarb in the 1995 WSOP, the tournament director said to him, "I knew you were going to win. Because when we brought out the $1 million and we brought out the gold bracelet, your opponent went up and looked at the gold bracelet and you fondled the $1 million." Dan admits, "a lot of people are there for the glory. I'm there for the money. You can keep the glory."

Even though he may be "there for the money," Dan says he doesn't get caught up in the throes of fear or greed. "I have more control than 99.9% of the people," says Dan. This is something that Dan considers to be key to winning at the game. He keeps his head under the stress of making what he knows is basically a business decision. "To Dan it is self-evident that a player must have the discipline to "keep [his] losses down" and not let these inevitable losses affect his play. He sees poker (and his related dealings in stocks and real estate) as a matter of character. "Character makes the whole difference," muses Dan.

What does Dan hope for in the future? "To borrow a line from Woody Allen," he says, "I don't want to become immortal through my work, I want to become immortal through not dying."

Major Poker Accomplishments

2004, Fourth place, WSOP, No Limit Hold'em Championship

2003, Third place, WSOP, No Limit Hold'em Championship

1996, First place, Four Queens Poker Classic, No Limit Hold'em Championship

1995, first place, WSOP, No Limit Hold'em Championship

1995, First place, WSOP, No Limit Hold'em event

Brian Haveson 

"I'm willing to take risks. A lot of players don't like to see me come to the table because they don't want to put all their chips at risk."

Personal Notes

- **Born in Trenton, N.J., 1964**
- **Studied Aerospace Engineering at University of Maryland**
- **Graduate degree in business from Purdue**
- **Former partner in NutriSystem**
- **Married with three children**
- **Resides in Newtown, Pennsylvania**

"I was very aggressive in business," says former executive Brian Haveson. "A lot of people who knew me in business would say I am one of the most aggressive businessmen they've run across." That aggressiveness, he adds, translated into success. In 2003, Brian sold off his portion in NutriSystem for seven figures. "I cashed out big!"

Now he considers himself a professional poker player. "I'm not doing anything else," he says. "I play all the big events." Brian's business aggressiveness carries over directly to the poker table. "I'm an aggressive player," he says. "In no-limit events I'm looking to move all my chips in against someone else in a 50-50 situation."

Brian remembers challenging Daniel Negreanu in just that way at the Sands tournament in 2003. "Two hands in a row I had Ace-King and he had a high pocket pair. So we put all our chips in. I'm willing to take risks. A lot of players don't like to see me come to the table because they don't want to put all their chips at risk. My feeling is that when the blinds are going up, I want to have the chips."

When asked whether his skills in business aid him in playing poker he says he believes the reverse is true: "I think the skills that I learned in poker helped me in business more than the other way around. Negotiating, bluffing, knowing when someone might come down in price on a

contract in business; being able to read people at the [poker] table and seeing that guy across the board room table—it's all remarkably similar." Brian also points out that he's been playing poker a lot longer than he's been in the business world. "I've been playing poker—literally—since I was three years old."

"When you get short-stacked in tournament poker, don't let the blinds and antes take you out of contention. You need to pick a hand and put your chips at risk, even if it's with a marginal hand."

-Brian Haveson

He says his parents were always gamblers, though they were never as good at gambling as he was. Consequently, they are "pretty excited" about their son's new career path.

Brian says he has a distinct advantage at the poker table on the tournament circuit: He's set for life financially, and he doesn't have the worry of having to win in order to pay the bills. "A lot of the guys who you think are great poker players—they are good players—but they're broke. They're playing for someone else. They're called horses. Someone else is putting up the money for them. I don't do that. I play for myself. I'm not worried about going broke because I sold my business for a lot of money."

Brian plays tournament poker purely for the sport of it. He loves the competitive aspect, something he thrived on in business and in sports before that. "One of my friends asked me what it is I like about playing poker," Brian remembers, "and I said, it's the same feeling you had when you were playing high school basketball; it's that same competitive accomplishment."

Brian says his aggressive style and his acute sense of competitiveness pays off for him in tournament poker, but he's much less aggressive when playing cash games. Consequently it's tournament poker that keeps him playing, and he loves to go heads up with other aggressive players like Phil Hellmuth, Mark Seif and Daniel Negreanu—guys who are willing to take risks.

Although aggressive in most situations, Brian never used to be very aggressive about telling friends exactly where he was going off to when he left town. "I wouldn't tell anyone I was leaving to play a poker tournament; I'd just say I was going on vacation," he explains. "But now I can tell everyone because poker's gone mainstream. No one thinks I'm a degenerate. Now when I tell people they are actually envious. They say, 'Oh, I want that kind of life.'"

Major Poker Accomplishments

2004, Ninth place, WSOP, No Limit Hold'em event

2003, Second place, Showdown at the Sands, No Limit Hold'em Championship

2003, Sixth place, WPT World Poker Finals, No Limit Hold'em Championship

Phil Hellmuth

"One thing you can't argue is that I'm the man in the public's eye in poker right now. They've heard stories about me for years and years."

Personal Notes

Born in Madison, Wisconsin, 1964

Married with two children

Author of *Playing Poker With the Pros*

Youngest player ever to win a World Series of Poker Championship bracelet

Known as the "Poker Brat"

Resides in Palo Alto, California

Phil Hellmuth is one of the most recognizable faces in the poker world today. Known as the "Poker Brat," Phil compares his much-deserved reputation to that of tennis's John McEnroe. "I hate losing, and I hate bad calls," he says, "just like John McEnroe. I'm a lot like him, but the difference is that McEnroe retired at 33. He never had a chance to grow up more." Phil, on the other hand, believes that he's matured over the past several years. "The brattish stuff is getting less and less," he contends.

The advent of televised final tables, however, hasn't done his image much good. "I might be a brat just one time during that whole tournament, but that's what's going to be played on TV. Most of the time when I'm at the table I'm fun to be with, although if someone's trying to push my buttons, I can get a little unpleasant with them. At the same time, if I berate someone, I always apologize. I'm a man. I know when I'm wrong. I know what my faults are," he says, adding that in the past 20 years of playing poker he's only got into one fistfight at the table with a fellow poker player.

Phil was introduced to poker when he was a student at the University of Wisconsin. During a pickup basketball game one winter evening, a fellow player mentioned that he was heading out to play poker later that night. Phil asked if he could come along. "I won a little bit that first time and won a little the second time," he remembers, "but the third time I got lucky and won $420, which was huge for those games."

Phil took his winnings down to the registrar's office to pay his tuition bill that semester, which meant that he returned to the poker game next time with empty pockets. "I had to borrow $100," Phil remembers. "He took my driver's license as collateral, and I lost all the money at the table." This time Phil returned to the registrar's office to drop all of his classes, and took a temporary job. But after he received his first paycheck, he went back to the poker table—this time he won and was able to return to school the next semester with more than $5,000 to his name.

But the night he won $6,500 he returned to the registrar's office once again to drop all of his classes—this time for good. He had decided that he would go to Las Vegas to continue his poker playing career. The reaction he received from his mother and father was less than supportive. "You can imagine what my father said when I told him that I was dropping out of school to play poker."

Phil's father, however, eventually warmed up to the idea of his son being a world-class poker champion. But, he says, "until my first World Series win, there was always some kind of pressure on me to return to school."

"In the right situation, say, when you have Jacks and the flop is 2-6-K, raise on the flop when it's cheap; and use that information later."

-Phil Hellmuth from Phil's *Poker Tip of the Week*

When Phil was 24 and already a financial success from his poker earnings, he approached his father with a proposal. "I asked him where in the world he'd like to go, and told him I'd take him there. I was hoping he'd say New Zealand or Australia. I had already flown my mother and my siblings to places of their choice, and now it was his turn." His father surprised Phil by saying that he wanted to join his son in Las Vegas to watch the World Series of Poker that year. "He asked me if I was going to win," remembers Phil, "and I said yes, I'm going to win the big one."

This was 1989. "I kept telling everyone that year I was going to win the World Series," he says. And win it he did—the youngest player ever to capture a World Series championship title. "Winning the World Series is every poker player's dream," he explains. "And when I beat Johnny Chan my hands went up in the air, and I was filled with pure joy." Phil says he looked around for his father. "He came running up the aisle and was stopped by the security guards because there was a million dollars in cash laying on the poker table. I told them to let him through, and I still remember hugging my dad right then and there."

Major Poker Accomplishments

Winner of nine WSOP gold bracelets

2001, First place, Austrian Masters, No Limit Hold'em Championship

1995, Hall of Fame Big One Championship

1989, First place, WSOP, No Limit Hold'em Championship

Juha Helppi 

"I have no fear."

Personal Notes

Born in Turku, Finland, 1977

Former casino dealer

World-class paintball player

Former soccer player

Online poker player

Resides in Littoinen, Finland

Known as "the kid with the purple glasses," Finland's Juha Helppi is one of the youngest and most formidable new players on the world poker circuit today. He made his world debut by winning the Ultimate Poker Classic in Aruba in 2002, taking first place in the amateur competition, and then going on to beat Phil Gordon (the winner of UltimateBet's pro tournament) in heads-up play.

Wearing shades that wrap around his face, the 26-year-old Juha (pronounced *you-haw*) appears as a sort of Scandinavian "Terminator," although he states emphatically that he has no ambition to ever run for governor of California. His motto at the poker table: "I have no fear."

Juha started playing poker when he was 21 years old. "When I was working as a casino dealer, my friends introduced me to all the different poker games and showed me that I could play online." He started small by making a deposit of $250 to Paradise Poker's online site and built up from there. But it was the book *Hold'em Poker for Advanced Players* that made him into a winner, he says. "Every year online, I've been winning bigger than the year previous." The first live tournaments he played were in Tallinn, the capital city of Estonia, across the Baltic Sea from Finland. "They were small," he says. "But I won."

Juha attributes his success at the poker table to his intensely competitive nature. "I have been playing all kinds of games all my life—like sports," he says. For 11 years he was a star on the soccer field, and he's played paintball (the only team sport in the world played with guns and goggles) for the past decade in Finland's National League. As team captain he led his paintballers to national victory last year.

Juha sees plenty of similarities between paintballing and poker playing: "Paintball is a game where we play seven against seven. As captain, I have to build a strategy around my team in order to know which way to break through. The same is true in poker. You play different ways at different moments, using different strategies. You have to know your opponents in both games."

> **"Cards are war, in disguise of a sport."**
>
> **-Charles Lamb**

Juha's first big tournament was on the beach in Aruba. "A lot of people were rooting for me there," he remembers, "because I was regarded as the underdog and the amateur. At that time I hadn't won anything big yet."

Over the past year, Juha has made a good living at poker playing, traveling for about four months of the year outside of Finland. When he first hit the tournament trail he thought the professional players he'd be up against would be much more challenging than they have been for him. This was a pleasant surprise. "They weren't nearly as good as I thought they would be," he says. "I can do pretty well in any game, no matter who I'm up against."

When Juha first started traveling to play poker, his girlfriend of nine years was a bit skeptical. "Now that I've been winning, she's OK with it," he says, "and she even travels with me some of the time." But not everyone back in Finland has been quite so understanding of his chosen profession. "People who understand how good I play poker think it's great that I travel to tournaments all over the world to play," he explains, "but my older relatives don't understand. They think it's all about luck, that there's no skill involved. Even my mother has told me that I should quit poker now while I'm ahead because I've won so much that I couldn't possibly win anymore—that my luck is running out."

When Juha meets people he's still reluctant to talk about his poker playing. "I tell them that I'm a dealer and that I play poker as a hobby," he says. Nevertheless, poker is no hobby for this Finn. It's an occupation that Juha Helppi fully intends to pursue. His parting words: "I'll be back."

Major Poker Accomplishments

2004, Fourth place, World Poker Open, No Limit Hold'em event

2003, Fourth place, WSOP, No Limit Hold'em event

2003, Fourth place, WPT Battle of Champions

2002, First place, WPT UltimateBet No Limit Hold'em Championship

2002, Fourth place, Helsinki Freezeout, Pot Limit Omaha

Randy Holland  

"I wouldn't be playing poker for a living if I didn't think that skill mattered."

Personal Notes

Born in Calgary, Alberta, 1951

Married with two children

Graduate of California State, Fullerton

Former attorney

Resides in Los Angeles, California

Randy Holland was introduced to casino poker quite by happenstance. When he was a practicing attorney living in Florida, he traveled to Las Vegas for a legal convention. "I didn't have a lot to do at the convention," he says, "so I played poker in the casino card room." Although Randy had played poker in home games for years, he was surprised that he was able to sit down at a casino and win, which is what he did that first time.

What really got him hooked on poker-playing, however, was the opening of casinos in Biloxi, Mississippi. That was a short drive for Randy, who was living and working in Tallahassee at the time. "I started going over there on the weekends," he says, "and I was very lucky in all those first trips." Randy started off playing low-limit games, but after his consistent wins, he moved up in stakes quite rapidly. "I don't think poker is rocket science," he comments. "I read how-to books, and I took the game seriously."

Randy had been working in his Tallahassee law office for seven years when he began to feel restless. "I was tired of doing the same thing," he says of his work as an attorney. "It was time for a change." Since Randy was doing well at the Biloxi poker tables, he decided to take a year off of work to play full-time. That one year has turned into more than a decade now. Still single, Randy spent the first year of his poker sabbatical playing in tournaments in Europe and on poker cruises throughout the Caribbean. He still recalls the delight of that first year as a rookie pro: "I was very enthusiastic. I was studying. I was focused, and I was really into it."

Randy was introduced to Laurene, his future wife, on the dance floor at Commerce Casino in Los Angeles. "We've been married now for more than five years," he says, "and the poker playing lifestyle works out for both of us. We can go on cruises. We can travel, and do different things, and it's great to have a companion." Although Laurene had never played poker before they married, she eventually started to play the game herself on those trips. "I try to get her not to take poker too seriously," he says, "but she does pretty well."

"In tournament poker always be mindful that you are walking a tightrope between aggressiveness and patience."

-Randy Holland

After ten years on the road playing the pro-circuit, Randy says the game has become a bit of a grind for him. "Poker has definitely lost a lot of its excitement for me over the years," he laments. "There's a lot of sitting around in playing poker. I think it's going to be hard for anybody to say it's not going to be a little bit of grind after ten years. For me, it's become a little more like a job than I would like it to be."

Even so, Randy says he's not about to return to a 9 to 5 job. "I can't imagine where I'd be able to make the same kind of income right now." The current poker explosion, however, has boosted Randy's enthusiasm in recent years. The infusion of new people and new money is refreshing, he says. "In L.A. you might have 400 or 500 people show up to play a $200 buy-in tournament," he observes, "whereas in years past there would be no more than a hundred players, and I would know virtually every one."

He's seeing a lot of new faces lately, and he attributes that primarily to the fact that televised poker has popularized the sport. "A lot of these new people probably didn't even realize that there was such a thing as professional poker players," he says. But TV poker not only brings new blood to the table, Randy observes. It also generates a lot of misconceptions about the game. For Randy, that's both good and bad.

For a professional poker player, there's more opportunity now in tournament play, not the least of which is bigger prize pools. Randy says that's good, but adds: "My odds of winning are going to be much lower now on account of the sheer number of people I need to beat. It's probably going to give me bigger swings—the ups and downs of the game." Nevertheless, Randy stresses that, in the long run, skill is still very important. "I wouldn't be playing poker for a living if I didn't think that skill mattered," he says.

Major Poker Accomplishments

2003, First place, LA Poker Classic, Limit Hold'em

2002, First Place, LA Poker Classic, Limit Hold'em

2002, Second place, WSOP, Limit Omaha

2001, First place, Legends of Poker, No Limit Hold'em event

2000, First place, WSOP, Seven Card Stud Split

1998, Legends of Poker, Overall Points Champion

1996, First place, WSOP, Seven Card Razz

Phil Ivey

"Tiger Woods is the best in his game; I'm not there yet."

Personal Notes

Born in California, 1976

Known as the "Tiger Woods of Poker"

Tied for the record of WSOP bracelets (3) won in one year

Likes to push his chips in

Resides in Atlantic City, New Jersey

California native Phil Ivey is arguably the fastest rising star in the professional poker scene today. He was just 26 years old in 2002 when he took home three gold bracelets from the World Series of Poker, tying the record held by Phil Hellmuth and Ted Forrest. Making his home now in Atlantic City, New Jersey, Phil is commonly referred to as the "Tiger Woods of Poker" for his looks, style and charisma—and, course, because of his incredible success in the game.

Typically attired in basketball jerseys at the table, Phil has a reputation of moving his chips in. He's not one to sit back and let the blinds eat away at his stack. That sometimes helps him steam roll right over his opponents. Yet at other times his impetuousness to play gets him into trouble, sometimes through no fault of his own.

Much has been made of the fact that for two straight years Phil suffered a bad beat in the main event at the World Series of Poker. After already earning a whopping three bracelets in 2002, Phil went up against an English bloke called John Shipley in the final No Limit Hold'em tournament. The two competitors saw a flop of A-3-x before they both put in $130,000 in chips each, Shipley going all-in. Phil showed pocket threes, giving him three of a kind. John turned over A-K for a pair of aces, giving Phil an incredible advantage. The turn, produced another ace, which meant that Shipley was still trailing behind Phil's full-house. The river, however, produced Shipley's dream card: the final ace. Phil never recovered and finished 23rd in the big one.

"I've always had confidence, but I never let my ego get to the point that I think I'm the superstar, because I know that ego has destroyed many a poker career."

-Jim Boyd

The next year Phil was one spot away from making the final table when he went head-to head with a virtual unknown by the name of Chris Moneymaker. Phil was holding a pair of pocket nines while Chris held an A-Q combo. Two queens on the flop gave Chris trips, but Phil stayed in the hand to play. The turn produced a nine giving Phil a nice full house. Chris Moneymaker pushes in $200,000 and Phil goes all-in. Just like the year before, Phil's opponent gets his dream card on the river. An ace sends Phil Ivey packing.

But bad beats like these haven't slowed Phil. He continues to slam dunk his opponents on his way to becoming one of the all-time best in the world of tournament poker.

There are those who feel the comparison of Phil Ivey to Tiger Woods is unfair—to Phil, that is. They see him not as the "Tiger Woods of poker," but as the "Phil Ivey of poker." His arrival on the poker scene as such a tough player at a relatively young age puts him in a class by himself. His looks, demeanor and style create a charisma that fosters a deep admiration and fierce loyalty from his fans. And considering how he compares himself to Tiger Woods, "Tiger Woods is the best in his game; I'm not there yet," you can add modesty to his other qualities.

Phil's play is consistent and steady, important attributes for a winner. His 2002 WSOP wins are evidence of these qualities. He won his three gold bracelets in three different events—S.H.O.E. , Seven Card Stud Hi-Lo Split, and the Seven Card Stud event; then he followed that feat with a 10th place finish at the 2003 WSOP main event.

Phil shuns the inevitable publicity that comes from being a world-class poker player. But he can't stop the growing respect that he engenders from both young, aspiring players and poker professionals. "Phil Ivey is the best up-and-coming player on [the World Poker] tour by far. He looks fierce and focused at any table;" and "watching Phil Ivey is a learning experience. . . he is . . . totally aware of all the psychology and head games at the hold'em table" are just a few of the thoughts from his fans. And the way Phil is playing, the comments can only get better and better. Another fan sums it up well. "Ivey is hot. There's nothing more to say."

Major Poker Accomplishments

2004, First place, Poker Championship at Turning Stone, No Limit Hold'em

2003, Third place, WPT Five star World Poker Classic, No Limit Hold'em Championship

2003, Tenth place, WSOP, No Limit Hold'em Championship

2003, Second place, WPT World Poker Open, No Limit Hold'em Championship

2002, WSOP, Winner of three gold bracelets

2002, Fourth place, WPT World Poker Finals, No Limit Hold'em Championship

2000, First place, WSOP, Pot Limit Omaha

Kenna James

"Poker is a temptation that can absorb you and really take up your life if you don't have other outlets."

Personal Notes

- **Born in Chicago, Illinois, 1963**
- **Graduate of Michigan School of Arts**
- **Former actor**
- **Newly wedded to poker pro Marcia Wagner**
- **Helped run Russia's first poker tournament**
- **Resides in Downey, California**

Poker playing and acting are probably two of the most difficult ways to make a living. "Only the top five percent in each profession make a decent living," says Kenna James, who's had a taste of the trials and tribulations of both. He started out as a teen actor studying on scholarship at the prestigious Michigan School of Arts, followed by several years of stage acting in regional theaters.

When the time came to decide between an acting career on the stage in New York or in film and television in Hollywood, he decided to make the move to Southern California. "I ended up doing some soap operas," he says. "and had some minor roles in films. I did one with Dan Haggerty and Troy Donahue, and another that didn't get released. It was tough going."

To make ends meet, Kenna took a job dealing cards at Hollywood Park Casino. He moved up through the casino ranks quickly, soon becoming a tournament director. "That's when I first got into poker," he says. That was in 1995. At that point Kenna had to make another career decision. He'd pretty much resigned himself to leave acting behind, but now he had to decide whether to stay at the casino where he says he could be promoted to a position such as floor manager. "It's more work and less exciting than playing," he comments of his casino job, so he decided to give poker playing a professional go.

"Poker is a good fit for my personality," says Kenna, who is known for his friendly and easygoing personality. His training as an actor, he says, was a double-edged sword. "My skills tend to help me at the table because I can understand the feelings of different people," he explains. "But my acting skills also can work against me because I learned to be so in tune with my emotions. That means things would effect me emotionally. As an actor that's important. In poker, if you are playing at a certain level it's going to effect you emotionally, and those emotions come out. I can sometimes be easily read or go on tilt. And when I'm running good I can get too "high."

Kenna found out quickly that the poker world is no less daunting than the world of Hollywood. Despite the fact that he has been able to travel the world, playing in tournaments in Australia, Europe, North America, and the Caribbean, he has the constant worry of going broke in this business. "I've done it two or three times a year over the past four years," he admits. "Last year I was fortunate that I didn't. The year before that I went broke three times."

"If you've dug yourself into a hole . . . STOP DIGGING!"

-Kenna James

Kenna likens his poker playing to a business venture. "It's like someone making a movie," he says. "You borrow money and charge up the credit cards to finance your career and try to recover, but some people never recover. That's the tragedy of the business."

When Kenna first started playing poker he had another dilemma—a moral one. He didn't like the idea of "taking" someone else's money. When he was playing in the lower limit games he had to struggle with the reality that he was at the table with people who were gambling with their rent money or their welfare checks. "I couldn't get past the guilt of taking that money from them; I was capitalizing on their vice." When Kenna began playing with the pros, he said his concerns evaporated. He was now playing with big boys who were responsible for themselves. "I also came to realize that I wasn't really playing against the other people at the table, I was playing a game against myself. Poker is actually a game about my own character. If I make myself a better person, I make myself a better poker player."

One of the brightest spots of the poker circuit for Kenna is seeing the sights of other cultures. He's helped organize a poker tournament in Moscow, for example, where he trained the Russians to deal hold'em. After taking third place in the $10,000 buy-in No Limit Hold'em tournament in Melbourne in January 2004 he stayed on in Australia for a bit of kayaking and whale watching. His favorite venue, however, is Amsterdam. "We play poker there until 4 in the morning when the casino closes, and then get up at 11, go have breakfast along the canal and look out over the flowerpots. There's balance there," he explains. "It helps when there's not poker 24 hours a day. The challenge is to have balance in my life with everything, especially poker. Poker is a temptation that can absorb you and really take up your life if you don't have other outlets."

Major Poker Accomplishments

2004, First place, California State Poker Championship, No Limit Hold'em Shootout

2004, Third place, Crown Australian Poker Championship, No Limit Hold'em event

2003, First place, Five Diamond World Poker Classic, Limit Hold'em

2003, First place, Four Queens Poker Classic, No Limit Hold'em event

2003, First place, Grand Slam of Poker, No Limit Hold'em event

Randy Jensen

"I can build up chips like nobody's business. My problem is keeping hold of them."

Personal Notes

- **Born in Casper, Wyoming, 1970**
- **Expelled from two colleges**
- **Married with two children**
- **Real estate broker**
- **Considers himself a "semi-pro" poker player**
- **Resides in Fort Collins, Colorado**

Randy Jensen says he has literally been playing poker since he was just a babe of five years old. By the time he got to junior high school, he was running games—in the classroom! "I'd push the seats together," he remembers, "and we'd play." By the time he entered college at Weaver State in Utah, he was regularly playing poker and for several years he'd already been helping his mother with her real estate business.

The night before his first day of classes at college, Randy drove 300 miles to Wendover, Nevada to play poker. "I missed my first day of school," he remembers. During his college years he says he won some and lost some—"probably breaking even." Oddly enough, Randy found himself winning at blackjack simply by "dumb luck." It was a game of billiards, however, that ended Randy's college career at Weaver State. Randy beat a classmate at the pool table, but when the loser decided he wasn't going to pay up on his bet, Randy's friends egged him on, and the night ended in a fight. "I'm just a little guy, but I kicked the hell out of him," says Randy. The next day he found that he was expelled.

He went on to the University of Boulder, where he allowed a friend of his—not a student there—to live in his dorm room and eat at the student cafeteria, all for free. "We got away with it the whole time, until the end of the year," he says. "When we were found out, they told me I had to pay my friend's room and board for the year or leave." That was the last college that would give him the boot. "Between poker and real estate, I was already making more money on my own than I would with a degree, so I decided to call it quits on college."

From there he moved on to Fort Collins, Colorado where he got involved in a private poker club. "That was my first experience with Pot Limit Hold'em," he says, "and Bill Duarte taught me how to play, although I play nothing like him. I play crazy, which makes a lot of players think I'm terrible."

"Money . . . M-O-N-E-Y. That's how you measure success. One dollar at a time. One chip at a time. That's how you keep score."

-Stu Ungar

After Randy broke up with a girlfriend in 1997, he decided he'd go to Vegas for a change of scenery and a challenge. Three days after arriving, he won $4,000 and started his bankroll. He went on to California, where he ran his bankroll up to $30,000 in just another two days in a $10-$20 pot-limit Omaha game. "I took all that money, hopped on a plane for the Four Queens in Vegas, and was broke within an hour of playing my first live game there. I was busted by O'Neil Longsen. I didn't even have enough money to get back to San Diego, where I'd left my truck. I borrowed $100 and was on my way.

In 2000 Randy started in on the tournament circuit. "I won a lot of the little tournaments," he says, but it wasn't until 2001 in Tunica that he won his first large tournament, a $500 limit hold'em, and he made four other final tables in that tournament. "I can look back at every tournament I lost," he says, "Practically every time I was up huge and then got busted. I can build chips like nobody's business. My problem is keeping hold of them."

Randy says he's fortunate to be married to a wonderful woman who believes in his poker playing abilities, and he credits her for his biggest win to date. For the past couple of years, Randy has limited himself to a $100,000 bankroll for each calendar year. The first tournament he played in 2004 was Binion's World Poker Open in Tunica, Mississippi in January. He lost his entire bankroll in the first ten days there. "I couldn't make a hand hold up," he remembers.

Randy flew back home, telling his wife he went bust, but she encouraged him to take another $20,000 back to Tunica so he could play in the WPT's $10,000 buy-in event. "She told me I couldn't lose it all in ten days and quit playing poker for the rest of the year." So back to Tunica Randy flew, knowing that he'd have to finish fifth in the big event just to break even.

"I was planning to quit poker at that point. I figured if I lost my bankroll that quick it meant I wasn't supposed to play." As it happens, Randy Jensen finished second in the big event, losing heads-up to Barry Greenstein. He returned to his wife with over $600,000. "My nickname used to be 'the minnow' because I got so little respect, but now it's 'the Dream Crusher,' because of my habit of crushing the pipe dreams poker players have at tournaments."

Major Poker Accomplishments

2004, Second place, WPT World Poker Open, No Limit Hold'em Championship

2003, Second place, Legends of Poker, Limit Hold'em

2002, First place, World Poker Open, Limit Hold'em

Chip Jett

"If I have two different things to do in the same day, that freaks me out. Poker is my total comfort zone, and it's there that I can really focus. For me, poker just happens."

Personal Notes

Born in Scottsdale, Arizona, 1974

Married with one daughter

Former lifeguard

Former poker dealer

Sometimes mistaken for Layne Flack

Resides in Las Vegas

One of the most common questions Chip Jett gets is about his name: Is it real? Or is it a poker *nom de plume*? "My name is unrelated to poker," he has to explain. "It's my real name. I was born 'Charles,' but I was 'Chip' even before I got out of the hospital."

Chip has considered himself a professional poker-player since age 18. "I mean from that time on I was earning at least eighty percent of my income from the poker table," he explains. He was working as a life guard at a pool in Arizona the summer after he graduated from high school when he started to play poker recreationally. That's also when he discovered how much more poker dealers were making than life guards. In a matter of weeks he found himself working as a professional dealer at a casino on an Indian reservation in Arizona."

As a dealer, I was playing more than I was dealing," he admits. "For two of the three years, I dealt no more than twenty [days] *per year* total. Most of the time I didn't even bring my dealer's clothes to work."

By the time he was 21, old enough to travel and play, Chip had three years of experience. At 21, he did start to travel to various venues, especially to Las Vegas, to play poker, but he didn't take it on as a full-time occupation until 2000. That's when Chip decided to leave cash games behind and to concentrate exclusively on tournament play. Now he plays somewhere around 300 tournaments a year, about as many as is humanly possible.

When Chip entered the poker-playing profession as a teen, his parents had mixed reactions at best. When he was 19, he says he paid cash for a new home. "When I look back on that," he says, "I probably shouldn't have done it because it took a big chunk out of my bankroll. One of the main reasons I did it was because I wanted my family to see that I was solid, that I was stable in what I was doing. They had the misconception that I was going to be a professional slot machine player, and that I was going to go broke because I had no chance to win."

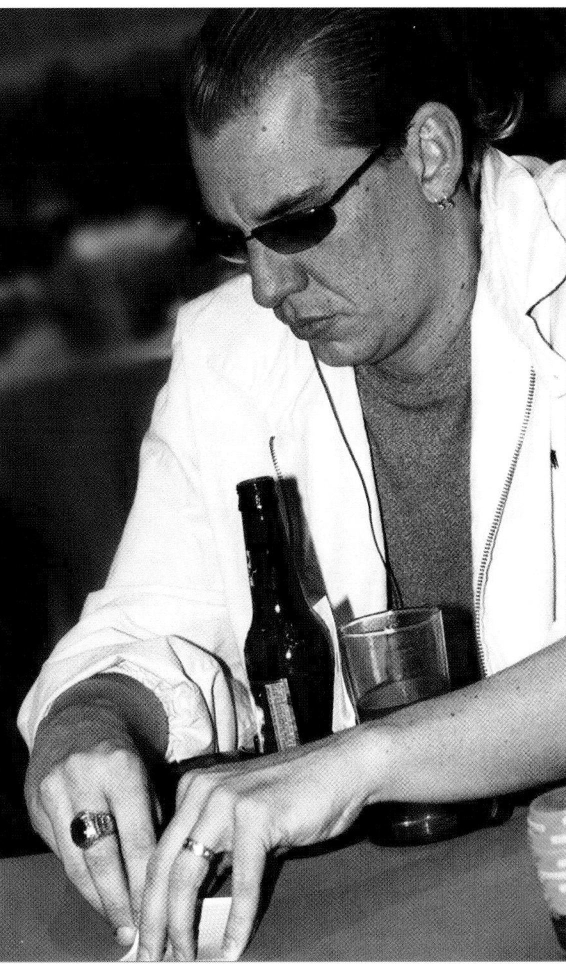

"Condition your opponents to react to situations in a certain way, then capitalize on it. When done correctly, it makes no-limit, no-problem."

-Chip Jett

At age 21, however, Chip once departed from his usually safe gambling habits. He flew up to Las Vegas to celebrate his birthday and blew half of his bankroll at the blackjack table. "I learned from that," he says. "I now have no desire to play any games other than poker. I don't bet. I don't play blackjack. I might find a way to blow my money, but it's certainly not going to be on gambling. There's plenty of other ways that are a lot more attractive."

Since Chip has become an all-star pro, his parents have changed their tune about their poker-playing son. "Now they tell all their friends when I'm going to be on TV; they must send out a hundred emails."

Chip's newfound television fame has given him a recognition-status in many places. "I still find it weird when someone wants my autograph," he says. "I'm recognized a lot more than I would have thought." Oddly, he adds, the first few times that he was recognized outside of a casino, it was not as Chip Jett but as Layne Flack. "They would say to me, 'oh, you're that poker guy. You're Layne Flack.' Layne has told me that people have mistaken him for me too. It's amazing what TV does."

In the past two years, his poker wins and TV appearances have attracted other interest. Many sponsors have approached Chip about being a spokesman for their products or services. "But I don't want to put my name behind something that's not right," he says. "I am not going to sell myself to just anybody who comes along. I'm interested in doing the right thing to maintain my own integrity and the integrity of the game."

Despite other opportunities that may arise for him, Chip says he wants to focus primarily on his poker playing. In that way, he says, he's single-minded. "If I have two different things to do in the same day, that freaks me out. Poker is my total comfort zone, and it's there that I can really focus. For me, poker just happens."

Major Poker Accomplishments

2003, Champion of the Year

2003, Fourth place, WPT Legends of Poker No Limit Hold'em Championship

2003, Second place, WPT Party Poker Million II, No Limit Hold'em Championship

2003, First place, California State No Limit Hold'em Poker Championship

2003, First place, World Poker Open, No Limit Hold'em event

2003, First place LA Poker Classic, H.O.E.

2001, Best All-Around Player, LA Poker Classic

Christer Johansson 

"My wife . . . likes to go with me as often as she can when I'm traveling and that is the best support I could ever have."

Personal Notes

Born in Sweden, 1970

Married with one daughter

Former electrician

Plays a lot of online poker

Runs a successful sports betting office in Sweden

Resides in Höllviken, Sweden

Chris Johansson was only ten years old when he realized that he may have a future in poker. The young Swede was playing poker with his father and some of his father's friends. They were playing 10 cent draw poker and his uncle tried to bluff him with a $50 raise. "I asked my father if I could borrow the money to call him," says Chris." His father replied, "Okay. [But] let this be a lesson to you." And a lesson it was—but not the kind that his father had imagined. Chris took home the monster pot with just a pair of Aces. Presumably his uncle was not amused!

Now Chris plays in more serious games; some live tournament action and some on the internet. And the pots he wins are "monsters" in the real sense of the word. His first tournament was in Vienna in 2000. He had more success there than he could have imagined by winning the opening event (Limit Hold'em), coming in fourth in the Pot-limit Hold'em event, making the Pot-limit Omaha final table, and capping it all off by winning the main event, the No-limit Hold'em four-day WSOP trial. "I had only played the Swedish Championships," says Chris, "and this trip proved to me that I really could compete against tougher international fields."

Chris credits his patience, courage and a good memory with helping him to be a top player. These traits, along with just trying to be himself as he plays seems to be an excellent formula for Chris. Superstition plays no part in his game and he doesn't consider his play to be unique in any way.

Chris admits that he enjoys the live tournament play more than he does playing online, though he has had great success at both. "Playing online is more of a grind and it's sometimes pretty boring," laments Chris. But since Chris subscribes to the "practice makes perfect" rule, he continues to play as often as he can. "You can't practice enough," Chris advises.

"Don't overplay your bankroll!"

-Chris Johansson

Chris's most well-known win to date has to be winning the WPT televised championship at the Aviation Club in Paris in 2003. On a WPT set that looked more like the back room of an elegant gentleman's club, Chris was facing other top European pros, Claude Cohen, Alain Hagege and Jacques Durand, as well as the United States' Allen Cunningham and Australia's trash-talking Tony G. It was a formidable lineup, fraught with perils, but Chris would see these poker aces fall one by one, as he played with a composed, deliberate demeanor.

When it got down to three-handed action, Chris began to show his stripes. He had lost quite a few chips in the hands before that, but, methodical thinker that he is, he was not about to let that get him down. Though he suffered a couple of big losses, he studied his opponents and went on the attack until he was heads-up against the daunting play of Claude Cohen.

The second-last hand they played crippled Claude Cohen leaving him with less than $30,000 in chips to Chris's $832,000. The following hand, Claude moved all-in with a 10-2. Chris called with K-2 in his hand. No ten came on the board and Chris Johansson was the WPT ACF No Limit Hold'em Champion.

With a wife who also plays poker, Chris finds that his professional and family life mesh well. In fact his wife Brigitta finished not too far behind her husband in the 2001 European WSOP four-day trial. "She has great patience with me playing," Chris states. "She also likes to go with me as often as she can when I'm traveling and that is the best support I could ever have."

Major Poker Accomplishments

2003, First place, WPT Euro Finals of Poker, No Limit Hold'em Championship

2003, Fifth place, WSOP, S.H.O.E.

2000, First place, European WSOP trial, No Limit Hold'em

Won over $1,000,000 in online poker tournaments

John Juanda  

"In poker, as long as you're willing to learn and adjust, you'll be alright."

Personal Notes

Born in Medan, North Sumatra, Indonesia, 1971

Graduate of Oklahoma State University

Has an MBA from Seattle University

Former award-winning salesman

Resides in Marina del Rey, California

It seems that John Juanda excels in more than just poker. From academics to sports, John has had incredible success. When he was in Junior High School, John was unbeaten in track events from 200 meters to 5000 meters. "For three years and in hundreds of practices and real competition, not once did I ever not finish first," says John with pride.

John admits that he is a very competitive fellow, and this itch for high level competition is what makes tournament poker so attractive to him. "I hate to lose," he says, "so every time I lose in a tournament, I go home and analyze my own play to find out what mistakes I made and make sure I don't do it again the next time." After doing this for awhile John says that he has pretty much identified any detrimental tendencies and the types of mistakes he makes most often. Then, "I try hard to avoid doing them."

It didn't take John long to make his place in poker. He finished 10th in his very first major tournament; in fact he almost made the final table, but played "way too aggressively" in his estimation. But John analyzed his play and was determined to learn from his mistake. In the very next tournament, he finished first! John says he learned a very important lesson that night. "In poker, as long as you are willing to learn and adjust, you'll be all right."

Learning from his mistakes was not the biggest obstacle John had to overcome in his poker career. Because he comes from a culture that does not view gambling as something respectable, he had virtually no moral support as he ventured into the poker arena. "I was afraid to tell even my mom about it," he recalls. "I didn't tell her until I'd had some major success and to my surprise, even though she would've preferred that I got a "real" job like everyone else, she could live with it. That lifted a big burden off my back."

John was not even introduced to poker until he made a plane

trip from Indonesia to the United States, "but I didn't play it seriously until around 1996 when I was doing my MBA," he admits.

"In big bet poker (pot limit and no limit) do not play a big pot unless you have a big hand."

-John Juanda

When asked to recall his most memorable poker experience, John modestly says that though he has many of his own, the most memorable moment he can recall was watching Erik Seidel beat Johnny Chan in their rematch at the World Series of Poker in a No Limit Hold'em game. "Up to that point, Erik had been taking a lot of heat about finishing second to Chan in their first match back when Erik was still a rookie," recollects John. "To see Erik, one of the nicest guys I have ever met in poker, get his rematch—and win—was just unbelievable. I remember thinking, 'maybe there is justice after all.'"

John credits persistence in the face of a short stack as one of his most successful tactics at the poker table. "A lot of top players that I know play extremely well when they have big stacks," observes John, "but not as well when they have small stacks. I think I play just as well when I have short stacks as I do when I have a big stack in a tournament."

Another talent essential to John as a poker player is his ability to deal with the players he faces. "First I observe them," he says, "and if I still don't find out what I want to find out, then I try to play a pot with them to see if I can bluff them, if they will try to bluff me, and so on." John plays each opponent differently. As an example, he says that he may bluff against a tight (scared) player, but he is more patient with aggressive players. Adaptability, he concludes, is essential.

John sees that it is vital to be motivated when a person plays poker, but he does not feel that ego plays into the equation. "I think ego is the most overrated thing in poker," John states. "To me, ego is doing something to show off, and every time you try to show off instead of using logic and common sense in poker, you'll be giving up something." Though he is not superstitious, John does like to wear certain shirts or shoes when he plays poker, but only because he feels comfortable in them.

When he first started playing poker, he says, he was living his dream. But now John envisions something more in his life. He has made the decision that poker is not something he wants to do for the rest of his life and sees himself playing only for fun sometime in the future. Retirement from poker? John says he's thought about it "almost every day in the last three years! I'd like to be a doctor in a third world country," John admits. That's John Juanda for you!

Major Poker Accomplishments

Winner of three WSOP gold bracelets

2002, Champion of the Year

2001 and 2002, Runner-up in Player of the Year

2001, First place, World Poker Open, No Limit Hold'em Championship

Winner of over 20 major tournaments

Mel Judah

"When you play with professionals you realize that if you're not playing seriously you are going to lose a lot of money to these people."

Personal Notes

Born in Calcutta, India, 1947

Former hair stylist and salon owner

Married with one son

Lived in Australia for years

Owns the World Poker Championship

Resides in London, England

You won't find too many professional poker players who are former hair stylists, but Mel Judah is one such man—and he was tops in that profession just as he is now tops in the poker world. After moving from India as a child, Mel took up the trade of his mother, who had owned and operated salons in both India and England. He started out on the artistic team with the highly fashionable Vidal Sassoon in the heart of London. While styling for *Vogue* magazine and Christian Dior collections Mel got to know the heads of stars and models such as Goldie Hawn, Mia Farrow, Julie Christie, and Beverly Sassoon, one of the early James Bond actresses. Once he left his position with Vidal Sassoon, Mel decided to stay high-profile by opening his own salon on Bond Street in London's West End.

Not too far off lurked the Victoria Club, and one day when his wife went to Australia for holiday with their son, he accompanied some of his friends to the casino. "They played roulette and all that," says Mel, "but I never gambled. I only played poker, and I discovered there was a poker room upstairs." Mel played Seven Card Stud there regularly for a few years before making his first poker trip to Las Vegas in 1981.

It's from that time onward that he's considered himself a bona fide poker player. "I moved with my family to Australia and got into the import-export business, but quickly found out that wasn't my forte, and I didn't want to get back into hairdressing again," Mel explains. "So I thought I'd do something different." Poker, he says, had always been very good to him, both in home games and in the card rooms. Once he discovered poker tournaments he realized that was the way he could make a lot of money.

"Patience at the table will give you the edge over other players who jump into a pot when they should be mucking their cards."

-Mel Judah

Mel made a habit of returning to Las Vegas each year for the World Series of Poker. He won his first World Series event in 1989 and another in 1997. "I've placed second four times," he laments, "and placed in the money thirty times at the World Series. I haven't won the big one yet, and now with so many more players, it's going to be a lot tougher."

Mel says his family never had a problem with his new chosen career path. "I was never a losing player," he says, "and the money was always coming in. When you play with professionals you realize that if you're not playing seriously you are going to lose a lot of money to these people, so you either do it professionally or you stay at home and play."

After years of tournament play, Mel says his profession feels more like a grind to him now. "I don't like playing poker as much now as when I started, and I'm already easing my way out." Mel's poker career has spawned several poker-related pursuits, including running tournaments. He helped put together the first tournament in Costa Rica and the first in Russia. Both tournaments have since taken off.

Mel's latest poker-related endeavor is the World Poker Championship, a new company he formed to compete with the WPT. "They've done a good job and we've got to come to that standard if we're going to succeed." Mel plans to televise more than just the No Limit Hold'em tournaments. The first WPC tournament is slated to be broadcast on Fox-owned Sky Sports.

"At the moment," says Mel, "the WPT has the monopoly. It's like saying, 'if you don't fall in line, then we don't need you.' But there's enough people to go around." Part of the problem with the current monopoly structure, he explains, is that too many players don't feel they are getting their fair share, especially since the WPT excludes sponsorship for players. "They want to be able to get their own sponsors, so that they can pay for all their tournaments for the whole year. It's a very expensive business to be in if you're not making money."

Mel sees the current system as "a very closed shop," and wants to see it changed. "I'm going on the other side of the fence to provide some competition. Maybe some day the WPT will take on the WPC for a sort of Super Bowl of Poker."

Major Poker Accomplishments

2003, First place, WPT Legends of Poker, No Limit Hold'em Championship

2003, Sixth place, WPT Five Diamond World Poker Classic, No Limit Hold'em Championship

1997, First place, WSOP, Seven Card Stud

1997, Third place, WSOP, No Limit Hold'em Championship

1989, First place, WSOP, Seven Card Stud

Chris Karagulleyan  

"They push all-in, and they try to bluff me, wanting to steal the pot. But I don't care if they want to waste their chips. People make mistakes so I get more chips."

Personal Notes

- **Born in Beirut, Lebanon, 1968**
- **Immigrated to U.S. in 1984**
- **Graduate of Hollywood High School**
- **Former bread baker**
- **Wears suit and tie at final tables**
- **Resides in Glendale, California**

Chris Karagulleyan saw it all when he was growing up in Beirut under siege during the war years of 1973-82—bombings, death, and all the other side effects of war. Of all these memories one stands out in particular. "There were a lot of casinos in Beirut," says Chris, "and everybody seemed to be passing their time there because everyone was out of work during the war."

But Chris didn't start his own poker and gambling career until he came to California, two years after the end of the Lebanon War. He and his family lived in Hollywood, where Chris attended the famous Hollywood High. It was during those high school years that he started sneaking into L.A.'s casinos as an underage gambler. "I started playing at Commerce, El Dorado, and Normandy," he says. "I didn't waste my time playing my friends in home games. I went straight to the casinos, and I made money there. Everybody knew me at those places, and no one cared that I was under 21."

Playing poker is easy money for Chris, he says. Especially these days. "I don't have a particularly mathematical mind, and you don't need to," he explains, countering the prevailing idea of most poker players that mathematics plays a large part in the game of poker. Instead, Chris says, "If you're disciplined enough there's enough fish out there." A good poker player, he says, simply needs to prepare himself for these fish—that's Chris's nickname for all the suckers playing poker at places like Commerce Casino.

Chris makes California his home now and has only great things to say about his favorite California casino—the Commerce. With as much enthusiasm as he can muster he unabashedly promotes the poker room there. "Commerce is the best poker place in the whole world," he says. "All kinds of people go there with all kinds of money. They love to gamble. They love to throw their money away." Chris says it's his job to be there to catch it. "These people love to gamble," he continues, "but they just don't have any skill. They're at the table to win, but they don't realize they're not good enough to win."

Chris says he spent a lot of time at the casinos watching the good players, learning not only from how they play but also learning from their mistakes. "That's the key to success," he says. According to Chris, many of the people who are playing No Limit Hold'em now have failed to do their homework. "They have no clue," says Chris—not of the seasoned pros, but of a lot of the new players who have flooded the tournament tables since the onset of poker TV. "They push all-in, and they try to bluff me, wanting to steal the pot. But I don't care if they want to waste their chips. People make mistakes so I get more chips."

Chris prides himself on his table appearance. He likes to dress up, wearing a suit and tie at final tables. "Girls like that," he says, "but it also makes you feel good about yourself—and you get all the compliments." Chris complements his dress with a gentlemanly presence at the

"Given enough time, the skillful player knows how to work around this thing called luck."

-Louis Asmo

table. "A lot of people like the way I play because I never get upset at the table. I'm friendly with everybody. If I win or lose a big pot I'll act the same. Either way, I want to be gracious to other players."

In 2003 Chris made it to 50 final tables, and took first place in the WPT tournament at L.A.'s Bicycle Club. Though Chris is a laid back player, final tables make him nervous, he says. "I don't want to disappoint myself, and when I'm in L.A. I have a lot of friends who come watch me. When I'm on a final table I have about 100 people watching me and rooting me on. That's extra pressure on me, but I always play my game no matter what." At the Legends of Poker Championship, Chris defînintely did not disappoint his supporters. He took home the first place prize of over $250,000.

In addition to final table nervousness, Chris readily admits to another fault. At times, he says, he can be reckless with money as gamblers tend to be: "For poker players, money comes easy, and that's why I have no respect for money. It's not right, but the reality is if it's easy money, you lose respect." Chris says he's reckless with money at the table, not away from it. "Many times I've taken $50,000 to a game, and I get excited and lose it all. I've done it many times."

One particularly rash incident came *after* he had just taken second in a big tournament, taking away a prize of $60,000. "I took all that money and walked by a blackjack table. I put it all down and lost everything in one shot. Sixty grand! I've done that sort of thing many times. It's difficult to win in blackjack, and I've never even been lucky at the game. It all comes back to discipline. Discipline is the key."

Major Poker Accomplishments

2003, First place, LA Poker Classic, Pot Limit Hold'em

2003, Fifth place, WPT Battle of Champions

2002, First Place, WPT Legends of Poker, No Limit Hold'em Championship

Phil Laak  

"I am either the smartest dumb guy, or the dumbest smart guy [the other poker players] have ever met."

Personal Notes

- **Born in Dublin, Ireland, 1972**
- **Former sports bet broker**
- **Part-time stock market speculator and real estate investor**
- **Splits his home base between San Francisco and Los Angeles**
- **Known as "the Unabomber" because of his hooded sweatshirt and sunglasses**

Phil Laak has so many interests that it is amazing that he has time to play tournament poker—and play it well! Besides taking a month or two off to travel to new and exciting places, Phil counts among his many hobbies and activities motorcycling, scuba diving, skydiving (which he highly recommends that everyone try at least once) and judo. This last activity saved him a lot of pain when he was involved in a serious motorcycle accident. "The whole thing was too crazy to be true," remembers Phil. "I actually flipped over the car, leaving the bike behind me and came out of the flip landing on my feet."

Phil's physical conditioning is not the only conditioning important to him. He is quite an enthusiast of the study of higher-order thinking and keeps abreast of current research in the often misunderstood area of higher-order mental capacities. He admits that when he broaches the subject to others he is often thought of as some sort of "quack." But Phil uses his techniques to establish a psychic connection with the other players. One technique he uses is "lucid dreaming." He replays hands over and over in these dreams so as to pick up on the other players' conscious or subconscious tells. "This is another example of my self training in higher-order mental functioning that gives me an edge at the poker table," states Phil. He considers that his "ace up the sleeve."

Like a lot of other players, Phil traces his poker roots back to childhood games, either with family or friends. He recalls a camping trip when he was seven years old, where he played cards with the heavily financed big guys (the 12 year olds). The game was called "between the sheets." Each player was dealt two cards and made a bet based on whether the next card would fall between the original two he was dealt. "Ridiculous, of course," he explains, "but what did we know?"

His family liked to play Tripoli for pennies when Phil was a youngster, and it was during these games that Phil realized that there was a lot of card logic involved. He carried this philosophy of logic to the college games he organized on Wednesday nights in his room, but it wasn't until 1999 that he was first exposed to big bet poker. When he was in New York city he played at an "underground" club and adapted to the game with ease. "That was really my baptism into poker," Phil admits. "From there, part of myself splintered off to be a part-time 'poker degeneratum'."

"Maintain a balance between freedom, fun, and fulfillment."

-Phil Laak

It wasn't long before Phil became interested in tournament poker. He saw that tournament poker involved competition, patience and implementing various strategies during different phases of the tournament and he was hooked! He could see that his hobbies, especially his interest in higher-order thinking and abilities of perception would play well at the poker table. "What I am talking about," Phil says, "is being able to pick up information from my opponent that is neither visual nor verbal. In other words, information that would not be called a tell."

Phil does not live and die for poker, though. Neither the fame nor the fortune are important to Phil. "Living well is all about optimizing, and achieving a balance between fun, freedom, and fulfillment." He tries not to become too involved in the outcome of a hand or a tournament. He simply wants to get up from the table knowing that he has played well.

He ranks his win at the LA Celebrity Invitational Tournament as one of his most memorable poker experiences. He sees his win with an Ace on the river as putting him not only even with the universe but actually handily ahead. "I, of course, drove extra careful that week, as I was not planning on letting the universe re-level the playing field."

Though Phil doesn't have any real superstitions when he plays he admits to having a few "quirks" about his money. For instance he doesn't like old hundreds, and tries to trade them in for new ones. "It is similar to someone who likes to start the day by making his bed," Phil muses. "It's no biggy if it does not get made, . . . it just makes for a happier mind." He also likes to have all of his money facing the same direction and ordered from the ones on up to the hundreds. But again, the order of his money is not essential to Phil; it is simply a preference. He sees poker as all about having fun. "When it stops being fun, I will hunt for something else."

Major Poker Accomplishments

2004, First place, WPT LA Celebrity Invitational

2003, 12th place, WPT Five Diamond World Poker Classic, No Limit Hold'em Championship

2003, Sixth place, Legends of Poker, No Limit Hold'em Championship

2002, First place, Bay 101 Uncle Louie Tournament, No Limit Hold'em

Howard Lederer 

"After playing for four days, you almost don't know what to do after you've been eliminated..."

Personal Notes

- **Born in Concord, New Hampshire, 1964**
- **Attended Columbia University**
- **Brother of poker pro Annie Duke**
- **Former competitive chess player**
- **Resides in Las Vegas**

Standing at an imposing 6'5", Howard Lederer is intimidating at the poker table. But it's neither his manner nor his height that's frightening. It's his poker expertise. He's a man to be feared both in side action and in tournament play.

The son of English professor Richard Lederer, the author of *Anguished English,* a look at the eccentricities of the English language, Howard is also the brother of poker pro Annie Duke—or, more accurately perhaps, considering he taught her to play, Annie is Howard's sister. His other sister, Katy, is a poet and the author of *Poker Face: A Girlhood Among Gamblers.*

Howard's math-peppered table chatter hints at the sort of analytical and mathematical mind that once made him a competitive chess player at prep school in his native New Hampshire before he headed south to attend Columbia University.

When he arrived in New York City, Howard found himself drawn to Manhattan's wide range of competitive chess clubs. Nor could he resist the lure of the city's underground poker rooms. "The allure is gambling," he once told the *Los Angeles Times.* Consequently, he left Ivy League academia in order to take up the profession of poker. Over the next decade

Howard cut his teeth in New York's poker world, preparing him to make a move to Las Vegas in 1994.

"Morals are an acquirement—like a foreign language, like piety, poker, paralysis—no man is born with them."

-Mark Twain

Considered one of the great high-stakes cash players, Howard has also had much success at tournament play. After a whopping 13 final tables appearances at the World Series of Poker, Howard earned his first gold bracelet in the 2000 Omaha Hi-Lo Split.

But it wasn't until 2002 that Howard decided to concentrate much of his time on honing his no-limit tournament game. He saw the writing on the wall: the World Poker Tour was going to be the next "big thing" for poker. Writing in his online "diary" of his experience at the 2003 World Series of Poker, Howard said that because he realized that the big scores in poker are to be had in No Limit Hold'em, he "vowed to go to all the major no-limit tournaments for at least a year and see what happens."

That turned out to be a fortuitous decision on Howard's part. He met with success in several of the WPT tournaments, taking first place at Connecticut's Foxwoods in 2002 and WPT's Party Poker Million II in early 2003, making him the first player to win two World Poker Tour events.

Howard says he saw the 2003 WSOP main event as the culmination of his yearlong effort in playing tournament No Limit Hold'em. "I was thrilled with the wins I had this year," he wrote in his online diary, "but I was determined to erase an embarrassing fifteen year run with zero cashes in the final event of the WSOP." Howard had finished fifth in his first try in 1987, but had gone south since then.

When Howard arrived for the tournament he found that it was the largest No Limit Hold'em tournament ever played. 839 players entered. He made it to day four, and the field was down to 45 players at starting time. Up against the likes of Freddy Deeb, Phil Ivey and Marcel Luske at his table, Howard got busted by Ivey, and finished in 19th place—an in-the-money win, but not as stellar a finish as he had hoped.

"I didn't feel anything. I was in shock," he said of the moment he was knocked out of the tournament. "I am sure that at that moment, every brain chemical responsible for aggression, focus, and feeling got drained out of my body. After playing for four days, you almost don't know what to do after you've been eliminated…I kept my mental and physical focus for four days, but the toll it took on me was felt for over a week afterwards." But Howard was sure to add that he "can't wait to do it again."

Major Poker Accomplishments

2004, First place, Five Star World Poker Classic, Pot Limit Omaha

2004, First place, Five Star World Poker Classic, No Limit Hold'em event

2003, Third place, WPT Battle of Champions

2003, First place, WPT Party Poker Million II, No Limit Hold'em Championship

2002, First place, WPT World Poker Finals, No Limit Hold'em Championship

2001, First place, WSOP, Deuce to Seven

2000, First place, WSOP, Omaha 8/OB

1987, Third place, WSOP, No Limit Hold'em Championship

Jim "Cincinnati Kid" Lester

"I was so good at the game at one time that I didn't even have to look at my cards."

Personal Notes

Born in Richmond, Virginia, 1960

Married with two children

Owns several contracting firms

Played $1,000-$2,000 poker when he was 13 years old

Semi-professional poker player

Resides in Cincinnati, Ohio

Jim Lester didn't earn the nickname "Cincinnati Kid" just because he's from the river city. He earned it—and early in life—because he was playing successful high-stakes poker by the age of 13. Moreover, his poker playing career resembles that of Steve McQueen's "Eric Stoner" in the 1965 poker blockbuster *The Cincinnati Kid.*

At 12 years old he started his first summer job. A neighbor had hired Jim to work on a construction site for 40 hours a week. On his first payday he pocketed $120, but didn't make it out the door before being sucked into a few hands of poker with the other workers—seasoned after-hours poker players. "I lost all my money in an hour," he remembers.

When he returned home that Friday night his dad asked him what he was going to do with all his hard-earned cash. "I lost it playing poker," Jim 'fessed up. His punishment? A 48-hour marathon poker lesson. "My dad sat me down and said, 'I'm going to teach you how to play, and I'm not going to let you get up until you fully understand the game'"—the mathematical and psychological aspects and everything else that comes with it. "It wasn't until Sunday at 7 p.m. that we got up from the table."

The following Friday Jim took his $120 paycheck again to the poker table. This time he broke every man there: "I made $1,100 that night, and I couldn't wait to tell my dad."

Jim returned each week to the same game and kept winning. "I never lost a night," he says. "I won every single week." A year later the owner of the construction company took the

13-year-old across the Ohio River to Newport, Kentucky, where he staked Jim at a $1000-2000 game. "It was back room type of action," he recalls. "The guys brought guns to the games, but they all liked me." He quickly earned their respect and the name "The Kid."

"Poker is the game closest to the western conception of life, where life and thought are recognized as infinitely combined."

-John Luckacs

Jim continued to play—and win—those Newport poker games until he was 22 years-old. By the time he was 18 he was making upwards of $600,000 a weekend playing poker. "I was playing with the same men for about 120 hours a week, and I could almost name you exactly what every man was holding, judging by their mannerisms. They thought it was the freakiest thing. At first, they thought I had to be cheating. I was flawless at the game for a long, long time. Every once in a while I had to lose on purpose in order to make sure the guys would keep coming back. I wanted this to be like a well."

Some of the most memorable poker games of his teen years were played with two men Jim describes as the biggest drug dealers east of the Mississippi. "They would come in with suitcases full of money and armed bodyguards," he remembers. "But they were the worst poker players in the world. They couldn't understand how a young kid could dominate a game."

The first time Jim beat these two out of $600,000 in a weekend, they told him they thought they'd never see him again. But Jim had a gutsy response: "I said, 'you guys are so bad that I'll bring back this $600,000 next weekend, and each of you has to match it.' I told them I'd put my money on the table, and told them that if I didn't double it by the time I passed out or fell asleep then they could have it all back." The others agreed, and Jim did double the $600,000 the next weekend.

Jim made the mistake, however, of taking his huge bankroll to Las Vegas. "Sixty days later," he lamented. "I was broke. I wasn't even allowed to be in the casinos because I was underage. But I guess they didn't care when they saw I had fistfuls of cash." Jim flew out there on several weekends and stayed in a presidential suite. "It was the life," he said, "while it lasted."

He kept playing the Newport games for several more years and eventually bought enough construction equipment to open his own contracting business at the age of 22. That's when he gave up playing full-time poker to raise his family with his wife Cathy.

Now Jim Lester's two sons are grown, and he's back at it. In 2002 he returned to playing poker and has been going gangbusters ever since. The "Cincinnati Kid" may not be as much of a kid anymore, but he's still a force to be reckoned with—and he still lives in Cincinnati.

Major Poker Accomplishments

2001, First place, WSOP, Limit Hold'em

2000, Third place, World Poker Open, No Limit Hold'em event

2000, First place, World Poker Open, Seven Card Stud Hi/Lo Split

David Levi  

"In Israel being a poker player is on par with being a drug dealer."

Personal Notes

- **Born in Tel Aviv, 1962**
- **Grew up in Israel**
- **Former paratrooper in Israeli army**
- **Former professional soccer player**
- **Professional poker player**
- **Resides in Las Vegas**

Back in Israel David Levi was known as a paratrooper and a soccer star. In the U.S. he's known as a poker hot shot. From 1981 to 1983, David jumped out of military airplanes during the Israel War with Lebanon. After that he played professional soccer, Israel's most popular sport, for several years before being sidelined by a knee injury. "Even after the war, the army kept calling me up while I was playing soccer," he says.

After his soccer career was cut short, he jumped at an opportunity to come to Los Angeles. That's where he first learned about the game of poker. After several trips to casinos in Las Vegas, a friend introduced him to the Bicycle Club in Bell Gardens, California. That's where he started his poker career, but he didn't get off on the right foot. David describes his first year of play as an expensive learning lesson: "I was playing big then because I had a lot of cash, but I didn't know anything. I was doing pretty bad."

By the time David realized that he didn't know much about the game, he had already lost most of his money at the poker table. "I had to start playing my cash games at medium level instead of for the big stakes," he explains. With discipline and tight money management, he was able to survive his many losing streaks. Then he started to win: "I wasn't making big scores at first, but just enough to live on."

Once he started doing well, David went back to playing for high stakes—$1,000-$2,000 games—but this time with financial backers. That's also when he started playing tournaments, in which he was successful right from the start. "I was missing that element of competition that I felt when playing soccer," he says. "Unlike playing cash games, the tournaments gave me that same sense of competition and accomplishment. If I make $1,000 in a cash game and $1,000 in a tournament, I feel like I really accomplished something in the tournament." In the cash games, it's just the money, he says.

"Poker is a fighting game, a game in which each player tries to get the better of every other player and does so by fair means or foul so long as he obeys the rules of the game."

-Karl Meninger

Tournament play also provides David with a challenging equivalent to what he had as a paratrooper and on the soccer field. "All three endeavors are very challenging," he says, "but, of course, they're also very different. When you are a paratrooper there are things you must do in the name of duty; there's no option. I like the freedom of poker playing: I can play whenever and wherever I want."

As much as David enjoys playing poker, he admits that it has become somewhat of a grind for him. "When I started playing poker tournaments, it was very exciting. It was new for me, and I didn't know anything. Now I look at it more like work. Sometimes I don't feel like playing, but this is what I do now. I'm a poker player, and so I play."

David had the most enjoyment while he was playing soccer. "Poker is much more stressful for me," he explains. "In soccer you can lose a game and still feel good if you played well. In poker you can be the best player in the world but get bad cards—and there's nothing you can do about it."

At the moment David has his life focused on professional poker playing. Since 1997 he's been traveling to all the major tournaments throughout the United States. But eventually he'd like to spend a bit more time at home base. His jet setting lifestyle makes it difficult for him to be a part of local soccer leagues. "I want to teach young kids how to play soccer," he says. "That's what I'm trying to get into, but right now I am in full-time poker mode."

David also comments that, in Israel, he would get much more respect as a soccer coach than as a professional poker player—no matter how good he is or how much he wins. "Israel is different," he says, comparing his country to the U.S. and Western Europe. "Gambling is illegal, and since people don't play poker in public, my family has a very different view of poker. It's hard for them to accept what I do. In Israel being a poker player is on par with being a drug dealer."

Major Poker Accomplishments

2004, First place, California State Poker Championship, No Limit Hold'em

2004, First place, California State Poker Championship, Seven Card Stud Hi/Lo 8 O/B

2003, First place, Legends of Poker, Seven Card Stud

2003, First place, California State Championship, Seven Card Stud

2003, First place, Grand Slam of Poker, Omaha Hi/Lo

2002, First place, Bellagio Poker Tournament, No Limit Hold'em Championship

2002, First place, Legends of Poker, Limit Hold'em

Kathy Liebert 

"…So I slapped him. I slapped him across the face, and he looked like he was going to hit me back."

Personal Notes

- **Born in Nashville, Tennessee, 1967**
- **Grew up in Poughkeepsie, New York**
- **Graduate of Marist College**
- **Antismoking (at the table) crusader**
- **Resides in Las Vegas**

Kathy Liebert recognizes that poker is a "man's sport," but that doesn't bother her. "I accept that," she says, "and I enjoy poker." Being a woman at the poker table has both its advantages and its disadvantages, she says. Some men are more friendly to her than to others, she believes, by virtue of the simple fact that they don't see that many women at the poker tables each year. Others think they can just run all over her. "Some don't seem to play their hands as hard against women," she observes, "and others try to bluff women players more or play us more aggressively." In the end, the advantages seem to even out the disadvantages, and Kathy sees herself playing on a level field with the men.

The seeds of Kathy's poker career were sown in 1991 when she moved to Colorado. Five dollar limit casinos had just opened up in Central City and Blackhawk. "I started out playing there," she says, "and then I got invited out to two regular home games." Three years later she found herself at the Gold Coast in Las Vegas playing her first tournament. "In my first event I went heads-up with a guy and made a deal to chop," she remembers. "A week later I went heads-up again. I was on a roll right from the beginning. Every time I played I would either win or finish in one of the top spots."

It was in these tournaments that Kathy first noticed that she was getting some respect for playing a solid game. "I picked my spots to play bluffs," she admits, "but overall I played solid and got a little lucky too. I was paying attention and focused. That was enough."

Since her first tournament wins, Kathy relocated to Las Vegas to take up poker as a full-time profession, one of the few women in the world to do so. But she's found that it's not the fact that she's a woman that has caused her the most problems. Rather, it's her aversion to smoking at the poker table, her single greatest pet peeve about the world of poker.

Smoking is one reason that Kathy prefers to play open events as opposed to the ladies-only events. "When they allowed smoking," she explains, "the women's events tended to be more heavily smoky. Not only do the women who play seem to smoke more than the men, they also hold their cigarettes higher and in your face. A man who smokes will typically keep his cigarette down by the ashtray." It's not that women are ruder, she clarifies, it's just a matter of style she says of the Virginia Slimmers.

"Shrug off beats and maintain your composure under pressure."

-Kathy Liebert

Kathy remembers one particular game in which a smoker gave her a bit of trouble. It wasn't a woman though. "I was playing in a Super-Satellite in a big tournament," she says. One of the players was good and drunk, playing aggressively, and blowing smoke in everyone's face. When he lost all his chips, he refused to leave. "He was still sitting there blowing smoke in my face," Kathy remembers. "I said something to him, not trying to offend him, but wanting him and his cigarette to leave the table."

He must have taken it the wrong way because he stayed and made a point to keep puffing smoke into her face while she was trying to play. Kathy finally had enough of the rogue smoker. She reached out and placed her hand on his face to turn it away from her. That just made him take another big drag from his cigarette and blow a blue cloud into her face once more. "So I slapped him," Kathy admits. "I slapped him across the face, and he looked like he was going to hit me back." The foreman came over to quell the disturbance, and Kathy received a penalty.

"There are some people who like to try to rub it in and become abusive," she says, "but it really doesn't happen all that often." After Kathy's $1 million win on the Party Poker Cruise tournament in 2002 it's much more difficult for the other players to be lacking in respect of her simply because she's a woman. She's proven she can survive in the man-infested waters of the poker world. "I believe that you must shrug off beats and maintain your composure under pressure to be competitive in poker. You have to be mentally, tough," insists Kathy. "and that's what I try to do."

Major Poker Accomplishments

2004, First place, WSOP, Limit Hold'em Shootout

2003, Third place, World Poker Finals, No Limit Hold'em event

2002, Sixth place, WPT Legends of Poker, No Limit Hold'em Championship

2002, First place, Party Poker Million, No Limit Hold'em Championship

2002, Third place, WPT Ultimate Bet Championship, No Limit Hold'em, Pro Division

Erick Lindgren 

"I'm just a really competitive guy and poker satisfies my competitive nature."

Personal Notes

Born in Burney, California

First WPT Player of the Year

Former high school sports standout

Former blackjack dealer

Resides in Las Vegas

The spirit of competition is something that has been with Erick Lindgren for some time. Back in high school, Eric was an All-League quarterback and MVP basketball player. He fully intended to continue in the sports competition when he entered junior college until he took a job as a blackjack dealer at a local casino. When he wasn't dealing the cards, he was playing them; at that time, mainly as a diversion from school and work. But Erick found that he was pretty good at the poker table and soon it became a full-time job for him. "I'm just a really competitive guy," Eric states matter-of-factly, "and poker satisfies my competitive nature."

Erick left school to become a "prop" player at the casino (someone paid by the casino to keep the games going or to get games started). He developed his poker skills by doing this for a while until he broke into the ranks of the poker professionals. And the rest is history!

With over $2 million in winnings to his credit, Erick has nothing to prove. He has won three major tournaments in just over a year, the latest being the Party Poker Million III, where the first place honor put over a million dollars in his pocket. But Erick is not likely to "rest on his laurels." He continues to play with the best and learn from them. Though he may come off as a bit arrogant on TV, his fellow players have a different opinion of the young man. Other than considering him a fantastic poker player, they describe him as friendly, fun and easygoing—well-liked by everybody.

When he's not playing in a live tournament, Erick plays online. The ability to analyze hands after the game by having a play by play description of the game emailed to him helps him to analyze any mistakes he may have made.

He told one interviewer that he sees himself as a student of the game, "constantly thinking, analyzing and honing his skills." The fact that many poker players just get up, sit down at the table and play with little or no preparation or study works to his advantage. He has read the books and analyzed the hands, played the game and focused mentally for the tournaments. He is ready for them. "Bring them on," he seems to say.

"He was about to gamble his life on that poker table, and the insanity of that risk filled him with a kind of awe."

-Paul Auster
from
The Music of Chance

When he sat down at the final table at the Party Poker Million III tournament held on the cruise ship MS Ryndam, Erick was focused. He told *Cardplayer* magazine that he never left the ship for any excursions on shore because he was focused on winning the tournament. But when it was over he was ready to party, so he bought drinks for everyone at the bar that whole night.

When it got down to heads up play at the tournament, he faced a good friend and great player, Daniel Negreanu. Though Daniel had said a win over Erick would be bittersweet, considering their friendship, Erick was not buying it. "I wanted to kick Daniel's butt," he admitted, "and I'm sure he felt the same way."

Though poker is his profession right now, Erick is far from a one-note fellow. He enjoys playing golf and basketball when he has the time and he is also involved with Full Tilt Poker, an online poker site where if you're lucky, you can play with this poker ace.

Erick is destined to satisfy his yen for competition at the poker table and poker fans are likely to see a lot more of this World Poker Tour Player of the Year. With a serious poker face or with a hint of playfulness in his eyes, Erick Lindgren is here to stay.

Major Poker Accomplishments

2004, Named the first WPT Player of the Year

2004, First place, WPT Party Poker Million III, Limit Hold'em Championship

2003, First place, WPT Ultimate Bet, No Limit Hold'em Championship

2003, Fifth place, WPT Euro Finals of Poker, No Limit Hold'em Championship

2002, First place, Five Diamond World Poker Classic, No Limit Hold'em Championship

Marcel Luske 

"It is hard to explain; but as a poker player you are looking for beautiful moments. It's the challenge that spices up your soul."

Personal Notes

- **Born in Amsterdam, 1953**
- **Married with two children**
- **One of the founders of the International Poker Federation**
- **Known as the "Flying Dutchman"**
- **Has a black belt in karate**
- **Resides in Almere, Holland**

For two out of the last three years, Marcel Luske has been the man to beat in Europe. He was ranked number one there in both 2001 and 2003. Not a bad record for a man who has only been playing tournament poker for five years. Putting to rest the insinuations early in his career that he may just be a "flash in the pan," Marcel has shown beyond a doubt that he is here to stay.

The man they call the "Flying Dutchman" embodies the competitiveness and cunning of a poker superstar without compromising his gracious and gentlemanly demeanor both at the table and away from it. Marcel is arguably the most likeable person on the international poker scene. Consider what he had to say when asked to share his thoughts on the current state of poker in the *Hendon Mob Diary*: "It is hard to explain; but as a poker player you are looking for beautiful moments. It's the challenge that spices up your soul. Funnily enough it is the bad beats that most of us talk about and not the joy that we have or we are supposed to have from meeting so many different kinds of people...Wouldn't it be great if all poker players, in the environment that we exist, all had mutual respect for each other and acted that way? If we only all treated each other the way that we would like to be treated, wouldn't that be great? I think that the key word is respect."

Barney Boatman, an international poker colleague and member of the Hendon Mob has written some good things about Marcel, whom he thinks personifies the best of the poker world. "Luske is here to stay," writes Barney. "Look at him ... in his immaculately cut suit, reddish blonde hair slicked back, only the finest links on his freshly starched cuffs.... Marcel is focused," he continues. "He's focused, relaxed."

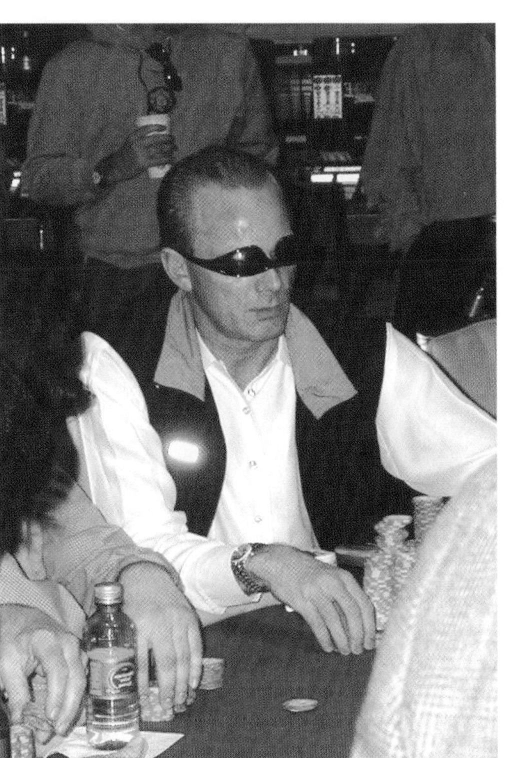

It is easy to see Marcel as the owner of a pub in Amsterdam, something he did before he became an international poker sensation. He enjoyed meeting a variety of people in that business, but he says that the "headaches" involved would test even the strongest person.

Now, Marcel travels the tournament circuit, mainly in Europe, but also throughout the world. His favorite card room is at the Concord Card Casino in Vienna. Why? "They have the best dealers," he says. He also feels very much at home in its peaceful environment. Perhaps he also enjoys the everpresent musical atmosphere of Vienna since one of Marcel's greatest pleasures is song; he loves to sing almost as much as he loves to play poker. But, be that as it may, Marcel also plays regularly in his native Holland at the Lido Casino in Amsterdam.

"You have to keep in control of your game."

-Marcel Luske

Though Marcel could probably take on anyone at the poker table with his black belt in karate, that's not likely to happen. Marcel maintains his gentlemanly image at all times. His mantra is "Treat others the way that we would like to be treated."

Reflecting this generous attitude, Marcel sees positive developments in the sport of poker in the form of television, sponsorships and advertisements. "The business world realizes that these are new markets," Marcel notes. "They are looking for material to show and things to get involved with. That means poker players—us!" He thinks that it is great that the business world is willing to invest in and sponsor poker. "By doing this they are showing that they believe in us and respect us."

Marcel has his preferences in play, as do all poker players. He prefers tournaments to cash games and his game of choice is pot limit play. But it seems that his greatest preference is to play with players that behave well. He is disturbed by those who are arrogant or insolent at the table, even the dealers, and he does not like to suffer the grumbling and muttering of the other players. He sees much to be changed in the poker world. "Very much," he emphasizes. But this does not deter him from his goal to "bring along your best mood and trust in yourself."

Marcel continues to make his mark, just recently placing 10th in the main event at the 2004 World Series of Poker and second in the Seven Card Stud event. In the main event Marcel locked horns with Dan Harrington after 13 hours of play. With a pair of fours he called Dan's A-J pre-flop raise. The flop was Q-8-6, all clubs. With a four of clubs in his hand Marcel went all in. Though Dan was ready to throw away his hand he took another look at his hole cards, finding that his Ace was an Ace of clubs not spades as he had thought. Bad news for Marcel. The flush did not develop, but a Jack on fourth street gave Dan the pot. Marcel was out on the bubble.

Things like this do not discourage Marcel. At least he doesn't show it. He maintains his outlook on the poker world which is represented well in this statement by Marcel. "I would like to . . . thank all the poker players that I have played and am still playing with as well as all the ones who try to make the poker environment better especially the ones who are poker smart and business serious."

Major Poker Accomplishments

Ranked number one player in Europe, 2001 and 2003

2004, Second place, WSOP, Seven Card Stud

2004, Tenth place, WSOP, No Limit Hold'em Championship

2003, First place, Victoria Poker Classics, No Limit Hold'em Championship

2003, 14th place, WSOP, No Limit Hold'em Championship

2001, First place, Euro Finals of Poker, Pot Limit Hold'em

2001, First place, Euro Finals of Poker, Pot Limit Seven Card Stud Hi/Lo

2001, First place, British Open, Pot Limit Omaha

2001, First place, Prague Open, No Limit Hold'em Championship

Tony Ma  

"I had something like a bolt of lightning open up my brain. I felt like I had just received a message, and I was so happy. It was a miracle: Play poker!"

Personal Notes

- **Born in Saigon, Vietnam, 1956**
- **Immigrated to the U.S. in 1975**
- **Married with two children**
- **Received thunderbolt miracle message**
- **Professional poker player**
- **Resides in El Monte, California**

On April 29, 1975, Tony Ma was 19 years old and in the South Vietnamese Navy. "I was out at sea on a cargo ship," he remembers. "That night we heard that the South had surrendered, and so the captain told us to keep going out to sea, and that's what we did." Tony and the rest of the crew never made it back to Vietnam. Instead they ended up in the Philippines, where the Americans were helping Vietnamese refugees from Communism. "There were about thirty people on the ship, including several civilians who had jumped on as we were pulling out of port that day. We all had to leave our families behind," says Tony. "It was a very rough time."

From the Philippines, Tony moved to Bristol, Connecticut where he had an American sponsor. In 1987 he moved to Southern California, where he was introduced to casino games. Tony started by playing Paigow and Dominoes, but after a few years he figured out he wasn't much good at either and gave them up. "I was getting older, and I knew I had to take care of my family," he admits. "I quit my gambling and went to work at a very tough job, because I didn't have any special qualifications."

A year later, Tony returned to a casino aspiring to make just $100 a day. That was the first time he noticed the poker tables, and he was drawn in right away—not to play, but to watch. "While I was watching them that day, a thought came to me," he remembers. "I had something like a bolt of lightning open up my brain. I felt like I had just received a message, and I was so happy. It was a miracle: Play poker!" Tony went home that night and told his wife: "I know what to do now. Give me some money." Tony told her that he was supposed to be playing poker. She believed him, and he left the next day with $5,000 in his pocket.

Tony won straight away. He started playing for small stakes, and he won a little money every day, pushing ahead of his $100 a day goal. "The more I played," he remembers, "the more I learned technical skill. I learned some techniques from the pros. I was making a good living for my family."

"Write down all your mistakes so that they won't be repeated."

-Tony Ma

In 1994, Tony was first introduced to tournament poker at L.A.'s Commerce Casino. He finished sixth place in that first tournament against some 300 players. "I went home frustrated that night, and I wrote down what I did wrong. I made some mistakes, and I vowed that next time I wouldn't make those mistakes."

The next tournament that Tony played, he made the final table again, this time finishing fourth. Although he pulled in some cash, he still wasn't happy with his performance. He went home again to write down his mistakes in order that he wouldn't make them again. It was in his third tournament that he went on to finish in first place. From that day on, Tony has been hooked on tournament poker. "I travel to all the major tournaments across the country now," he says.

In 1996, Tony Ma played in his first World Series of Poker tournament. The first event he played was the $5,000 buy-in Limit Hold'em event. Again, he made the final table. And although he didn't realize it at the time, the other men sitting at that final table were some of the biggest names in poker: T.J. Cloutier, John Bonetti, Johnny Chan, and Peter Vilandos. When it came to the final four players, the other three wanted to chop, but Tony refused. "I wanted to play, and I wanted to win first place," he says. Tony's response irritated the other three players. "When I said no, they looked at me and said, 'who's this guy anyway?' Nobody knew me. I was a rookie. I had no fear if only because I didn't know much. I just wanted to keep playing and win."

When the table got down to three players, the other two again proposed a chop, but Tony refused. "Now they were more than a little upset," he remembers. "That just made me want to win all the more. There was no way I was going to let them beat me." Tony went on to knock out Johnny Chan, leaving him heads-up with John Bonetti. "I told him again that I didn't want to split the money. I felt like I was going to win, and seven hands later I had him beat. It was a $236,000 win. After that, my name really got out there. They had a lot of respect for me after that."

Major Poker Accomplishments

2001, First place, World Poker Open, Pot Limit Hold'em

2000, First place, WSOP, Limit Hold'em

2000, Third place, WSOP, Limit Hold'em

1999, First place, Rio Carnivale of Poker, No Limit Hold'em Championship

1999 Player of the Year

Tom McEvoy

"A lot of the time you have to go with your instincts, and you had better be right because No Limit Hold'em is a cruel and unforgiving game."

Personal Notes

Born in Grand Rapids, Michigan

Author or co-author of ten poker books

Graduate of Ferris State University

Former accountant

Aruba is his favorite tournament venue

Resides in Las Vegas

Tom McEvoy got tired of working for other people. That's one reason he left his accounting job in Michigan and moved his wife and three children to Las Vegas in 1979. Another reason was money. "I used to play poker in home games over the weekends," he says, "and a lot of times I was making more money at these games than from my 'real job.'"

Since Tom's Independence Day—the Fourth of July in 1979—he's never had to look for another job. Poker playing and authoring books on poker became his full-time occupation. Many of his friends and relatives back in Grand Rapids, however, thought he was manic. "They thought I'd lost my mind," he says. His parents, in fact, were quite ashamed that their son was going to seek his fortune as a gambler. It wasn't until four years later, when Tom won first place at the World Series of Poker in 1983, that his mother "finally 'fessed up" to her friends that her son was a professional poker player. "She had no choice," says Tom. "I appeared on the front page of the local newspaper sitting at the table with the money I won."

The biggest misconception about professional poker players, he says, is that they are a bunch of sleazy lowlifes who hang out in smoke-filled backrooms. Conceding that there are, of course, sleazy, lowlife poker players, Tom says that's not typically the kind of person you find among the world's top players—especially the best tournament players. Tom tries to clarify his point with friends by explaining the nature of professional poker. Certain games, he says, are purely skill-based—tennis, golf and chess, for example—and in most cases the best player will

win. Other games are pure gambles, based on the luck of the draw: blackjack, craps, slots, and most other house casino games. Poker, however, is a combination of skill and luck, he emphasizes, and the skill factor in tournament poker is high enough that the best players can make a living off the game. "If skill was not a factor," he adds, "no one—including myself—could make much money off the game."

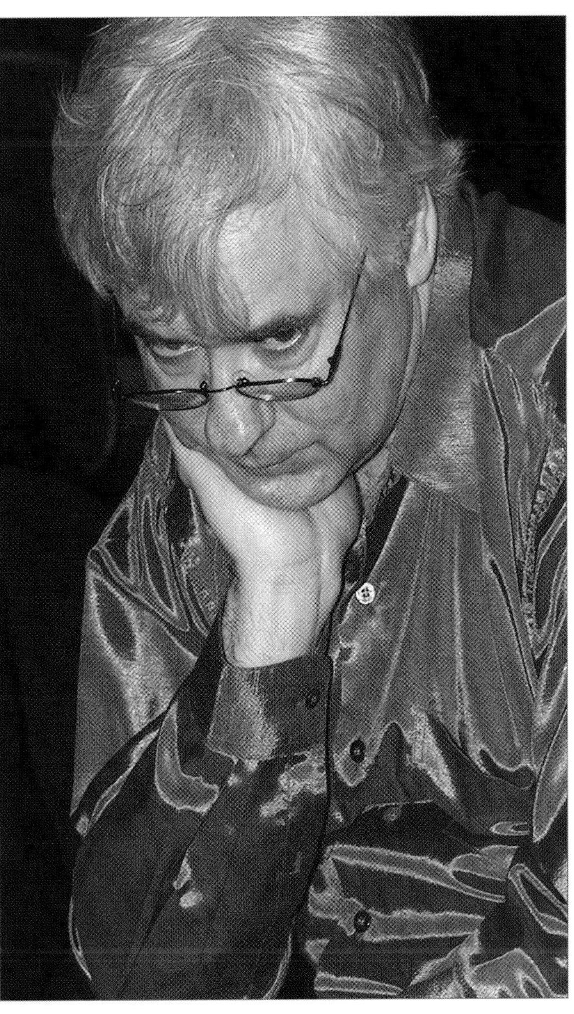

"Poker is probably the toughest way to make an easy living."

-Tom McEvoy

Tom likens professional poker playing to the ministry in one way: "Many are called, but few are chosen." What he means is that a lot of people would like to earn their keeps playing poker in international tournaments, but that in reality very few people are capable of succeeding. "Poker is probably the toughest way to make an easy living," he says, voicing the oft-repeated cliché, "but playing tournament poker is even tougher."

In addition to having the skill to play poker at the highest level, Tom says he has succeeded because he knows how to handle failure—a natural part of the game. "When I play," he explains, "I'm looking for the big money, which usually means placing in the top three spots. Most of the time, even the best tournament players are going to be beaten 80% of the time. That means they aren't going to 'cash.'" Tom compares this to baseball: "If a major league player hits .300, he's a superstar. No one bats .300 in tournament poker. If you hit as high as even .250 then you're a superstar."

Given the fact that poker is often a losing proposition, his favorite piece of advice to aspiring pros is a popular quotation from Winston Churchill: "Never, ever, give up." In nearly every tournament he's ever won, Tom says there was always a point at which he seemed to be in a hopeless chip position. "I often had the shortest stack, but I came back."

The highlight of Tom's career was his 1983 win at the World Series of Poker. "There's nothing that will ever be better than winning the World Series," he says. Since then he's made it to three more final tables at the WSOP. In addition to table play in tournaments such as the World Series, Tom says he likes the fringe benefits too. "I get to travel the world and see foreign countries and exotic islands." But his favorite place to play poker is his own living room in front of his computer, where he's never more than sixty seconds away from a game. "Some days," he says, "I never even get out of my pajamas."

Major Poker Accomplishments

1992, First place, WSOP, Omaha Limit

1986, First place, WSOP, Seven Card Razz

1983, First place WSOP, Limit Hold'em

1983, First place, WSOP, No Limit Hold'em Championship

1983, First place, Irish Championship

Chris Moneymaker 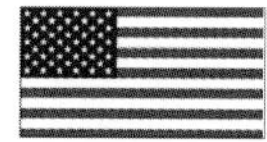

"I have no fear. I don't care if I get eliminated. I play to win, not to lose."

Personal Notes

- **Born in Atlanta, Georgia, 1975**
- **Married with one daughter**
- **Graduate of the University of Tennessee**
- **Professional accountant**
- **Learned to play hold'em in 2000**
- **Resides in Nashville, Tennessee**

He's got the perfect name for a man who walked away from the World Series of Poker with over $2 million in prize money. His name is Chris Moneymaker, an accountant from Nashville, Tennessee. His first place win in the main event at the 2003 WSOP was unprecedented in that it was the first major live tournament Chris every played in his life. In fact, he won his seat in the $10,000 buy-in via a $40 tournament online.

It was just a few years ago that a friend taught Chris the game. "The first time I played hold'em was at a friend's house in Nashville," he says. "We usually played Chase the Queen, but a buddy brought back a new game he learned at a casino: Texas Hold'em." Chris explains that at first he didn't really like the game much. "It was too slow," he says. "Since we played dealer's choice, my buddy always chose hold'em, and he always won." Finally, Chris decided to try to learn the game, so he traveled down to the Goldstrike Casino in Tunica, Mississippi. "I lost my entire bankroll that trip," he remembers, "but I left loving the game."

Chris didn't play poker tournaments at that point. He was a cash game player. He only got into tournament play through sheer boredom. "I started playing tournaments online for a change of pace," he explains, "something to do while wasting time." Chris typically played in $5 to $100 tournaments. When he entered the $40 tournament in an effort to win the WSOP seat, Chris had not yet sat down at a live tournament table, nor had he ever read a book on tournament poker. Coming into the Horseshoe Casino to take his seat in the $10,000 event, Chris Moneymaker's name was recognizable to no one. His face was just another in the field of obscure newcomers. "I was happy to make it through the first day [of the tournament]," he says. "The rest was gravy."

Up until that day Chris says his life was pretty "normal." He had been an accountant in several Big 5 firms and had got used to frequent business travel. Unlike most other top-notch pro poker players, Chris didn't quit his day job to pursue poker full time; he simply took a new post, one that affords him a bit more

"Always bet the same amount (in proportion to the blinds) pre-flop and on the flop 'til you figure out how to manipulate your opponents with your betting strategies."

-Chris Moneymaker

time to relax. "Now I work a 9-to-5 job as an accountant for a small restaurant, and I love the people I work with." His new job doesn't require him to travel at all. "The best part," he says, "is being able to stay close to my family; this is the main reason I have decided not to go 'pro' in poker."

With Chris's second place finish in the 2004 Bay 101 Shooting Star tournament, he may want to reconsider that decision. Though naysayers wanted to chalk up his 2003 WSOP win to incredible luck, it appears that this young man is not just a flash-in-the-pan. Chris really loves the game of poker and plays as often as he can. His matter-of-fact approach to the game reflects well not only in his play but in his encounters with all of those would-be players who want to shake his hand and get his autograph.

Poker analysts have commented on the fact that the 2003 WSOP win by this "amateur" player will give the tournament an even larger audience in the future. He has made it "everyman's" game and polished the image of the poker players with his down-home humility and his unassuming celebrity. And he has joined other poker stars by donating $25,000 of his WSOP winnings to cancer research.

Chris Moneymaker also projects a sportsmanlike manner at the table. He shook the hands of all of the players whose luck ran out and it is not hard to imagine that if he were the one to be leaving the table, he would still be shaking the hands of those he left behind.

When the field of play had been narrowed down to the final two players, Chris and the more experienced Sammy Farha, Chris demonstrated the same calm attitude that had gotten him to that point in the tournament. He was not intimidated by his opponent's calculating, aggressive play and in the end he was the one to take home the $2.5 million prize. Not a bad day for an "amateur."

Major Poker Accomplishments

2004, Second place, WPT Bay 101 Shooting Star, No Limit Hold'em Championship

2003, First place, WSOP, No Limit Hold'em Championship

Carlos Mortensen

"I thought, 'hey, this is better than working a job.'"

Personal Notes

- **Born in Ambato, Ecuador, 1972**
- **Moved to Madrid, Spain at age 15**
- **Married with no children**
- **Former chess and pool player**
- **Resides in Las Vegas**

At the age of 29, Carlos Mortensen took home $1.5 million when he won the $10,000 buy-in Championship Hold'em event at the 2001 World Series of Poker in Las Vegas. That's when he put both himself and Spain on the poker map. Ever since then, he and his wife Cecilia have been traveling the world together, visiting all the major tournament hotspots in Europe and North America from their home-base in Las Vegas.

Aside from the fact that he came out on top in that tournament, Carlos says the heads-up play in that main event against Dewey Tomko was the most exciting moment in his poker career. At the start of the final hand, Carlos outchipped Tomko two to one. Carlos was holding a king and a queen of clubs when he called his opponent's $100,000 bet. The dealer laid out a jack of diamonds, and a 10 and 3 of clubs. Tomko went on to raise the pot to $500,000, and then Carlos moved all in. When Dewey Tomko turned over his two aces, Carlos felt his stomach drop to the floor. The dealer showed a 3 of diamonds on fourth street. Carlos needed an ace or a nine to make a straight or a club to make a flush, otherwise it looked as if Tomko had him beat. Fifth street: a nine! "It was just incredible," says Carlos. "Incredible!"

Although born in Ecuador (his mother is Spanish and his father is Danish), he and his family moved to Madrid when Carlos was fifteen. It was in Spain that he was introduced to poker. "I used to play chess in a club," he remembers, "and one day they started up a poker game. One of the guys had just come back from America where he learned to play."

"Poker is a microcosm of all we admire and disdain about capitalism and democracy."

-Lou Krieger

Carlos couldn't resist the urge to join in the game. He'd never played any kind of poker before that day, and he lost. "I lost the equivalent of seventy dollars that night, and it really bothered me," he remembers. In fact, it bothered him so much he could hardly sleep that night. He kept trying to understand exactly where he had made his mistakes. The next day he returned to the club to play again. This time, he won. "And the day after that and the day after that," he says, "I won again and again—four straight days."

The $1,000 he earned in winnings over the course of those days got him to thinking a lot more about poker. "I thought, 'hey, this is better than working a job.'" Carlos was working in a pub at the time, and he was already heavily competitive at pool and chess. It was this third game—the game of poker—that really held his interest.

Outside his club, Carlos found that in Spain poker was not regarded so highly. "When I started playing," he says, "I could only play in home games. Playing poker wasn't legal back then."

Carlos then discovered tournament poker, and he and his wife began their years of world traveling—first touring Europe, and then going to Las Vegas, the epicenter of gambling culture. It was there that the Spanish couple would remain. They moved to Las Vegas and bought a house, which they regard as the home-base for their travels, which takes up much of their time throughout the year. "Right now," says Carlos, "we spend about two months a year in Spain. We go from there to the major European tournaments like Vienna, Paris, Amsterdam and London." The rest of the year they're in the U.S.

Both Carlos and Cecilia say they miss Spain when they're away but admit that "we like what we do right now, and we are very happy."

Major Poker Accomplishments

2004, First place, LA Poker Classic, No Limit Hold'em

2003, First place, WSOP, Limit Hold'em

2003, Fourth place, WPT Poker Open, No Limit Hold'em Championship

2003, First place, WSOP, Limit Hold'em

2001, First place, WSOP, No Limit Hold'em Championship

2001, First place, LA Poker Classic, Limit Hold'em

John Myung 

"I'm just getting started, and my name isn't out there yet, but it will be."

Personal Notes

- **Born in New York City, 1974**
- **Graduate of Cornell University**
- **Gave up medical school to work on Wall Street**
- **Worked for Morgan Stanley in the World Trade Center**
- **Beat Lenny Dykstra heads-up**
- **Resides in Rockville, Maryland**

John Myung was born into a family of bright doctors, but after beginning his studies at Cornell Medical School in Manhattan, he decided to give up his medical career for a career in the stock market. "I didn't want to spend another six years in school," says John. "I just didn't think I could do it. I always liked business and trading stocks so I decided to go in that direction."

In 1999, John took a job working for Morgan Stanley on the 73rd floor of the World Trade Center in downtown New York. On September 1, 2001, John left his job at Morgan Stanley to take a new position on Wall Street. On September 11 terrorists flew two hijacked airliners into the twin towers. One of them hit just two floors above his office at Morgan Stanley. "It was too surreal," says John. "I was there every day, Monday through Friday, for two years. I used to get there about 8 in the morning, so if I had still been working there I would have been in the building at the time of the crash."

Several of John's co-workers didn't make it out of the building alive. Fortunately, he adds, many others hadn't arrived for work just yet that morning. As fate would have it, John wasn't due to start at his new Wall Street job until the following week. He was safe and sound in his apartment on East 66th St. at the time of the calamity. "From my building, I could see the smoke billowing into the sky." Two of his friends, in fact, ran all the way from downtown to John's apartment. "They weren't in the towers at the time," he explains, "but they were very close. When they got to my place they were covered in soot from head to toe."

Most of John's family and friends were not yet aware that

"Give it your best always; whether you're up or down, keep focused and strong."

-John Myung

he had quit his World Trade Center job, and many expected that he was in the building at the time. "I had something like 400 calls on my cell phone that day," he remembers. "They were all calling to see if I was still alive."

The whole ordeal hit just a little too close to home for John. "I needed a vacation," he says. "A bunch of my friends wanted to see me so we met on the beach at Ocean City, Maryland, and we hung out away from any big cities." John realized quickly that he didn't want to return to New York, so he quit his job and moved to Rockville, Maryland. "That's how I got started playing poker."

From Rockville, John traveled regularly up to Atlantic City to play poker at the Taj Mahal and the Sands Casinos. It wasn't the first time he'd played poker, but it was the first time he played without having a 'real job.' He did so well there, he decided that he wasn't going to bother looking for another job. When he won the million dollar no-limit tournament at the Sands in 2003, he knew he'd found his calling. "It was only the fourth no-limit tournament I ever played," he says, still amazed.

John not only plays the tournaments, he dabbles in cash games too. One of the most memorable, he says, was playing heads-up against Philadelphia Phillies all-star Lenny Dykstra. "I kept beating him at the table and Lenny said, 'hey, let's play heads-up.' We did, and I beat him real bad." In the end Dykstra lost so much money to John he handed over his Rolex watch. "He wrote me a check at first," John explains, "because I let him borrow money to play me. I didn't want to take more money from him, but he just kept insisting. I suggested that we just go hang out and drink a few beers, but he kept insisting. In the end, he said, 'I'll give you a deal: rip up the check, and I'll give you the Rolex.' I took him up on it because the Rolex was worth a lot more than the check."

With an early million dollar win and a successful track record otherwise, John Myung appears to be an incredible poker star rising off the horizon. "I'm just getting started," he says, "and my name isn't out there yet, but it will be."

Major Poker Accomplishments

2004, Third place, LA Poker Classic, Omaha Hi/Lo 8 O/B

2003, First place, Showdown at the Sands, No Limit Hold'em Championship

2002, First place, World Poker Finals, Limit Hold'em

Daniel Negreanu  

"For the most part I think my game is entertaining for the other players, but there is always that one guy who resents my success and wants to dispel it as pure luck."

Personal Notes

- **Born in Toronto, Canada, 1974**
- **Known as a "wild man" of poker**
- **Professional poker player**
- **Resides in Las Vegas**

"I wasn't going to make it in the NBA or the NHL," says Daniel Negreanu, "so tournament poker satisfied my competitive urges." In fact, he says that he doesn't play tournaments primarily for the money. Daniel plays them for the challenge and because it's just plain fun. He relies on side games, he says, to pay the bills. "That's where I go to 'work,'" he explains, "the tournaments are just a fun little treat, if anything."

That doesn't mean that Daniel hasn't had some success in tournament play—far from it. In fact, the first World Series of Poker event he ever played, he won. That was at age 23, and came to Daniel as a shock. What was perhaps even more memorable for Daniel was his showing at the World Poker Finals at Connecticut's Foxwoods Casino, where he chalked up wins in back-to-back events, beating T.J. Cloutier heads-up in the second event. "I did that on virtually no sleep, and lots of hot tea," he says.

Daniel started playing poker for fun when he was a kid. Sitting in his basement with friends, he says he cut his teeth on all kinds of bizarre wild card games like Follow the Queen, Kings and Little Ones, Fiery Cross, and Ponzai. "I didn't have a clue what was going on, but I knew I liked the game [of poker] right away."

Daniel started his tournament career in his hometown of Toronto, Canada, where he says he was lucky to have some success. "The first tournament I ever played in, I finished fifth out of a sixty player field." When he moved on to play major events south of the border in places like Las Vegas, it took a while before he made a final table. But when he finally did, he took first place. "In fact," he adds, "the first eight final tables I made, I won all eight!"

"Keep good records and don't play long hours."

-Daniel Negreanu

One of the reasons that a career as a professional poker player appealed to Daniel was the freedom. He was never one to like authority. "I hated going to school when 'they' wanted me to go," he explains. "I like doing what I want, when I want. No boss, no deadlines, no headaches. Poker offers me that luxury."

Daniel doesn't deny that poker can be a rough profession sometimes. There's the ups and downs of the game, for example, which one must constantly deal with. "There is no choice as far as I am concerned," he says. "You have to avoid emotion." Daniel has been playing tournament poker for more than a dozen years now. He's seen everything, he claims, and there's little that comes his way that he can't handle. "I approach the game as a business," he explains, "and I understand that short term results are meaningless. I just focus on making the right decisions and let the results take care of themselves. I don't get too high with the highs, and I understand that the lows are just a temporary situation and don't really sweat it."

That includes going flat out broke, which Daniel has already experienced. "If a poker player tells you he never went broke, he either plays extremely small limits or he's lying! Virtually all the greats have gone broke at least once in their careers, and I'm no different," he admits. "The key is to learn something from the experience and grow as a poker player."

Aside from being known as a "wild man" at the table, Daniel is very personable. "I basically have a good understanding of human nature," he says. "Combine that with an aggressive competitive spirit and you have the tools to do well in poker." That aggressiveness, however, sometimes comes off as cockiness, he says. "For the most part I think my game is entertaining for the other players, but there is always that one guy who resents my success and wants to dispel it as pure luck. I can't tell you how many times I've heard, 'that kid's just lucky.'"

Major Poker Accomplishments

2004, First place, Championship at the Plaza, No Limit Hold'em

2004, First place, WSOP, Limit Hold'em

2002, First place, LA Poker Classic, Omaha Hi/Lo Split

2001, 11th place, WSOP, No Limit Hold'em Championship

2001, First place, Legends of Poker, Seven Card Stud

1999, First place, US Poker No Limit Hold'em Championship

1999, Third place, Player of the Year

1998, First place, WSOP, Pot Limit Hold'em

Men "The Master" Nguyen

"I'm a hard worker, and I work hard at playing poker."

Personal Notes

Born in Phanthiet, Vietnam, 1954

Escaped from South Vietnam in 1978

Has three daughters born on the same date (December 22), in different years

Financed the building of two schools in Vietnam

Resides in Bell Gardens, California

Poker wasn't the first thing on Men Nguyen's mind when the Communists took over his country in 1975. For three years afterwards he lived in South Vietnam under conditions he compares to Castro's Cuba. "They made living there very hard," he says. That's why in 1978 he sneaked onto a 30-foot long fishing trawler on its way to Malaysia. The trip lasted five long days, he remembers, but he made it. After six months in Malaysia he went to Los Angeles, where he lives to this day.

"I came to this country empty-handed and without knowing any English," he says. "It was tough to live. I was a refugee." At first he worked as a furniture delivery man for $10 a day. "It was hard to make a living like that, but I had no choice."

A few years later, he got work as a machinist making $11 per hour, and was part-owner in a dry-cleaning business. That's also when he started to play poker. "I was working three jobs at the time," says Men. "I would get up at six and get to the machine shop by seven. Then at four in the afternoon, I would leave there to get over to my dry-cleaning business. After I closed up the store, I'd go home, shower and change before going over to the Bicycle Club to play stud."

Men got turned onto poker when he took a $30 junket to Las Vegas one weekend. He watched the pros playing Seven Card Stud at Caesar's Palace before he sat down with them at the table. "In my country, we used to play Five Card Stud: one down, four up—easy to read; and we played with only 28 cards, eights to aces," says Men, "so this game they were playing was new to me, and I lost $3,200 that weekend. To learn the game was kind of expensive."

For a few years after that, Men continued his "expensive poker lessons" until they began to pay off for him. Men worked in Los Angeles and played at the Bicycle Club during the week, but come Friday he would fly to Las Vegas to play poker there until he returned on Sunday evening. "Sometimes," he says, "I stayed over until Monday morning and would fly back early and go straight to work."

"It is very important to be patient. Don't go on tilt when you lose a pot."

-Men "the Master"

Men says he learned everything he knows about poker just from watching others play. "I'm a quick learner," he says, "Anything you show me I can learn." One quick lesson he learned was at the Dunes in 1985. "I went into the poker room there and saw a sign for 'stud,' and sat down there because that was my game. The first hand I played I had a full house—aces full of eights. I kept raising another guy, who looked like he might be holding a flush. Finally I laid down my hand to show my full house and started to take the chips. But they told me this is hi/lo split. Then they had to explain to me what that meant; I'd never heard of that game."

Men says he stayed at that table all weekend and lost all his money. But week after week he kept returning to the same game. Six weeks later he says he had it mastered. "I beat the game good, but I paid for my lessons."

By 1990, Men realized he was making a lot more money from his poker playing than from his other two jobs combined. A year later he quit his machinist job and sold off his dry-cleaning business. "That's when I became a full-time poker player. I won so many tournaments that it's hard for me to count."

It was in the early 1990s when Men was giving poker lessons to a man who started to call him "the Master." Since a lot of people in the poker world were using nicknames, Men kept that one, he says, because of his ability to master a game just by watching how it's played.

It was in 1996 that Men scored big. That year he won four gold bracelets and took home a sizable paycheck each time. "I had always said if I made a lot of money doing this, I would do something for the children back in Vietnam," says Men. He fulfilled that promise by donating more than $20,000 to build two new schools in the poorest areas of his native country. "I never thought I'd become a full-time professional poker player, but it just happened that way," he says. "Now that I have the resources, I want to keep giving to the children in Vietnam who have almost nothing."

Major Poker Accomplishments

2004, First place, Bay 101 Shooting Star, Limit Hold'em

2003, First place, World Poker Challenge, Pot Limit Hold'em and Omaha Hi/Lo

2003, First place, World Poker Finals, Limit Hold'em

2003, First place, Legends of Poker, Mixed Games

2003, Fourth place, WPT Celebrity Invitational

Winner of six WSOP gold bracelets

1997, Player of the Year

1996, Fourth place, WSOP, No Limit Hold'em Championship

Scotty Nguyen  

"And when I get to the final table, it's all over, baby."

Personal Notes

- **Born in Nha Trang, Vietnam**
- **Came to the United States when he was 14 years old**
- **Ranks among the highest-earning tournament players of all time**
- **Often visits his large extended family in Vietnam**
- **Resides in Las Vegas**

Don't be fooled by the big smile on Scotty Nguyen's face when he is playing poker. He is known as one of the most talkative and friendly guys at the table; but he is also one of the deadliest when it comes to poker. According to Scotty, when he reaches a final table he has about an 80% win rate. "I've been there so many times," Scotty says without a hint of pretention, "that I'm relaxed. I know the players and I know what to do." And Scotty has the credentials to back him up on that.

Scotty is ranked among the highest earning tournament poker players of all time. He has won a countless number of events, including "the big one," taking home the gold bracelet in the main event of the World Series of Poker in 1998. Though he works hard at his wins, you would never know it from his demeanor. He is as easygoing as they come, even up until the moment he takes his opponent down.

When Scotty won the World Series Championship, it came down to the final hand with Kevin McBride. He said to Kevin, "You call this one and it's all over, baby." Kevin called and was beaten by Scotty's higher full house. Scotty credits his confident style along with his friendliness at the poker table for his ability to win, though he admits that his aggressive style can sometimes pose problems for him.

Scotty has always been one to take charge of his life and the direction it was taking. When he was 14 years old, he came to the United States under a sponsorship program. After one winter in Chicago with his sponsor, Scotty took matters into his own hands and asked for a different sponsor. He was moved to a family in Orange County, California where he was much happier.

Never the scholar, he relied on copying answers from a friend of his whenever there was a test. After his friend caught on

"It's not enough just to have a poker face. You have to have poker shoulders and poker hands."

-John Vorhaus

to what he was doing, he pulled a fast one on Scotty by turning his paper upside down so Scotty couldn't read the answers properly. When the test grades were handed out, Scotty was dumfounded. He had an F and his friend had a B! With all the bravado of a reckless teen, he told his teacher that it was impossible that he got an F. When she asked why, he simply pointed to his friend and said. "Well, he got a B." He said the class just "cracked up" with laughter.

Scotty was also inventive when it came to finding a way back and forth from school. Every day he and his friends would steal a different bike to ride home, then bring it back the next day. "I was very bad back then," he says sheepishly. Scotty didn't even graduate from high school because he was missing a few credits at the end of the year. Not to worry. He and his friends broke into the principal's office and stole about 300 diplomas and passed them out around school. One can see where Scotty's fearlessness at the poker table has its roots!

Family is very important to Scotty, as well. He brags that it would take "about three years" to talk about all of his relatives. He supports them in Vietnam where money goes a lot further than it does in the States. He bought his mother one of the biggest houses in her area and when she walks on the street, he says people whisper, and say, "There goes Scotty Nguyen's mother." He is proud to be helping his mother and the rest of his family.

Scotty realizes that he has changed a lot from the time he lived in Vietnam. He says his friends sometimes treat him as if he were an alien. "They think I'm going to eat differently, and things like that but I'm not," he tells them. Since he won the World Series, he says that he dresses differently and maybe talks a little differently, but he is the same old Scotty.

As to all of his winnings, Scotty admits to being a bit of a spendthrift. "He calls his money management skills "horrible. If I have $10,000, I will spend $9,000. I just go out and have fun." And Scotty always looks like he is having fun. The smile, the twinkle in his eye, the offhand comments always peppered with his signature word "baby," give Scotty Nguyen a unique presence that puts his opponents off-balance and that's the whole idea!

Major Poker Accomplishments

2004, Sixth place, WPT Party Poker Million III, No Limit Hold'em Championship

2002, First place, LA Poker Classic, Seven Card Stud Hi/Lo Split

2002, Sixth place, WPT Five Diamond World Poker Classic, No Limit Hold'em Championship

2002, Third place, WPT Ultimate Bet Championship, No Limit Hold'em, Pro Division

2001, First place, World Poker Finals, No Limit Hold'em Championship

Winner of four WSOP gold bracelets

1998, First place, WSOP, No Limit Hold'em Championship

Frankie O'Dell 

"You can't control the cards even if you know how to play the game well."

Personal Notes

Born in Denver, Colorado, 1971

Repentant ex-gang member

Hangs out in Hollywood

Former poker dealer

Professional poker player

Resides in Long Beach, California

When Irish fans look around for Frankie O'Dell to wish him well before a tournament, they're surprised to find that he's Chicano—not Irish. "The Irish love me," says Frankie. "They don't seem to care that I'm not Irish. They invite me to visit their country anyway."

Frankie explains that his father was adopted by an Irish-American family whose ancestors hail from the city of Dell, located at the northern tip of the Outer Hebrides. "I've thought about opening a Mexican restaurant there," he jests. "They'll love the O'Dell burrito special."

Frankie was actually born to Mexican-American parents in Denver, Colorado. His father was a traveling casino employee, and Frankie often traveled with him. "He took me to the World Series when I was about eleven," he remembers, "and while I was watching at the rail, Johnny Moss winked at me. My dad told me he was one of the best players in the world, a guy who helped define the profession of poker. I remember thinking that maybe that wink was a sign."

Frankie says he was "thrust into poker" because it was his father's business. "He always said I had a knack for playing poker," he says of his dad. "He said to me once that I was ten times the player that he was at my age. He told me I had ability and talent." Ability, explains Frankie, is being able to wait for the good cards and knowing when to move in. Talent, he adds, is knowing how to read the other players at your table.

In addition to working poker games at casinos, Frankie's father also ran his own poker room in Denver. When Frankie was 15 he started dealing at these games—not by choice but more out of necessity. "In the course of the night my dad would usually get drunk and pass out. Then it would be up to me to run the games."

At 19 he was traveling to Las Vegas to play poker in the casinos.

"I just hoped the places wouldn't card me," he says. "But I got kicked out a few times for winning too much money. When you win a lot of money, people notice you. Otherwise they wouldn't have cared how young I was."

"Hold'em is to stud what chess is to checkers."

-Johnny Moss

Frankie is also noticeable because of the tattoos he wears on his arms and fingers. One, which reads "Naked," is written in black script across his right forearm. "I had a brief marriage when I was 16," he explains, "and this was a kind of wedding ring." His left fingers bear the marks of the Denver street gang he ran with from the time he was 12 on through high school. "I was foolish and naïve then," he admits. "I thought I had a lot of power because I was a gang leader. Later I figured out that wasn't the kind of power I wanted."

Frankie says his life changed drastically for the better when he became a Christian. "I found religion, and it's helped me a lot. Once I found Jesus my heart opened up to emotions and normal behavior. I was pretty bad when I was younger, but not anymore. There are some pro poker players who know me from when I was a teenager, and they can't believe how much I've changed."

When Frankie used to play poker he would be filled with anger that got expressed like fireworks. "I used to get mad when I got a bad beat, and I used to get angry at people who played poorly and just got lucky," he admits. "I realize now that you can't control the cards even if you know how to play the game well. My hot, heated days are over."

Although there is an element of luck in the game of poker, Frankie says the key is to put yourself in a position to get lucky. "You play well and then, boom, you start getting lucky. You have to be able to play well to get to the point where you can catch the wave of luck."

Frankie started his tournament winning streak at the Horseshoe Casino in Las Vegas in 1997. "My dad was still alive then to see me win that one," he says. "I was 26 years old at the time, and the veterans called me a 'rising star.' They recognized that I had talent, but they also said I need to refine it and develop it. That's what I've been working on."

Major Poker Accomplishments

2003, First place WSOP, Omaha Hi/Lo Split

2003, First place, World Poker Open, Omaha Hi/Lo Split

2003, First place, Legends of Poker, No Limit Hold'em event

1997, First place, Hall of Fame Poker Classic, Limit Hold'em

Pascal Perrault

"I do not care about the fame or the money, but the challenge. You can spit on the money!"

Personal Notes

Born in Paris, 1959

Father of five

Graduated from Paris University with a doctorate in pharmacy

Favors the WSOP as his favorite tournament

Known to others as "P.P. the Bandit"

Resides in Brazil and Paris

Pascal Perrault has a lot of support for his poker career. He sees his family as his greatest fans. In fact, his girlfriend Lise Vigezi is the "Pink Lady" of the European "Late Night Poker" show who appears in the beginning of the show for the introduction. His 16-year-old son is so enamored of his father's life that he wants to follow in his father's footsteps as a pharmacist . . . "so he can play poker!"

Tournament poker became a part of Pascal's life as he attempted to forget about the tragic loss of a loved one. He found that immersing himself in tournament play was a good way to help him recover from the loss. Though he plays some cash games, he much prefers tournament play and has made a name for himself as "P.P. the Bandit" in European circles—a man who will take your money and show no mercy.

He quickly won many European tournaments which gave him the incentive to travel to Binion's Horseshoe in Las Vegas for his first World Series of Poker. His dreams of winning the main event were quickly destroyed, however, when he was eliminated within two hours of starting play. "I decided that I had a lot more learning to do," Pascal admits. The WSOP is still his favorite tournament event, though, and he hopes one day to be a gold bracelet winner at the tournament.

Before televised poker burst onto the scene in the U.S.A., Europe had its own "Late Night Poker" show and Pascal has had the honor of appearing in every season of the show. In fact, his most memorable poker experience was being the first to be on "Late Night Poker," the pioneer of all televised poker series. Pascal sees that television has given poker the legitimacy of a sport. "TV makes it look more like a sport, which is the view that I have always had on the subject."

There is one drawback that he sees to popularizing poker on television. He says that the audience thinks that "what you win is really strictly what you win, without realizing that you must pay for expenses, other entry fees into other tournaments, etc." Yet he would not give up poker unless he became the world champion. Even then, he admits that he might want the challenge of becoming a back to back winner the next year.

This attitude reflects Pascal's entire philosophy of poker. He plays for the challenge, not the money. "I do not care about the fame or the money, but the challenge. You can spit on the money," he comments.

"Focus your mind completely on the tournament at hand without any distractions from any outside source."

-Pascal Perrault

Pascal has a number of qualities that he feels are important to tournament play. He tries to maintain a good attitude at all times, and feels that he is able to adapt to others' play to his advantage. One of the ways he is able to do that is by "putting his ego in his pocket" when he plays. "You can't focus on getting your chips back from a particular player once you've had a bad beat," he advises.

For a man so focused on his techniques for the game, Pascal also admits to having some superstitions. His biggest one is that he does not want a player who has just been eliminated from a tournament to talk to him. He sees that person as having a bad aura and he wants nothing to do with it! Pascal also foresees some major developments in the psychology of poker in the next couple of decades. This includes the debatable subject of extra sensory perception as it applies to the game of poker. He sees a scientific explanation for having a good hand and feeling that he will still lose with the hand . . . and he does! "On the other hand sometimes with bad cards you know that you are going to win with them and you do," states Pascal. He looks at the action of the mind as having an influence on chance and feels that study in this area will help players to understand how it influences poker ability.

Though he loves to play in America, there is one area of stateside poker that Pascal questions. He does not understand why American dealers use two hands to deal the cards. Europeans use a blackjack shoe where the cards are pulled out with one hand. With two hands, it is easier to cheat, he says. It is the only thing that he would change about American poker, but it won't stop him from competing at the WSOP for his dream win.

Pascal is not giving up his day job just yet, however, and he advises new players to do the same. "So many people, especially the young ones will win one huge tournament; then they have a bad period, they won't be able to go back and they will be broke." He also advises playing in live tournaments, not just on the internet, and starting out small, building up from there. Other than that, Pascal refuses to give away any of his poker secrets. When asked what makes his game unique he replies that he wouldn't tell us if there were something! Got to have some secrets.

Major Poker Accomplishments

2003, 14th place, WSOP, No Limit Hold'em Championship

2003, Fourth place, European WSOP, No Limit Hold'em Championship

2002, First place, Euro Finals of Poker, Pot Limit Omaha

2002, First place, Austrian Masters, Pot Limit Hold'em

2002, First place, European Poker Classics, Pot Limit Omaha Hi/Lo

2001, First place, British Open, No Limit Hold'em Championship

2001, First place, Euro Finals of Poker, Limit Omaha Hi/Lo

2001, Winner of Best Poker Personality, European Poker Awards

Young Phan

"One thing I've learned about getting involved in poker is that you better not be a gambler."

Personal Notes

- **Born in Nha Trang, Vietnam, 1958**
- **Immigrated to U.S. in 1975**
- **Graduated from California Polytechnic**
- **Former supervisor at Bicycle Casino**
- **Professional poker player**
- **Resides in Irvine, California**

Young Phan is as gregarious as they come, but you wouldn't know it from watching him play poker. "When I'm on the table," he says, "you won't hear a word from me." Young, who considers himself a conservative poker player, believes that one of his greatest assets is his patience. "I'm tight," he says, "because I can be. I like to wait."

Unlike many other poker players on world tour, Young Phan isn't too much concerned with "having fun" while playing. "For me," he explains, "it's usually a grind. Poker is not gambling, but work, for me. I treat it like a business, and I work hard at it."

In this business, Young is a real-life jet setter, flying at least thirty times each year. It was his first airplane trip, however, that was his most memorable. "I flew out of Vietnam on a C-20, a U.S. military plane that carried tanks and other military vehicles." This was in 1975, the year the Communists took over South Vietnam. "I was lucky," he says. "Two of my sisters worked for the American Embassy in Saigon, and they spoke English well. If it wasn't for them, I probably wouldn't be in the U.S. today."

The Communists had already captured two-thirds of his country, and he saw his neighbors killed in many ways. "It was horrible there," he remembers. "We left because we knew we couldn't live with the Communists. We were among the last who were able to escape." After a layover in Guam that lasted several weeks, Young and his family flew into Camp Pendleton, California. "St. Christopher's Catholic Church in Covina helped us get on our feet," he remembers. "They helped us with food and clothes for three years."

Young went to school in Southern California for twelve hours a day just to learn how to read and write in English. He then went on to study at UCLA and graduated from Cal Poly in San Luis Obispo. He landed his first job as a casino supervisor at Bicycle Casino, where he was introduced to the game of poker.

"My favorite player was Johnny Chan," he says. "He played real high,

"Win or lose, take it like a man or a woman. Don't embarrass yourself."

-Young Phan

and I liked his style. I learned a lot from him. He's one of the biggest reasons I got turned onto poker." Once Young started to play he was hooked. "I decided to turn professional. Everything I went to school for just went out the window. I was making a lot more money playing poker even though I made pretty good money working at Bicycle."

Despite the fact that Young made good money playing poker, he says he fought against a financially crippling gambling addiction for almost fifteen years. "There wasn't a casino game that I didn't play," he says, "and I was losing about five times more than I was making." A decade ago he gave it all up cold turkey. "One thing I learned about getting involved in poker is that you better not be a gambler."

Five years ago Young got into playing the big tournament games, and that's when his family discovered he was a poker player—and not everyone was understanding of the fact. "I have three brothers and three sisters, and there's my mom," he explains. "Some of them wanted to disown me when they found out I was a professional poker player." They found out when his youngest brother, a California dentist, saw a television interview with Young on the Discovery Channel. "That interview was broadcast over and over," he says. "I had kept my poker playing from my family up to that time because I knew they didn't approve of gambling. When my brother saw the interview he videotaped it—and then showed it to my mom."

Young won a tournament in Reno in 1999; the payoff was around $370,000. "I even kept that from my mom," he says. "That shows you how my family feels about gambling." But things are changing now, he says, even with his mother. "Because of televised poker programs, many of my family members are coming to accept that I play poker for a living."

Major Poker Accomplishments

2004, Seventh place, WSOP, No Limit Hold'em event

2004, Sixth place, WPT World Poker Challenge, No Limit Hold'em Championship

2003, Second place, WSOP, Limit Hold'em

2001, First place, LA Poker Classic, No Limit Hold'em Championship

David Plastik

"I'm very excitable when I play—at times, a bit too excitable, but all in the art of competition."

Personal Notes

- **Born in Queens, New York, 1964**
- **Graduate of University of Hartford**
- **Former music photographer**
- **Former textile salesman**
- **Partied with Madonna and the Rolling Stones**
- **Resides in Las Vegas**

During his high school and college years David Plastik was living out every teenager's American dream. With a 35mm camera in hand he traveled the U.S. with his rock and roll idols, making a living as a freelance photographer. "I shot everyone from the Rolling Stones and Metallica to Madonna and George Michael," he says, "and sold my photos to whoever would buy them"—that includes the big music magazines like *Billboard* and *Rolling Stone.*

He also attended the American Music Awards and the Academy Awards in Hollywood. "It was good work for a kid," he says, "but the magazines didn't pay well. They took advantage of me, thinking that standing in the front row at a concert was enough to make me happy."

Partying with the icons of rock and roll also meant descending into a life of serious drug use. For a time, David worked as the personal photographer for comedian Sam Kennison. "I became very good friends with him, and he introduced me to all these famous people. He was a pretty extreme partier, and he got me into all that. It was a crazy life, and after a while it got ugly."

After moving to Los Angeles David decided to "clean up his act" and "straighten out his life." He worked as the sales representative for his father's textile business and became quite successful. The textile business, however, wasn't his only success. Commerce Casino was in the neighborhood, and David decided to drive over there during his lunch hour one day. "I had played poker in home games before but never in a casino," he says. "I sat down at a table and won."

He attributes that first win to beginner's luck because he wasn't that good at the game—No Limit Hold'em—just yet. He quickly became a regular at the poker room at Commerce and honed his play. "I just learned the game and liked it."

In 1997 he discovered poker tournaments. "I liked the competitive aspect of it because

"I've read every poker book ever written, but the only way to get better at the game is to go out and play with people who are really good. The problem is, you stand to lose a lot of money doing it."

-Mike from *Rounders*

I'm an extremely competitive person." One manifestation of David's competitiveness is his table manner. "I'm very excitable when I play," he readily admits. "At times a bit too excitable, but all in the art of competition." Although he may not be the biggest "brat" on the professional poker circuit, David compares himself to John McEnroe, known for throwing tantrums on the tennis court. "Like McEnroe," he says, "I get very excited when I win and very distraught when I lose."

David's poker career really took off when his business collapsed. When his father passed away, the company he worked for disbanded, and David went to work for another company owned by his father's partner. For a few years he was highly successful, bringing in as much as $25,000 a month. But when his mother died, he lost interest in the business and was cut loose. "I didn't know what I was going to do," he remembers. "Finding another job as a salesman meant I would have to start all over at the bottom. It wasn't worth it."

David had some money saved up and decided to try his hand at playing poker for a few months. He had just won his first tournament and his confidence was high. He flew out to Atlantic City to play at the Taj Mahal. On his third day there he made it to the final table of the big event, which was broadcast on ESPN. "I thought, 'Wow, I'm getting good at this.' I made $100,000 in my first month on the road."

The next month he scored again in Vegas. "I had a lot of money, and I owned a house. I was a single guy and had no dependents and no commitments, so I decided to keep doing this. I had the desire to go forward with it—and I did."

Poker is a game of ups-and-downs no matter how good a player might be, but for David it's nothing compared to the financial ups-and-downs he's experienced outside of poker. He invested most of his poker winnings and his business savings in high tech stocks on the market. "I thought I was safe. I thought I was being prudent, that I was investing my money wisely." Then came the big crash of high-tech stocks. "I lost everything—including my house," he says. "My bankroll is now very short." When times are tough financially, David says it affects his game. "I tend to become gun-shy. In poker, you can't be gun-shy."

Major Poker Accomplishments

2004, Seventh place, WPT Bay 101 Shooting Star, No Limit Hold'em Championship

2003, Second place, Five Star World Poker Classic, Limit Hold'em

2002, Second place, Hall of Fame Poker Classic, No Limit Hold'em event

2000, First place, Legends of Poker, H.O.S.E.

2000, Second place, LA Poker Classic, Limit Hold'em

"Amarillo Slim" Preston 

"I haven't anything left to prove."

Personal Notes

- **Born in Johnson, Arkansas, 1928**
- **Former professional billiards champion**
- **Member of five Halls of Fame**
- **Former bookmaker**
- **Kidnapped in Colombia by drug lord Pablo Escobar**
- **Resides in Amarillo, Texas**

Amarillo Slim is arguably the most famous poker player of all-time. He's known, however, not just because of his long and successful poker career, but because he's been in the public eye for a variety of accomplishments. Habitually dressed in his cowboy hat and cowboy boots, Slim is more the ultimate icon of the gambling world than just a simple poker face.

His illustrious career started out in the billiards halls of Texas, and Slim at age 16 became the youngest player ever to play in the World Billiards Tournament. "Uncle Sam sent me all over the world," he explains. "In fact, I held the title of Goodwill Ambassador for this country." During his twenties Slim traveled to every military base in the world. "They would hold a pool tournament prior to me getting there," he remembers. "Whoever won it would have to play me. If he could beat me, he got a $100 war bond and a three-day pass. But I didn't let anybody win it."

At age 26 Slim decided it was time to give up the international billiards routine. He was traveling too much and wanted to settle back down in Texas. He returned to the Lonestar State as a bookmaker. Along with longtime pal Doyle Brunson, Slim says he booked sports for 23 years. "We went all over the country playing poker during that time too," he adds. "When we hit town, we looked like a vacuum cleaner, sucking up all the money in sight."

Poker was a natural offshoot from bookmaking, says Slim, and his poker career was to outlast his bookmaking career by decades. "When Bobby Kennedy became the United States Attorney General, Doyle and I got out of booking sports because he had made it a felony to transmit sports information over state lines. When they started talking about incarceration, I said 'enough.'"

Slim never limited his wagers to poker. The more exotic wagers garnered not a little attention from the media. He once bet a million dollars that he could hit a golf ball a mile—and won. He challenged Bobby Reese, the number one tennis hustler in the world to a ping pong match, under one condition: Slim would choose the paddles. Reese agreed, and Slim chose iron frying skillets to be used as the paddles. Guess who won? Yep, Slim. These types of exotic wagers got him onto *The Tonight Show* eleven times and onto *60 Minutes* a record-breaking three times. So colorful has been the life of Amarillo Slim that his life story is being adapted to the silver screen.

"If you have a strong hand, don't check, then raise. It may scare your opponents into throwing hands away early."

-Amarillo Slim

But Slim's experiences haven't all been butter and roses. He's feared for his life a number of times—both at the poker table and off. His most memorable experience playing poker happened in Houston, Texas. "I played in a real bad game," he explains. "Everybody in the world asked me not to go. No sensible person in the world would have played in that game. It was at the headquarters of the banditos. But I went. At one point the bandito boss looked up at me and said, 'Cowboy, I've noticed that every time a big pot comes up it's me and you.' He said, 'I'll tell you what, you've won them all so far and now I'm thinking seriously of calling you. If I call you and you've got my hand beat, you'll never leave this room alive.'"

Slim knew the boss was serious. The banditos had a bad track record. They'd done it before—shot poker players who won too many pots. "I didn't even have a toothpick with me," he remembers. "So I had to do something. I looked over at him and didn't even blink. I said, 'Let me tell you something, asshole, it takes a tough son of a bitch to whip me, but it sure doesn't take him long.'" That made him laugh, and soon the whole room was laughing. For the rest of the night, no one bothered Slim.

But that's not the only time Slim sweat bullets. In the mid-1990s he was playing poker in a casino in Cartegena, Colombia when a man came in with a sawed-off shotgun and shot a woman's head off right in front of him. "The last time her heart beat, blood squirted out the top of her head and got all over me," he remembers. Another 40 gunmen came into the place with Uzis. He soon found out they were a part of Pablo Escobar's Medellín drug gang. When they discovered Slim was American, they stripped him naked, wired his hands together, and flew him in a helicopter to Medellín. "I was trying to figure out how to fly with my hands tied behind my back," he says. "I thought they were going to drop me into the jungle."

Fortunately an acquaintance explained to Escobar who Amarillo Slim was, and the Colombian drug kingpin (later assassinated by the CIA) released the naked Texan. No one can say the life Amarillo Slim has led hasn't been colorful. After it all, says Slim, "I haven't anything left to prove."

Major Poker Accomplishments

Winner of four WSOP gold bracelets

2001, Second place, World Heads Up No Limit Hold'em Championship

1972, First place, WSOP, No Limit Hold'em Championship

Greg Raymer

"I only appear to be wacko; in reality I'm much worse."

Personal Notes

- **Originally from North Dakota**
- **Patent lawyer by occupation**
- **Likes to collect fossils and uses them as card protectors**
- **Plays a lot at Foxwoods in Connecticut**
- **Resides in Stonington, Connecticut**

Greg Raymer is not a name that was widely known before the 2004 World Series of Poker. But after his mega-win of $5 million dollars at the main event in 2004, it is not a name that is likely to be forgotten. Before this big win, Greg's best tournament finish was third in the main event at the World Poker Finals in Foxwoods, Connecticut in 2001.

Greg "Fossilman" Raymer is a corporate patent attorney by trade. He loves to play poker, especially at the Foxwoods casino which is near his home. But he also plays online poker where he won his entry into the World Series at pokerstars.com. He says he entered a $160 double Shootout about a week before the main event started, though he would have paid the $10,000 entry fee himself had he not won it. This was the Second World Series of Poker that Greg has entered. The previous year he paid his way into the tournament. And he is the second consecutive online player to win the tournament.

The "Fossilman" gets his nickname from his passion for collecting fossils. It became a poker nickname when he began to use fossils as card protectors. One can imagine that the fossil he used in his World Series win will become his lucky charm.

Greg played nickel, dime poker in college and only started playing seriously after he entered a charity game in Chicago. It prompted him to do some studying of the game, which he did through books and practice. He says that he has been playing poker seriously now for 10 years.

Greg's wife and daughter accompanied him to Las Vegas this year to see him defeat a field of 2,575 people from all over the world. He not only won the largest cash prize in poker to date, but also beat the largest field of entrants, up from 839 the previous year. Greg felt that everything went right for him from day one of the tournament. He claims that he didn't even feel the effects of playing in a tournament that lasted for seven days. "For some unknown reason, I was very calm and very focused all week long," states Greg matter-of-factly. "I made very few plays that I thought were mistakes at the time the decision was made." He admits that he would like to know what it was that kept him on an even keel during the week of the tournament. "[Then] I could ensure to repeat it every tournament."

"Practice for free or for small stakes, and work your way up by winning your way up."

-Greg Raymer

Seven hours after the finals began, Greg, who had the chip advantage over his opponent, David Williams, matched David's all-in call. They both had full houses but Greg's eights over twos beat David's fours over twos and his name went down in the World Series records as the 2004 winner. Though understandably, Greg was jumping for joy over his victory, he modestly admitted, "I played well but I was the luckiest."

Pictures of Greg playing poker with his sunglasses on beg the question as to how he ever decided to wear something so bizarre at the poker table. "Two years ago," he answers, "I was on a family vacation to Disney World, and saw them in the Tower of Terror gift shop, about a month before the main event. I just had to wear them at the table, and did so." To some degree this reflects his motto: "I only appear to be wacko. In reality I'm much worse."

According to one commentator it would be difficult not to like this "amusing, intelligent and affable player," who is "a credit to the game." Another describes his play at the final table as "relentless," and goes on to say that "he raised pots and was not afraid to come over the top with spectacular re-raises as well." Let's not forget that he also outlasted the respected 1995 WSOP champion, Dan Harrington at the final table, not to mention the host of other memorable players who did not make it to the finals. The odds on Greg before the tournament (according to Pokertropolis) were 400-1. Mathematically speaking they will probably be a lot better next year!

Greg Raymer has shown everyone that he is no longshot when it comes to outlasting the best. When Benny Binion established the World Series of Poker, it's probably safe to say that he could not have seen, in his mind's eye, his winner facing a field of 2,576 entrants or winning a prize of $5 million; and he certainly would not have imagined the part that computers would play in getting the winner to the tournament. Greg Raymer has accomplished what Benny Binion could never have envisioned and he is to be congratulated for his success.

Major Poker Accomplishments

2004, First place, WSOP, No Limit Hold'em Championship

2000, Third place, World Poker Finals, No Limit Hold'em Championship

Chip Reese 

"If you never play someone on the next level you don't even know that level exists. It's almost another dimension."

Personal Notes

- **Born in Dayton, Ohio**
- **Graduate of Dartmouth College**
- **Planned to become a lawyer**
- **Highly regarded cash game player**
- **Resides in Las Vegas**

When other legendary poker players put someone at the top of their lists of the best poker players ever—yes, ever—he must be doing something right. That someone is David "Chip" Reese, the youngest player ever to be inducted into the Poker Hall of Fame. When Chip began to play serious poker in Las Vegas, he was not the stereotypical poker player. Chip was actually on his way to Stanford to enter law school after graduating from Dartmouth with a degree in economics. A chance entry into a Seven Card Stud tournament in Las Vegas, where he won over $60,000 put an abrupt halt to his legal ambitions.

He never made it to Stanford. But he did make it into the big time poker circles. The story has it that Chip's parents did not realize for almost a year that their son had taken a detour on his road to Stanford and continued to send him checks for his schooling and expenses even as he was becoming known as one of the top players in Las Vegas.

Chip had played poker before, just not professionally. When he lived in his hometown of Dayton, Ohio he was already playing poker for baseball cards when he was six years old. Some of the other pros who originated from the same city, like Mike Sexton and Danny Robison, remember playing with Chip back then and recognizing his extraordinary ability to win.

Now, Chip Reese makes Las Vegas his home. It's there that he takes part in some of the biggest games around. No longer playing for baseball cards, Chip takes part in games with the other legendary cash players like Doyle Brunson, Billy Baldwin, Lyle Berman, etc. He plays in games where it's not uncommon to win (or lose) at least seven figures.

For an intelligent man like Chip Reese, it's the mathematics of the game that intrigues him. "Like backgammon, it's a very simple game, Chip states. "But it's also highly mathematical. If you never play someone on the next level you don't even know that level exists," he continues. "It's almost another dimension."

Though Chip only turned pro after he made that life-altering stop in Las Vegas in '75, he had played in Las Vegas many times in the '60s. His recollection of poker in the '60s is worlds apart from what he sees in poker today. "In the '60s," he remembers, "someone bit a dealer's ear off." In the '70s, someone urinated on a dealer at the Stardust. But that was then. Today, casinos take a no-tolerance approach to bad behavior. People who misbehave get thrown out for two weeks, a month, maybe forever."

"In a game of poker, I can put the player's souls in my pocket."

-Beausourire

Gambling magnate Jack Binion says of Chip, "He's the premier poker player in the world right now. . . Since turning pro [about] 29 years ago, the Dartmouth economics grad, has consistently managed to remain among the highest rollers."

Maybe it's fitting, then, that Chip Reese made his first appearance on the World Poker Tour televised final table at Jack Binion's World Poker Open in Tunica. It was a pleasure to finally be able to see this gifted player in action. Though he did not place first in the event, just watching him play was enough for most fans, though probably not for Chip!

When he was interviewed for the show, Chip imparted some words of wisdom that apply to poker and to life in general. "What really separates top pros from good poker players is when things are going bad," Chip mused. "It's like life. It's a long road that doesn't turn. It's how you handle the adversity in a poker game that matters."

It's not likely that Chip regrets his decision to stay in Vegas instead of entering law school. At one time he told an interviewer, "Law doesn't have the same monetary incentive as poker." When Chip came to Las Vegas he partnered with his buddy Danny Robison another poker great, and they took the town by storm. But poker is not Chip's only forte. He is also a world-class backgammon player and gin rummy aficionado.

Aside from being a great poker player, Chip Reese is also known to be a genuinely nice guy. He commands the respect of the gambling community not only for his prowess at the games he plays but also for his affable manner. It would be a shame not to see more of Chip on TV at a WPT or WSOP final table!

Major Poker Accomplishments

2004, Fourth place, WPT World Poker Open, No Limit Hold'em Championship

1991, Youngest member ever inducted into the Poker Hall of Fame

1982, First place, WSOP, Seven Card Stud

1978, First place, WSOP, Seven Card Stud Split

Lucy Rokach

"The goal is not necessarily to win this hand, or this night, but to come away winning overall at the end of the year."

Personal Notes

Born in Cairo, Egypt

Left Cairo for England in 1960

Paved the way for ladies on the European scene

Has no superstitions as a poker player

Former history teacher and car dealer

Resides in Stoke-on-Trent, England

Lucy Rokach is a one-of-a-kind poker player well-known throughout Europe. Considered to be Europe's top female pro, she received the Lifetime Achievement Award at the 2003 European Poker Awards, a ceremony akin to the Academy Awards.

It's not that Lucy loves the limelight. She admits to never really thinking that poker is an exciting pastime. "People say to me, 'don't you get a high or something?' . . . and I don't think so. But you come [to the United States]," she continues, "and all of a sudden they win a pot and they get all excited. I think it's downright rude, to be truthful." Lucy keeps her adrenaline surges to a low even after winning a tournament. She admits to maybe feeling some adrenaline when she is bluffing but, she says, "I hope nobody can tell."

A realist at heart, Lucy prefers the fortune to the fame in poker. "I want the fortune, thank you. You can keep the bracelets and the awards." Lucy does appreciate that poker is a challenge, however. After losing her poker bankroll once, she re-financed her house and borrowed money to continue. "It's succeeding. It's a challenge. I have to know that I can do this," she says. And Lucy apparently does it well now.

Lucy learned early on that life can hand you some unexpected obstacles. Though Lucy was born in Cairo, she had to abruptly move with her family to England when the Suez crisis broke out in Egypt. All Europeans were "given marching orders," remembers Lucy. Since her mother had a British passport, they went to England, her home ever since.

She recalls with a certain sadness that her two brothers were over 18 at that time and so they separated from the family to go to Israel. She didn't see them again for nine years.

Worse yet, her mother had to leave all of her brothers and sisters, who scattered throughout the globe. Lucy did not even learn English until she was nine years old.

Lucy started out as a history teacher, but moved on to what she calls "greener pastures" in the automobile sales business. Seventeen years ago she began to play poker in local casinos and card rooms in England before she gradually moved on to bigger venues.

Lucy's aggressiveness at the table leaves no room for her opponents to take advantage of her. Her self-belief and discipline have served her well in that regard. "You have to know that what you're doing is right even though you haven't won that day, or that hand," Lucy cautions. "You have to know you're playing the right way and that it will win more times than it will lose. You need to be disciplined about your goal and very focused. The goal is not necessarily to win this hand, or this night, but to come away winning overall at the end of the year."

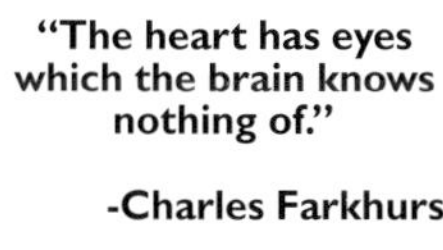

"The heart has eyes which the brain knows nothing of."

-Charles Farkhurst

The path has not always been free of twists and turns for Lucy, but she persevered as is her nature; and consequently she has paved the way for women on the European poker scene. Along the way she has learned some valuable lessons and techniques that have stayed with her throughout.

She views courage and resilience in the face of defeats as her strongest and most valuable characteristics. She is never afraid to stand up and voice her opinion when she sees something wrong. Her respect for the other players is reciprocated by her opponents at the table.

It's almost strange to think of a poker player, who spends hours or days playing a tournament or a cash game, as taking the time to eat, let alone cook. But away from the table, Lucy likes to cook as well as pursue her newest hobby of gardening. With amazement she says that her garden is not only surviving but flourishing. "I'm amazed," Lucy happily admits. "They are so beautiful."

And if Lucy ever decides to retire from the poker tournament circuit, she won't have to look far to find another vocation. According to Lucy she enjoys the art of painting and is quite good at it. Of course, with winnings of more than a half million Euros, in the past 5 years, it may be quite a while before Lucy will be found behind the easel.

Major Poker Accomplishments

2004, First place, British Open, Pot Limit Hold'em

2003, Lifetime Achievement Award, European Poker Awards

2003, First place, Irish Winter Tournament, No Limit Hold'em Championship

2003, First place, Midlands Meltdown, Pot Limit Hold'em

2003, First place, Euro Finals of Poker, Pot Limit Hold'em/Omaha

2001, First place, Aviation Club Winter Tournament, No Limit Hold'em Championship

2001, First place, Irish Winter Tournament, No Limit Hold'em Championship

Ron Rose 

"It was the kind of game I liked to play. Eleven top WPT champions, no dead money and a prestigious title along with 'bragging rights'."

Personal Notes

Born in Vancouver, Washington, 1944

Graduate of the University of Massachusetts, BS in Mathematics

Married with three children and four grandchildren

Former member of American Stock Exchange

Former Captain in the U.S. Air Force

Life Master in duplicate bridge

Resides in Dayton, Ohio

Ron Rose started dreaming about competing with professional poker players when he was a young man playing penny ante games at his grandmother's dining room table. "I could see myself playing with the poker pros I had heard about, and this thought stayed with me for years," says Ron. "I liked the challenge and competition, even at a young age—and I was good."

He was determined to fulfill his youthful dream of competing with the greatest poker pros—and beating them. His poker education began in 2000 with the biggest event in the world of poker: the World Series of Poker at Binion's Horseshoe. "My ambition to actually play with the aces of poker was realized when I entered a No Limit Hold'em event," he says. "I wound up at one of the final four tables with a host of gold bracelet players like Berry Johnston, Phil Hellmuth, and Mike Sexton." Out of the eight satellite tournaments he entered, he won five of them; and although he didn't place in any of the major tournaments, he did well enough to want to continue playing poker. "I felt I could become good enough to compete with the best," he says. "I reasoned that I only needed to get some experience, seasoning, and focus."

Ron entered several more tournaments in the U.S. and did well in many of the events. Then he moved on to Europe. "If I was going to be serious about playing poker," he explains, "I had to learn how the Europeans played." His first stop was the Aviation Club in Paris. "I was thoroughly impressed by the level of play in Paris," Ron remembers, "and the competition seemed to raise the level of my game as well." Ron made three final tables during that December 2000 tournament.

In the summer of 2001 he returned to the Aviation Club, where he would not only win his first tournament, but win three of them in just one week. Understandably, Ron was tremendously pleased. "The most remarkable thing," he remembers, "was that I was named best all-around player for the 2001 Summer Tournament. " In 2002 he returned to Paris and took his fourth win—again at the Aviation Club. "I was beginning to think that I should move to Paris," he jokes. A few months later he would take his fifth win—again at the Aviation Club.

© 2003 World Poker Tour

"Never give your opponent a 'free' card."

-Ron Rose

The inauguration of the World Poker Tour in late 2002 gave Ron an added incentive to pick up his first win in America. "Poker was going in new and exciting directions, and now I had another goal," he explains, "to be one of the six people at a WPT final table." He entered the first WPT tournament, which was at Foxwoods. All the big names in poker were playing in that three-day event, and amazingly enough, Ron made it to his first final WPT table. But Ron realized quickly that he had set his goal just a bit low. He had wanted to get onto TV—and he did. But he was the first to be eliminated and finished sixth. "I was not at all happy with my play that day," he says. "I dreaded seeing myself on television later in the year. But it was a good experience, and the next time I played on TV I was prepared to win."

The next time came in Reno, Nevada at the 2003 World Poker Challenge. This was Ron's second WPT final table, and he was determined to win this one. "I had to redeem myself after that defeat at Foxwoods. I put my heart and soul into playing with these formidable opponents. I played with a patient and determined attitude; I stayed focused, read my opponents well, and in the end I won the tournament!" With confidence from the Reno win he went on to the 2003 WSOP. It was there that Ron won his first World Series gold bracelet in the Senior's No Limit Hold'em Championship event.

But Ron had one more event to look forward to in 2003. This time he was playing in an invitational that would be televised on NBC before the big game on Super Bowl Sunday. "It was the kind of game I liked to play," he says. "Eleven top WPT champions, no dead money and a prestigious title along with 'bragging rights'." Called the Battle of Champions, the event pitted all the winners of the first season of the World Poker Tour. "I was competing with champions from seven different countries," he says. "I could hardly maintain my enthusiasm." Two days later, Ron emerged as the first Champion of Champions. "I think that I was happier with that win than any other in my four years of tournament play."

Major Poker Accomplishments

2003, Winner of the WPT Inaugural Battle of Champions

2003, First place, WSOP, Seniors No Limit Hold'em

2003, First place, WPT World Poker Challenge, No Limit Hold'em Championship

2002, First place, Aviation Club Summer Tournament, No Limit Hold'em

2002, First place, Aviation Club Spring Tournament, No Limit Hold'em

2002, First place, Hall of Fame Poker Classic, Pot Limit Omaha

2001, First place, Aviation Club Summer Tournament :
- **Pot Limit Omaha,**
- **Pot Limit Hold'em**
- **Pot Limit Omaha Hi/Lo**

2001, Best Overall Player Award, Aviation Club Summer Tournament

José Rosenkrantz

"I just like the game. I play for the sport of it."

Personal Notes

Born in Frankfort, Germany, 1946

Married with five daughters

Retired clothing manufacturer

Member of the "Costa Rica Connection"

Wears his "lucky yellow shirt" at the poker table

Resides in San José, Costa Rica

Although he's been called the "Costa Rican Madman," José Rosenkrantz is as laid-back as they come—at least away from the table. A retired shirt manufacturer from Costa Rica's capital city of San José, he is a member of the "Costa Rica Connection," the group of outstanding Central American players who regularly finish well in tournaments on the international poker circuit.

Before his serious poker playing years, José was a star pool player. "My hobby was three cushion billiards," he explains. "I was the champion in Costa Rica. It's a game that requires a lot of concentration and discipline, and I carried that over into poker."

Back in 1985, José—along with Humberto Brenes—started a home poker club in San José. At first there was little interest beyond about a dozen men. At the time, says José, Costa Ricans viewed poker players similar to how they viewed drug dealers. "Even today, poker is not really accepted in my country like it is in the United States," he adds.

José, however, emphasizes that the Costa Ricans he plays with each week back home are all very nice people—most of them accomplished professionals like himself. Although the group started small, a trip José took with Brenes to Las Vegas changed all that. "That was when I saw hold'em played for the first time," he says. The next week he returned to Costa Rica and taught the game to others. Since then, his poker club has grown to nearly 80 regular players.

The year 2003 was defining for José as a tournament player. He took first place in the World Poker Tour's Casinos Europa tournament on his home turf, and later went on to finish second at the WPT's Champion of Champions invitational at the Bellagio.

Jose's appearances at two of the World Poker Tour's televised events have elicited favorable comments from those involved in the show. Shana Hiatt, the official spokesperson for the WPT credits Jose's high energy and good nature with getting him to the final tables of these events. "Away from the table, Rosenkrantz is happy and energetic," Shana noticed. "It seems like this high energy is what pushes Rosencrantz through to final tables." Vince Van Patten, the WPT co-host, has this warning for Jose's future opponents. " Don't let his pearly-white smile fool you because he is a poker piranha who is always looking for fresh meat."

"Poker's the only game fit for a grown man. Then, your hand is against every man's, and every man's is against yours."

-Somerset Maugham

Although José has been playing poker since he was 15 years old, he says he's never considered himself a professional poker player because he's never lived off the money he made in poker. "I am a semi-professional at best," he says. "I just like the game. I play for the sport of it."

Now that he is retired from his clothing manufacturing business—the company makes dress shirts that are distributed throughout Central America—he also enjoys traveling outside of Costa Rica to compete in the big tournaments. "I used to only travel to two tournaments each year outside of Costa Rica, but now I go to about six," he says. "Sometimes my wife travels with me, and sometimes we even bring our five daughters along for a vacation. I'm supported by my family, and that helps. Some wives might not be so understanding of their husbands playing poker late into the night."

While traveling, José says he sticks with tournament play and avoids the side games—what he calls "the dark side" of poker, where one can lose a fortune in just one night of play. Not at all interested in losing his shirt in the game, he sticks to the more prudent path: "I have a bank account just for poker," he says, "because I know I can't come out ahead every month."

Along with a passion for the game, discipline, he says, is the key to his success in poker. "I know, for example, when to fold my cards." In Vegas, he adds, there are probably dozens of people equal to him in the bare skills of the game. "What they don't have," he says, "is discipline. Discipline is what I need if I want to keep playing poker for the rest of my life." And that's exactly what José Rosenkrantz intends to do.

Major Poker Accomplishments

2003, Second place, WPT Battle of Champions

2003, First place, WPT Costa Rica No Limit Hold'em Championship

2002, First place, World Poker Open, No Limit Hold'em

Eric Seidel 

"With the advent of poker TV, I think the game will become a little more circus-like as the years go on."

Personal Notes

- **Born in New York City, 1959**
- **Grew up in Manhattan**
- **Married with children**
- **Former professional backgammon player**
- **Formerly worked on Wall Street**
- **Makes his home in Las Vegas**

At first look, Eric Seidel appears cautious—both at and away from the poker table. But looks can be deceiving. The mild-mannered Eric Seidel can sometimes be unpredictable. "I'm not a big fan of showing my hole cards to a television audience," he complains. "It gives away too much of my game." Before TV poker, Eric prided himself on having a style of play that isn't readily identifiable. "I had a friend once," he recalls, "who called me the tightest player around." Just a few months later another friend called him a maniac. "He thought I was too aggressive and said he doesn't know how I ever win." Eric was happy to hear it. He says it's an indication that he's doing a good job. He believes that the conditions of each game should dictate how he plays and the kind of strategy he uses.

Eric has been one of the most successful players on the poker circuit over the past several years. He was ranked as the all-around best tournament player for the combined season 2002-2003 at philhellmuth.com. Humility leads Eric to point out, however, that the most successful tournament players aren't necessarily the best all-around poker players in the world.

Born and bred amidst the hustle and bustle of Manhattan, Eric has played games all his life. Before he took to the poker circuit, he traveled the world as a professional backgammon player for eight years. Backgammon tournaments were smaller and the winners less well paid than in poker nowadays. Nonetheless, he says it gave him great experience in the art of tournament play. Moreover, he sees many parallels between the two games. "Both are similar in that the best player doesn't necessarily win each time," he explains. "There is both luck and skill involved with both games."

After playing both backgammon and poker professionally, Eric says he prefers poker. "It's more fun, and the pay is much better." But poker didn't always pay well for him. When he was in high school he played poker with his friends. "I was so bad," he admits, "that I got killed every week, and then I just stopped playing."

> **"The dollar you keep from losing on a losing day is the same dollar you add to a win on a winning day."**
>
> **-Mike Caro**

Years later, in 1985, he was reintroduced to poker at Manhattan's exclusive Mayfair Club. "Poker was so popular there at one time it almost became known as a poker club," he says. He started out playing No Limit Hold'em, and was fortunate enough to play others who were just as inexperienced as he was. For that, he was grateful. "Otherwise," he explains, "I don't know how quickly I would have picked up the game."

At the same time that he was learning to play poker at the Mayfair Club, he was busy trading stocks on Wall Street for Paine Weber. Just as he sees parallels between backgammon and poker, Eric sees plenty of parallels between playing poker and trading stocks. Again, both involve an element of skill and a certain amount of luck. But unlike poker, there are plenty of people on Wall Street, he says, that have great reputations solely because they were lucky. "In poker," he concedes, "I can't think of many players who have great reputations who are bad players."

Once Eric "perfected" his poker game, he and his wife decided to make the big move away from Manhattan and out to Las Vegas, where he'd have to travel much less to get to big events. "I love New York," he says, "and I didn't know if I'd be able to live outside Manhattan." After living in the neon-lit Nevada desert for eight years he's grown to like it there, and he especially appreciates that there's not the kind of pressure in Las Vegas as one feels in New York.

Once a cash game player, Eric says he is now concentrating on tournament play. "At times it can all be a bit stressful," he admits. "The hours are long, and the pressure increases the closer I get to the final table." The biggest pressure he feels in tournament play, he says, is simply to play as well as he can. "I feel really disappointed in myself when I leave a tournament and haven't played as well as I could have." Despite all the pressures, Eric Seidel is a winning man who may well go down in history as one of the best poker players ever.

Major Poker Accomplishments

Winner of six WSOP gold bracelets

1999, Fourth place, WSOP, No Limit Hold'em Championship

1988, Second place, WSOP, No Limit Hold'em Championship

Mark Seif  

"Bluffing is like using a sledge hammer to crack open an egg. You can do it if you land the hammer on the egg just right, but you risk demolishing the thing."

Personal Notes

- **Born in Cairo, Egypt, 1967**
- **Raised in southern California**
- **Graduate of UCLA and Loyola University Law School**
- **Former prosecuting attorney**
- **Loves water skiing**
- **Resides in Monrovia, California**

Mark Seif was banned from playing poker for 12 years—by his father! He was just a boy of six when he sat down with his family to play a friendly game of poker one night. His father had taught him to play just a few months earlier, and Mark liked the game. "One of the things I liked most about poker was bluffing," says Mark. That night Mark bluffed his dad out of a big pot. "He made me show him my hand," he recalls, "which I didn't have to do because he didn't call."

When six-year-old Mark turned over his hole cards, his dad saw the bluff. "He was mad—really mad," Mark says of his dad. "He sent me to my room. He made me give back all my winnings, and I was banished from playing poker for the rest of my childhood."

Thirty years later, Mark Seif is known as one of the biggest bluffers in the game. "I've turned out more huge bluffs than probably anybody else in poker right now," he brags. The key to pulling off a bluff, he says, is being able to have an accurate read of the situation. "You almost have to be in your opponent's realm of being. You have to become your opponent for a moment—be in his mind and exploit the weakness of his hand when you find it."

But Mark is quick to admit that his greatest strength can sometimes be his greatest weakness. "Bluffing is like using a sledge hammer to crack open an egg," he explains. "You can do it if you land the hammer on the egg just right, but you risk demolishing the thing." Mark knows well that poker players can destroy themselves by bluffing, and he's done just that. "I've had tremendous chip leads in big situations, and I've bluffed away all my chips."

Mark says he honed his bluffing skills in his former career as an attorney in Southern California. During law school at Loyola University in

Los Angeles, he was a prosecutor for the district attorney's office, working mainly on murder and dope cases. "I assisted on a motion in the O.J. Simpson case," he says. "That's my claim to failure."

"You have to become your opponent for a moment—be in his mind and exploit the weakness of his hand when you find it."

-Mark Seif

Mark later went on to work for a high profile employment and labor law firm in Newport Beach, California. There, he cut his legal teeth on cases concerning sexual harassment, age and race discrimination, and employment contracts. Mark sees many connections between his work as an attorney and his poker playing. "In both you have to understand the likelihood of success and failure." As an attorney he was constantly weighing the costs and benefits of situations that were not exactly cut and dried, constantly making judgment calls. In both professions, he explains, you need the ability to think on your feet; you have to be able to deal with pressure and adversity; and you have to know how to bounce back from defeat.

"As an attorney, I had to be looking at the jury and at the judge in order to get a feeling for what they were doing, where they were going—what they were holding in their hands, so to speak." As a poker player, Mark does much the same thing: "I am constantly assessing, for example, if the other person is bluffing. It was the same when I was negotiating contracts: the other person would invariably say, 'This is all we can afford to pay; this is all we can do.' I had to assess whether or not they were serious. I had to decide if I should call their bluff and continue the game."

As much as Mark loved practicing law, he says he's left the legal world behind for a while in order to pursue his career as a professional poker player. It's a decision he probably will not regret, since Mark has quickly worked his way to the top of the pack. Although he was able to make the transition from law firm to poker room with ease, his family had a hard time accepting the fact that he was no longer going to use his Juris Doctor degree. "It was very troubling for my parents at first," he remembers. "They thought I was crazy." Over time, however, Mark's parents, like many others, have lessened their perception that professional poker is played out amidst a seedy underworld.

"The televised poker tournaments have helped a lot," he says. "They show us as pretty decent individuals. We've gone from the idea of poker as something that happens in the smoke-filled back rooms of pool halls to the mainstream. The public watches and goes 'wow!'"

Major Poker Accomplishments

2003, First place, WPT Poker Open, Seven Card Stud

2003, First place, Festa al Lago, No Limit Hold'em event

2003, First place, Sport of Kings, No Limit Hold'em event

2003, First place, World Poker Open, No Limit Hold'em event

2002, Fourth place, WPT Legends of Poker, No Limit Hold'em Championship

Mike Sexton

"Poker is not as exciting for me to play anymore. During the years I played, I truly *loved* playing poker. I couldn't get enough."

Personal Notes

- **Born in Shelbyville, Indiana, 1947**
- **Attended Ohio State University on a gymnastics scholarship**
- **Former ballroom dance teacher**
- **TV commentator for the World Poker Tour**
- **Host and consultant for PartyPoker.com**
- **Resides in Las Vegas**

At 12 years old Mike Sexton used to get out of bed at 4:00 a.m. every morning to deliver the *Journal-Herald* in Dayton, Ohio. On Friday nights, he'd go door-to-door collecting subscription money from his customers. "When I would get back from collecting," Mike remembers, "Danny Robison—considered by many to be the best Seven Card Stud player of all time—would be shuffling a deck of cards on my back porch. He and I would then play poker, and seemingly always he would beat me out of all of my newspaper money."

Getting kicked in the teeth again and again was good for Mike. It molded him into the solid pro poker player he later became. After a stint as a competitive college gymnast and a ballroom dance instructor, Mike settled into a long and successful career at the poker table. By the late 1980s he got interested in tournament play.

His great thrill in poker came in 1989 when he won his first bracelet at the World Series of Poker. "It was Eight or Better Stud, which was the game I was playing everyday for a living at the time." Up to that point Mike had not entered the $10,000 No Limit Hold'em championship event at the World Series, so the Eight or Better Stud tournament was his world championship, so to speak. "I sincerely felt I played perfect poker that day," he says, "which made my victory that much more satisfying. To this day, it was the best tournament I have ever played."

"Pay attention and don't play in games that you can't afford."

-Mike Sexton

Mike's patience, discipline, and perseverance even in the face of a short stack made him into a consistently successful tournament player, and once he got into the no-limit hold'em scene, he made waves. He went on to win five major championships in No Limit Hold'em events.

His 25 years of poker success landed him in the pilot seat on the World Poker Tour's televised series, which has appeared on the Travel Channel and NBC. As chief commentator along with Vince Van Patten (pro poker's chief ambassador in Hollywood), he calls the shots at final tables from Paris to San Jose, from Reno to Aruba.

Consequently, Mike Sexton has become the most recognizable face in pro poker to the television public. His superb commentary has educated millions on how to play what he calls "the Cadillac of poker," No Limit Hold'em. And he is singularly responsible for coining a memorable phrase that has almost become WPT's unofficial motto regarding the game: "It takes five minutes to learn but a lifetime to master."

After a quarter century of sitting at the poker table, Mike says he feels more comfortable now behind the microphone. "Poker is not as exciting for me to play anymore. During the years I played, I truly *loved* playing poker. I couldn't get enough," he says. "I have now moved to the business side of poker, and I'm thoroughly enjoying that."

One of Mike's business interests is as host and consultant for the largest online poker cardroom, Party Poker. He is also the host of Party Poker's spring cruise, where the WPT holds its Party Poker Million championship. But celebrity has not gone to the head of this Ohio native. He is as down to earth and caring as they come. For instance, he will never harshly criticize a WPT final table player, knowing that it might hurt the family or friends of the player who are watching. And he doesn't hesitate to praise the particularly skillful moves he is sure to see at each tournament. Mike Sexton is a champ in every sense of the word!

Major Poker Accomplishments

2003, First place, Heads-up Euro Finals of Poker, No Limit Hold'em

2000, First place, Euro Finals of Poker, No Limit Hold'em Championship

2000, First place, Aviation Club Autumn Tournament, Limit Omaha Hi/Lo

2000, First place, Aviation Club Autumn Tournament, Pot Limit Omaha

Four Best All-around Player Awards

In the top five all-time for "in-the-money" finishes at the WSOP

1989, First place, WSOP, Seven Card Stud Split

Charlie Shoten 

"Being a better poker player has to do with being a better person."

Personal Notes

Born in Bronx, New York, 1937

Former insurance man

Internet business consultant

Owns wwpo.com

Graduate of University of Alabama, Tuscaloosa

Resides in Glendale, California

When Charlie Shoten first started playing poker tournaments in California—at places like Commerce Casino and the Bicycle Club—he suffered from an identity crisis. "I didn't want anyone to know that I won a lot of money," he explains, "so I used a *nom de plume*: 'Scotty Warbucks.' I have no idea where the name came from, but I didn't want anyone chasing me home."

For 14 years Charlie was "Scotty Warbucks." It wasn't until he started to become highly visible in the poker world that he extended his poker name to encompass his given name. That was in 2001 when Charlie first started playing the most popular poker game on the tournament circuit: "Until then I never knew how to play No Limit Hold'em," he says. "That's the big game, and it was a big question mark for me." As it happened, the first time he played a No Limit Hold'em satellite at L.A.'s Hustler Casino he took first place, earning himself a $3,000 buy-in for the tournament's main event. "All of a sudden I just sat at the table and knew how to play," he claims.

Charlie says that it's primarily his philosophy of life that paved the way for his poker successes. That philosophy is tied closely to issues of personal identity. "It's a Zen kind of thing," he explains, "because becoming a better poker player is a question of self-mastery. Being a better poker player has to do with being a better person." What is key to being a better person (and a better poker player)? Charlie says you first need to quit being someone you're not and "live the real you." That entails getting rid of all the distractions that prevent you from playing your best poker. "The more relevant data that you can bring in at the table, and the less distractions that you have internally, fears, doubts, preconceived ideas about your own abilities, the better decisions you are going to make.

Extending this philosophy to his entire life, Charlie says it helps him to see the opportunities that the universe brings him. "There is no difference between becoming a great poker player and becoming a more wholesome, happier person," he asserts. "The path that I've taken in life to liberate myself is to eliminate the things that keep me from enjoying life or fulfilling myself as a person." Forget religion, he says, forget positive thinking, trying harder, or reading self-help books. Charlie says the key is "cleansing—continuous cleansing of the mind."

"Read my article, 'Play Winning No Limit Hold'em and Life' and do the nine steps 24/7."

-Charlie Shoten

This process of cleansing, he says, is a gift that he wants to impart to all: "All I have to do is notice my distractions and have the intention that I want to transmute them. And then leave it up to the same forces that regulate my breathing and my blood pressure. This stuff will get transmuted automatically by your own life force."

Deep thoughts? Maybe. But Charlie says that *thinking* is the worst thing you can do. He relies more on what psychologists call the subconscious. Charlie calls it 'instincts,' and he doesn't question his—especially when it comes to playing No Limit Hold'em, a game that he sees as a metaphor for life. "In no-limit," he observes, "if you lose your chips, you're dead—you're out of the tournament."

When Charlie's playing no-limit he's engaging in what he calls a life struggle. "It's like I'm walking down a dark alley, and I'm very alert." He's played so many hands of poker in his lifetime that he instinctively knows what to look out for. He says that through his "life force" he knows how to avoid being sabotaged.

In 1990, Charlie's "life force" was telling him it was time to get out of New York City, where he had lived nearly his entire life—first in the Bronx, where he was born, and later in just about every neighborhood in Manhattan. "This was New York before Giuliani. The city was really a mess," he remembers. Charlie decided to move to Southern California, first living in Santa Monica and later moving to Sherman Oaks and then to Glendale.

If it hadn't been for that life move, Charlie may never have entered the world of tournament poker. "The insurance business has been good to me," he says of his former profession, "but I'm making a lot more money on the poker tour. I feel like one of these pro basketball players, playing in a different city each month." It's a great retirement, he says, and a chance to be visible. "The more visible I can get and the more constructive I can be, the happier I'll be."

Major Poker Accomplishments

2003, Second place, California State Poker No Limit Hold'em Championship

2003, Second place, WPT Poker Open, No Limit Hold'em

2004, Sixth place, WSOP, Seven Card Stud

2003, Top 10 Ranking Player of the Year

2003, made 19 final tables in major tournaments

Barry Shulman

"I don't consider myself a professional poker player or even a semi-pro. I consider myself a businessman who plays poker."

Personal Notes

- **Born in Seattle, Washington, 1946**
- **Father of two sons**
- **Publisher of *Cardplayer* magazine**
- **Former real estate developer**
- **Resides in Las Vegas**

"I don't consider myself a professional poker player or even a semi-pro," says Barry Shulman. "I consider myself a businessman who plays poker." That's quite a modest claim for a man who plays between fifty and a hundred tournaments each year, including the World Series of Poker and the major World Poker Tour events.

Although Barry can often be found on the tournament circuit, his major contribution to the world of poker is as publisher of *Cardplayer* magazine. "When I bought the magazine five years ago it was geared toward the hardcore poker players," he says. "Now that poker has expanded, *Cardplayer* is more mainstream and more professionally written." Barry and his family have grown the magazine in both size and appeal as it's focus has turned more toward general interest about the poker world. "We publish more articles now that would appeal to the average guy who watches poker on television," he explains.

Barry played poker when he was a teenager, but took an extended break from the game after graduating from the University of Washington. For twenty years Barry worked in the business world in his native state, before moving to Las Vegas. Golf was his game at first, and only later did he takes some breaks from the golf course to sit at the poker table.

But Barry says he's not the type to spend much time away from the business world. "I wasn't psychologically suited not to be working very hard," he explains. "I was fascinated by poker, and I was pretty fascinated by the business aspect of the magazine." *Cardplayer* wasn't for sale when Barry approached the previous owners and made them an offer.

Since taking over the magazine, *Cardplayer* has grown to 126 pages per issue with a circulation hovering around 50,000. "We are the number one print media in poker," says Barry. "And we want to stay the number one print media in poker. We're certain that poker is so popular that mainstream publishers will soon be interested in coming out with a poker magazine. We have to have the kind of magazine that appeals to the mainstream reader. That's why we're getting more professional writers. Every photo is now in color… That's a significant change."

"You must have a strong reason to start a hand in early position; you must have a strong reason not to start a hand in late position."

-Barry Shulman

As important as the print magazine is to Barry, he believes that the *Cardplayer* website is just as important, if not more. Cardplayer.com had only one page when Barry bought it. From there, he developed it into the monster site that it is today. "The website is bigger than the magazine now," he says. "We have 10,000 people a day coming to the site, whereas it used to be just 800 a day."

You'd be hard-pressed to find an internet-savvy poker player who does not have the *Cardplayer* website bookmarked. It is an invaluable source for information not only on the game of poker, but also on the players who make the game interesting. A number of poker aces write regular columns for the readers, making the sport more personal to each and every reader.

Barry's *Cardplayer* website is revamped every year to keep it current technologically, just as the magazine has undergone changes to keep up with the type of readers it attracts since poker has become a worldwide television phenomenon. "People are learning how to play poker by reading *Cardplayer*," Barry realizes, "and we are sensitive to that. That's why we are going to have a lot more beginning type of articles."

Barry acknowledges that television, the internet and the popularity of tournament-style poker has changed the game in the past five years. But there are other changes he considers just as important, such as behavior at the table and a no-smoking rule. *Cardplayer* magazine wrote a significant article directed at some of the old pros who like to cause a lot of trouble at the table. It got the message out to the players that it wasn't very cool to be a grump and it shouldn't be tolerated. "We're anti-smoking and anti-grump," Barry says. "We're trying to be good citizens. Those kinds of things are important to us."

Barry is not alone in his ventures with *Cardplayer* magazine. His son, Jeff, a stand-out poker player in his own right runs the magazine on a day-to day basis. This leaves Barry with the time to devote to the website. "I've been fascinated with this internet thing in the past year and I've been spending all my time on that," remarks Barry. Between the two of them, this father-son team has done its share of getting poker to the public.

Major Poker Accomplishments

2003, First place, Five Diamond World Poker Classic, No Limit Hold'em event

2003, Fourth place, WPT Ultimate Bet, No Limit Hold'em Championship

2002, Second place, Overall Best Performance, LA Poker Classic

2001, First place, Four Queens Poker Classic, No Limit Hold'em Championship

2001, First place, WSOP, Seven Card Stud, Hi/Lo

2000, First place, Vienna Spring Festival, No Limit Hold'em event

Jeff Shulman 

"I had only been playing for a few months at the time, and I really didn't understand how important of a tournament it was."

Personal Notes

- **Born in Seattle, Washington, 1975**
- **Graduate of the University of Washington**
- **Former real estate investor**
- **Publisher and editor of *Cardplayer* magazine**
- **Resides in Las Vegas, Nevada**

Jeff Shulman likes to know why people do what they do at the poker table. "I think that's because my brother used to lie so much to me as a kid," he says. "I would first have to figure out if he was lying, and then figure out what he was trying to achieve." Poker requires similar skills, he observes: "If you know *why* then you can figure out if the person has a hand or not."

Jeff's poker playing started in 7th grade at B'nai Brith summer camp. "I used to win about five dollars a day, which was huge at the time." He partly attributes his success, then and now, to his aggressive personality in life. "If I like something, I do whatever I can to get it." He's tough in business just as he is in poker. In the business world, he says, "I won't do a deal unless I think it is a win-win situation for both parties."

Jeff doesn't have such a big heart at the poker table. There, he's looking for a win-win situation for himself. A few years ago he reached the final table in the first World Series event he ever played.

"I was chip leader with seven people left," he recalls. "I called an all-in from Chris Ferguson. He had a pair of 6's and I had a pair of 7's. If I won the hand I would have well over half of the chips with six players left." Unfortunately, Jeff lost on the river. "I had only been playing for a few months at the time, and I really didn't understand how important of a tournament it was."

"Develop your own style; do what is comfortable and works for you."

-Jeff Shulman

Away from the table Jeff spends most of his time managing the day-to-day affairs of *Cardplayer*. He got involved with the magazine when his father became publisher. At the time he had no publishing experience whatsoever. "I learned how to run the magazine from my great employees," he says.

Thus far Jeff is exceedingly happy (his nickname, by the way, is "happy") with the progress he and his father have made since taking over *Cardplayer*. "I see us now and in the future as the information source for poker," he says. "We are the only magazine now, and I expect our distribution to increase exponentially in the next few years."

The mission of *Cardplayer* magazine is simple: to bring readers a well-written, interesting, accurate, and informative magazine that will tweak a person's poker interest, knowledge, and comportment to make poker more enjoyable for all. The success of the magazine attests to the fact that they are doing just that. Between the cardplayer.com website and the print publication, Jeff and his father Barry have provided both an informational and enjoyable place for poker players to go to learn more about the game, the results of tournaments, the champions of poker and the general environment of the poker world.

Jeff Shulman is a man in the know about poker. He doesn't just write about it. He is a seasoned player in his own right. When he is able to break away from his writing or editing obligations with the magazine, Jeff can be found at the poker table sharpening his poker skills. His column which can be found in every issue, often highlights his experiences at the table. It is informative, enjoyable and always entertaining, whether he is talking about the latest World Series of Poker Championship or the pros and cons of wearing sunglasses at the game. Jeff Shulman, whatever his endeavors, is one happy man!

Major Poker Accomplishments

2003, First place, LA Poker Classic, No Limit Hold'em event

Final table at WSOP, first time played - seventh place

2000, Second place, Legends of Poker, No Limit Hold'em Championship

Dewey Tomko

"I just played poker and slept. That's all I did."

Personal Notes

- **Born in Glassport, Pennsylvania, 1946**
- **Married with three children**
- **Graduate of Salem College in West Virginia**
- **Former pro golfer**
- **Former kindergarten teacher**
- **Owns a casino in San Jose, Costa Rica**
- **Owned Florida golf course and orange groves**

Dewey Tomko started making a living as a poker player in the pool halls of Pittsburgh when he was just 16. In fact, his game was so good, he worked his way through four years of studies at Salem College in the late '60s by beating the G.I.s coming home from Vietnam.

Once graduated, he took a low-paying job teaching Kindergarten to ghetto kids in Winterhaven, Florida. "Florida probably had the best poker action in the country at that time," says Dewey. "And my job was fitted perfect for a poker player." Just about every evening Dewey would sit down to play poker—all night long. "I'd come into school at 8:00 a.m. straight from the poker room, not having slept a wink all night," he remembers. "After lunch I'd run the kids around outside in the steamy Florida weather and get them all good and tired. Then I would take them back into the air-conditioned trailer for nap time." Once the lights went out, everyone went to sleep—including Dewey. "I had the parents trained to come pick up the kids from the trailer while I was still sleeping. Sometimes when I would wake up there'd be nobody there but me."

Although Dewey was making a mere pittance of $6,100 per year teaching Kindergarten, he loved the job and stayed on for six years. It was only when the school transferred him to teach P.E. that he decided to move on. "I taught P.E. for the first three days of school that year," he remembers. "Then on Labor Day weekend I went out to play 18 holes of high-stakes golf, and lost around $20,000. I decided to quit my teaching job right then and there."

The teaching job, he says, was actually costing him thousands of dollars because he was leaving poker games where he could win as much as $10,000 a night. Since he didn't like teaching P.E., he decided it was time to move on. "Once I quit my job I became a professional gambler, and I played nothing but poker," he says. From the age of 22 to 30

Dewey played poker every day. "I just played poker and slept. That's all I did."

"People will pay a hundred dollars for a bottle of wine; to me that's not worth it... So if a guy wants to bet twenty or thirty thousand dollars in a poker game, that is his privilege."

-Jack Binion

During the 1980s Dewey played a lot of tournament poker. He was famous for finishing second. In fact he placed second in 15 major tournaments, including the World Series of Poker, before he won the Grand Prix and the Irish Eccentric back-to-back. "From thereon out I was never a great poker player." Dewey explains that he always wanted to be the greatest poker player in the world. "Whether I was or not doesn't really matter," he says, but he noticed that once he started winning tournaments his fellow poker players began to treat him differently. "On my way up everyone always seemed glad to see me, but once I reached a certain level all the people who once cheered for me were now getting jealous."

Dewey says he thought he would feel elated when he won the Grand Prix at the Golden Nugget Casino in Vegas. "I had just spent twenty years of my life playing poker to get to that spot, but it wasn't like I expected it would be. I felt like there was nowhere to go from there." Consequently, Dewey lost all interest in poker for the next 15 years, limiting his tournament play to the World Series of Poker each year.

Dewey had made a good living and saved quite a lot through his years of poker playing. He invested it in a golf course, a sports book and some orange groves. Then he concentrated on his other sports love: golf. At the same time, he remembers being relieved that once finished with his full-time poker career, he was able to spend more time watching his three sons grow up.

It was his oldest son, Derek, who got Dewey back into the tournament poker scene several years ago: "Derek wanted to play poker, and he started drilling me with questions. When I was teaching him to play, I found I was getting interested again." In 2003 Dewey finished second at the WPT tournament at the Bellagio and made the final table at the WPT's Casinos Europa tournament in Costa Rica, where he recently bought a small casino. Now Dewey feels he's got another goal in poker worth shooting for: he'd like to go heads-up with his son at a final table—and beat him! "Derek's a good player. He's a better player now than I was at his age," Dewey concedes. "More power to him. Maybe he'd beat me."

Major Poker Accomplishments

2003, Second place, WPT Five Diamond World Poker Classic, No Limit Hold'em Championship

2001, Second place, WSOP, No Limit Hold'em Championship

1985, Back to back wins, Grand Prix and Irish Eccentric Tournament

1984, First place, WSOP, Pot Limit Omaha

1984, First place, WSOP, Deuce to Seven Draw

1982, Second place, WSOP, No Limit Hold'em Championship

1982, Second place, Super Bowl of Poker

1982, Second place, Grand Prix of Poker

1979, First place, WSOP, No Limit Hold'em event

An Tran

"I don't have any favorite venues. It's all the same to me. As long as there is a game going on, I can win."

Personal Notes

Born in Saigon, Vietnam, 1952

Escaped from Vietnam in 1975

Former lieutenant in the South Vietnamese Green Berets

Karate Master and former teacher of karate

Resides in Las Vegas

Five card stud was the game back in Vietnam, says An Tran. "I only played poker for fun there, and I never learned the other games like No Limit Hold'em until I came to the United States."

An Tran was a 23-year-old Green Beret, trained by the U.S. Marines, in the South Vietnamese Army during the fall of Saigon. The year was 1975; Communists from the North had taken over his country. "I had to run away by boat," he says. After several other brief stops, he ended up in the United States. "I had a sponsor in Houston," he says, and that's where he first lived in his new country. It was there that An Tran opened a Karate Studio to teach the martial arts.

Just a few years later, in 1980, An Tran got into playing tournament poker and eventually decided to close his karate studio and move to Las Vegas, where he could play poker every day of the year. Seven years later, An Tran made his first final table in the World Series of Poker. "My claim to fame," he says, "is that I have made it to 32 final tables in the World Series since then. I made it to seven final tables in one year alone."

An Tran says his style of play is unique. "Some people are always aggressive," he observes, "while others are always tight. But I can't play just one style. I play different every game. It depends on who I'm playing with and how I'm doing with my chips." And An Tran doesn't care how the others perceive him in his play.

An Tran isn't one to be intimidated by any other player at the table. "When I play against good players," he explains, "it doesn't matter. I just have to study them. When I sit down at the table with someone I can tell how they play after a couple of hands."

Nor is An Tran intimidated by the ups and down of the game. "I go broke all the time," he says, "but that doesn't make any difference. It doesn't bother me. I've lost a lot of money on the stock market. I bet on the options, and sometimes I go broke. There are plenty of parallels. It just doesn't matter much to me." This easy-going attitude works for An Tran. His "it doesn't make a difference to me" outlook saves him a boatload of frustration.

"If, after the first twenty minutes, you don't know who the sucker at the table is, it's you."

-Unknown author

An Tran doesn't seem much concerned with *where* he plays poker either. "I don't have any favorite venues. It's all the same to me. As long as there is a game going on, I can win." Winning was one of the things on his mind at the 2004 World Series of Poker when he added another final table appearance to his resume bringing him to a personal best of final table finishes numbering 33.

In the $5,000 Limit Hold'em tournament it came down to heads up play between An Tran and John Hennigan, with An Tran having the chip lead. When Hennigan beat An Tran's king-high flush with an ace-high flush, he won a monster pot, giving him a significant chip lead. According to the report on pokerpages.com, An Tran went into a tailspin from which he would never recover. This 1991 gold bracelet winner placed second in the tournament after many grueling hours of play.

Yet Hennigan had only good things to say about An Tran's play in that tournament. "I don't look at it like I had his number. An Tran is a great player. He's won a lot of big tournaments. A few freaky hands came up, like the spade flush, and I got lucky enough to win some of the big pots." Obviously, An Tran comes off to others as a seasoned veteran whose play is taken most seriously.

An Tran's unpredictable play makes for an interesting table, a factor that has brought a lot of enthusiasm to televised poker. What does An Tran think of this recent development? "I think it's a good thing that poker is growing, getting bigger," he replies. "The fact that poker is now televised doesn't matter to me. It makes me look good on the TV. It makes things more exciting. It's a positive development."

An Tran has been nicknamed "the Boss." Whether it is because his table moves are so decisive, or the fact that he seems to call everyone "Boss," is a matter of opinion. What can't be disputed is An Tran's record at the poker table, especially at all of the World Series of Poker events since he began playing in 1980. He is most certainly a force to be reckoned with.

Major Poker Accomplishments

2004, Second place, WSOP, Limit Hold'em

2003, First place, Four Queens Poker Classic, No Limit Hold'em event

2002, First place, Four Queens Poker Classic, No Limit Hold'em event

1991, First place, WSOP, Pot Limit Omaha

Numerous finishes at the WSOP final tables

Simon "Aces" Trumper

"I love the people. I love the fact that poker is nondiscriminatory. It's fantastic. I can't think of anything else like it."

Personal Notes

- **Born in Kensington, England, 1963**
- **Father of four**
- **Former owner of a drainage company**
- **Most successful player on the *Late Night Poker* shows**
- **Resides in Guilford, England**

You're not likely to see any of Simon Trumper's daughter's at a poker table in the near future. His daughters, ranging in age from 13 to 21, don't even revel in Simon's celebrity as a European television poker star. Simon relates a time when he was on holiday with his children in Rhodes. At dinner one evening, a man sitting near him asked to have his picture taken with Simon. He said, "Is it all right if I take my photo with you, because my mates back home won't believe it?" His daughters just sighed and said, "Oh, not again." His son, however, loves it.

Simon Trumper has all the fame and fortune that goes with being one of the most successful players on the *Late Night Poker* Series. "There were six series," Simon explains, "and I won series two and came in second in series four." *Late Night Poker* has been good to him, he says. The first time he played in the World Series of Poker was courtesy of that show. "Binion's put a $10,000 entry to the main event on top of the [money] for first prize." Simon won and was on his way to his first WSOP main event.

Simon boasts that he was born for television! When asked to fill in for a presenter for television poker on the psychology of poker tells, he quickly agreed to do it. In addition to a nice check for his work, the director told him that he came across well on television and that he was likely to become a star as a result of that series. "Now, if that's the case, all these things have got to add up," he surmises, "so eventually all the hard work I've put in and all the money that I've lost to get this far will come back to me tenfold."

Hard work was not foreign to Simon even before he started playing poker professionally. When he was only 25 years old he ran a successful company with a staff of 42 people. In a couple of years, Simon left that company to start his own business and grew it fivefold in only seven months. But like all entrepreneurs, he became bored. That's when Simon began to play poker in earnest.

"One of the biggest things is that when you are doing something all the time, like playing with your chips when you are bluffing, keep doing it every time. Or it will become a tell."

-Simon Trumper

He had learned to play the game from a friend of his who took him to a small tournament in England. "I played for two or three months and I lost every single time," he says. But a talk over breakfast one day with a fellow who was writing a book on mathematical probability in Hold'em and Omaha changed his luck. This fellow told Simon in no uncertain terms that he didn't have a clue as to a good starting hand. "I didn't even know what he was talking about," Simon admits. But after the statistician was through with him, Simon began to see the light. "The key thing that I did was to start using the button correctly, and I began playing starting hands correctly. I ran all over them."

Simon has also written articles giving his readers insight into the real world of poker. He had the vision to see that there would be corporate sponsorship and televised poker. "Everything that I predicted came true," he points out. The opportunities for some players who can do more than just play poker are endless according to Simon. "Whereas, most players are only capable of playing, I'm capable of doing a lot more. I've done live commentary on radio, television and in front of a live audience," he says. "What I'm trying to do is to create Simon "Aces" Trumper as a brand and as a well-known celebrity within the poker world."

When Simon first started playing poker it was only for the fun of it. When he realized all the subtleties of the game, it became more of a challenge—and for a guy like Simon, challenge is what it's all about! He also sees that the sport of poker is played on a level playing field. "I love the people. I love the fact that poker is nondiscriminatory," Simon says with satisfaction. "I can't think of anything else like it."

Simon admits to his limitations with no apologies. "I'm hopeless at Pot Limit Hold'em," Simon acknowledges. "For some reason I just can't adjust. No Limit Hold'em suits my style a lot better." And Simon never stops trying to adapt to the game and its players. "If you classify it as a sport," he says, "then I can't think of another one like it."

Major Poker Accomplishments

Made 26 final tables in the last four years in Europe

Won more No Limit finals than any other player in Europe

2003, First place, Aviation Club Winter Tournament, No Limit Hold'em event

2002, Fourth place, WSOP, No Limit Hold'em event

2001, First place, Aviation Club Autumn Tournament, No Limit Hold'em event

David "Devilfish" Ulliott 

"I'd swim across shark-infested waters with a pork chop hanging around my neck in order to play the best poker players in the world."

Personal Notes

Born in Hull, England, 1954

Married with seven children

Owns a jewelry business

Banned from all betting shops in England

His orange-tinted shades are prescription glasses

Speaks with a nearly impenetrable Yorkshire accent

Known as one of the fiercest No Limit Hold'em players in the world today, David Ulliott struggles little to live up to his nickname, "the Devilfish." Just like his deadly poisonous namesake, David has an aggressive style that makes him one of the most feared opponents in the game. His table appearance—suit, coat and tie, slicked back hair, orange-tinted glasses, and enormous finger jewelry—also makes him one of the most recognizable poker personalities of all time.

His unique nickname was coined by a poker opponent from Birmingham, England, during a game in October, 1996. "He said, 'you're a devilfish,' and we all just laughed," says David. "When I asked what a devilfish was, I was told it is a poisonous fish that can kill you if it's not properly prepared."

David's friend Gary Whitacre was standing behind him, watching him play that night. A few months later he was with David at the Four Queens tournament in Las Vegas, the first major tournament he ever played outside England. "I ended up heads-up with Men 'the Master' Nguyen. His friends were chanting, 'go on the Master,' and Gary yelled back, 'go on the Devilfish.' The headlines the next morning read, 'Devilfish devours the Master.'" Later that year, David won a gold bracelet at the World Series of Poker. "I put 'Devilfish' on the bracelet for a bit of fun—and the name stuck."

Devilfish started his poker career by playing cards with his friends on the flat tombstones in a cemetery near their school. Thinking he was quite good, he decided to play his mother and his father, but when he started winning too much at home his dad got furious with him and kicked him out of the house for a time, refusing to ever play with him again.

That was the beginning of a long string of lockouts. "I started playing poker seriously when I was 15," says Devilfish, who at the time was working for a shieldmaker. "We used to play Five Card Draw on our lunch hour. I beat everybody so much, no one would sit down with me anymore."

"If you want to show a profit at the end of the year, one or two rebuys [in a tournament] is enough."

- "Devilfish" Ulliot

That's when he met Jack Gardner, owner of a local casino. Gardner took him to the poker tables in there, where he proceeded to clean out everyone he played. "It got to a point where I couldn't get a game," he says. "No one wanted to take me on anymore."

When Devilfish was playing local cash games in his hometown of Hull in northern England, he was still running his jewelry business, playing home games once or twice a week. One night he arrived for a poker game only to find that no one but the host had showed up. The host sat him down at the poker table and told him that he'd just received a phone call. No one would be coming to the game because they knew Devilfish would be there. "After that," he says, "the guys started moving the games around from house to house, and holding them at erratic times so I wouldn't be able to track them down."

Devilfish took up poker full-time when he got "banned" from the local games. He first played in Leeds, which was about 70 miles from his hometown, and later started playing at the Victoria Club in London. From there he went to Vegas with stops at other poker hotspots in North America and Europe.

Being a world-class winner is part of the reason why Devilfish is known everywhere he goes, from the streets of Hull to the casinos of Vegas to the beaches of the Caribbean. "Most of the people in my hometown are quite familiar with me," he says, especially the twenty-somethings who come home a bit drunk from the pub to watch BBC's *Late Night Poker* show, the only television venue for poker in Great Britain. "I was walking along in Hull one night and a dozen guys on the opposite side of the road started chanting, 'Devilfish.'"

It's not only in his hometown where the Devilfish gets attention. He was sunning himself on the beaches of Aruba during WPT's Ultimate Poker Classic when three bikini-clad women came along yelling 'Devilfish.' Once they got his attention, they dropped their tops and flashed him. Such is the price to pay for stardom, he says.

Major Poker Accomplishments

2004, First place, British Open, No Limit Hold'em Championship

2004, First place, World Heads Up Poker Championships, Pot Limit Omaha

2003, First place, WPT World Poker Open, No Limit Hold'em Championship

2002, First place, World Poker Open, Pot Limit Omaha

2000, Second place, WSOP, No Limit Hold'em event

1998, European Omaha Champion

1998, Second place, WSOP, Pot Limit Hold'em

1997, First place, WSOP, Pot Limit Hold'em

Amir Vahedi  

"Although poker is largely a game of skill, the beauty of the game is that at any skill level it's possible to walk into a poker room and beat the champion on a particular day."

Personal Notes

Born in Tehran, Iran, 1961

Smokes Cuban cigars

Served in the Iran-Iraq war

Taught Ben Affleck to play No Limit Hold'em

Escaped as a refugee to West Germany in 1981

Resides in Sherman Oaks, California

Before Jennifer Lopez accused Ben Affleck of having "a gambling problem," she bought poker lessons as a gift for her famous ex-fiancé. The instructor: Amir Vahedi, a leading light of the poker world. According to Amir, approximately thirty percent of the game is knowledge of the fundamentals—and that can be taught. "But it's the other seventy percent" he says, "that distinguishes the good player from the excellent."

It's also the most difficult aspect of the game to teach, adds Amir, and probably his own greatest asset: the ability to "read" other players. "It's a gift," he says, "the way that I can perceive people's personalities—and not just in poker games. Even when I was a car dealer, within the first five minutes of meeting somebody I could tell you if that person was decent or degenerate. I could tell if he was angry or hostile towards me. That comes in handy in poker."

Amir was born in Tehran in 1961, and joined the Iranian army during the Iran-Iraq War. He saw combat against the Iraqis for nineteen months before getting a three-day pass to visit his mother. "She cried for the entire three days," Amir remembers. "She wanted me to leave the country with my brother-in-law because she thought I'd be killed in action. There were enormous casualties in that war."

Amir's mother gave him an ultimatum: if you don't leave now, you are no longer my son. "She pushed me," he says. "I didn't want to go, but she was so adamant." Instead of returning to the battlefront, Amir left for Pakistan with his brother-in-law. This marked the beginning of his refugee days. From Pakistan he moved on to Afghanistan, where he was imprisoned for a few months for being an undocumented alien. "From Afghanistan I was able to get to East

Berlin with a false passport," he recalls. "I stayed there for a day, and then escaped to the west side of Berlin through an organized underground network." The minute he set foot on West German soil he received refugee status. After five days detention in West Berlin, he stayed with relatives in London and Paris before joining his brother in California.

"Be a good money manager away from the table."

-Amir Vahedi

Amir eventually opened his own business in the U.S.—first a restaurant and then a limousine service and a car dealership. Things went well for a few years, but then he was forced to file bankruptcy. "It was around that time that I started playing casino games in Vegas on the weekends," he says. "After my business failed I started to work for a former employer. I remember the first paycheck I received from him; I lost it all in a casino."

Then Amir discovered poker. He started off by playing in a few of the smaller tournaments and won quite a few of them, enough to know that he had found his niche. "Then I started winning some big ones," he says. His first big win came in his own back yard at Bicycle Casino's Legends of Poker tournament in 1997. Three years later he won his first major Vegas tournament, the Harrah's Carnival of Poker, elevating him to the status of a world-class competitor.

But life hasn't exactly been a breeze for him since then. "This business has been hard to survive," he admits. "I've seen my ups and downs." Amir says he's gone broke more than a few times. In 2003, on the night before a $5,000 no-limit tournament he had to borrow $50 from a friend just to meet basic needs. A few days later he pocketed a quarter of a million dollars in winnings from the tournament. Soon thereafter he won another $270,000. "This is how it goes in the poker life," he says.

Amir is careful to point out that he doesn't lose a lot of money in poker. In fact, poker is his one mainstay, and feels he can always survive financially from his superior poker skills and instincts. "I need to be smart with my money," he says. Learning from his own mistakes, he advises poker players, above all, to be good money managers away from the table. "If you're in the meatpacking business, you don't go into trucking," he cautions. "The same goes for poker. If your business is poker, then don't touch any other sort of gambling."

Poker is a game of skill, he contends—a game in which you need to be intelligent and play intelligently. On the other hand, playing casino games like blackjack and craps is always a gamble. "It's even less than a 50-50 proposition," he says, "and a good way to lose all the money you earn in poker. If you're a poker player, stick with poker."

Major Poker Accomplishments

2003, Sixth place, WSOP, No Limit Hold'em Championship

2003, First place WSOP, No Limit Hold'em event

2003, First place, World Poker Finals, No Limit Hold'em event

2003, First place, World Poker Open, Limit Hold'em

2003, First place, World Poker Finals, Omaha Hi/Lo 8 O/B

2003, First place, Legends of Poker, Limit Hold'em

2003, First place, Poker Challenge Cup, No Limit Hold'em Championship

2003, Second place, Player of the Year

2001, No Limit Hold'em Player of the Year

Ram Vaswani

"It's always nice to hit the final of any event, but the world championships are something special"

Personal Notes

- Youngest member of the Hendon Mob
- Former snooker player
- Manages his brother's professional snooker career
- Nicknamed "Crazy Horse"
- Resides in England

Ram Vaswani is a man with many monikers. He is often dubbed "the quiet one" of the Hendon Mob. But his nickname on the poker circuit is "Crazy Horse," a testament to his ability to play carefully or with abandon, depending on the circumstances of the hand. He has also been called "The Looks," in an article in Esquire magazine, presumably because of his appeal to the women.

Whatever he is called, Ram is a solid poker player with the credentials to prove it. Like his other three cohorts in the "Mob," Ram has won a number of prestigious tourneys, like the Dutch Master Classic in 1999, the European Superbowl in 2000 and the French Championship in 2002. And the wins just keep coming. One poker analyst notes that he plays the large stack particularly well and has a very cool temperament.

A former snooker player, Ram has adapted the "moves" necessary for a good snooker match into the "moves" for a winning poker career. Since partnering with Prima Poker for the Prima Poker Tour, Ram has had several wins, even winning back to back tournaments, a feat every poker player wants to have on their resumés. And Ram was named the best over-all player on the Helsinki leg of the Prima Poker Tour. Primapoker.com boasts that Ram is "widely considered to be Europe's greatest tournament player." He hasn't let them down in living up to that name.

Ram had an auspicious start to his poker career when he was 12 or 13 years old and on a school trip to Wales. As Ram tells it, he organized a penny-ante card game with friends to make some extra spending money to satisfy his sweet tooth. Ram says that even at that age he was doing pretty well. "I was picking up on everyone's tells and it wasn't long before I was cleaning up." That is until one of the teachers popped in and stopped the game, telling them that they could not play for money. Always the thinker, Ram's brain went into overdrive to figure a way to satisfy his sweet tooth. The next night, the boys were playing with candy instead of money. Ram says, " When the teacher walked in again, he looked straight at me knowing I had cleaned up the night before, and he gave me a big smile before leaving us to finish our game." The stakes are higher now, but Ram is just as intent on winning.

"Poker is a sport. Train for major tournaments by exercising and practicing your moves."

-Ram Vaswani

At the 2004 World Series of Poker, Ram related his feelings on World Championship events in the Hendon Mob Diary. He had this to say: " It's always nice to hit the final of any event but the world championships are something special." The particular tournament of which he spoke was the $2,000 Pot Limit Omaha game in which he finished a respectable seventh. "The monster fields and huge buy-ins guarantee massive prize pools," he writes. "Then you have the razzmatazz of all the TV cameras and journalists surrounding the final table. . . It was about 4 a.m. before the last hand was dealt on day one of the No Limit Hold'em [tournament] with rebuys and it already felt like I'd done enough to win a tournament."

At this same tournament Ram had more to contend with on the final day than the oppponents at his table. As he tell readers of the Diary, he was doing quite well in the event. He made the final table but was facing some strong competition in the guise of Howard Lederer, Daniel Negreanu and John Juanda. All he wanted after that 4 a.m. finish was a good night's sleep.

That was not to be, however, since only one hour into it, he awoke to find that his stomach was feeling less than perfect. "Somehow I'd managed to catch some bug and found myself vomiting about fifteen times before it was time to leave for the casino," writes Ram. "As we got underway I felt a little better, especially when I won a couple of pots; but I made sure my girlfriend was standing by with a plastic bag just in case!" Ram fought off his opponents and the bug until he finally finished seventh in the tournament.

Like other poker pros he sees the bigger fields as a double-edged sword. Of course the number of players these days, particularly in worldwide tournaments such as the WSOP, give the winners a huge payout. Just the same, surviving the field to make it to a final table is brutal. Maybe that's why Ram tries to exercise to maintain stamina for the big tournaments, something he advises all players to do. Even fighting the flu bug, it works for him!

Major Poker Accomplishments

2004, Third place, WSOP, No Limit Hold'em event

2004, Fifth place, WSOP, Pot Limit Hold'em

2004, Seventh place, WSOP, No Limit Hold'em event

2004, Fourth place, Five Star World Poker Classic, Pot Limit Omaha

2003, First place, Poker Classics, Pot Limit Seven Card Stud

2003, First place, Midland Masters, No Limit Hold'em

2002, First place, Euro Finals of Poker, No Limit Hold'em Championship

Dennis Waterman 

"For some reason there's an emotional intensity in tournaments that is unsurpassed."

Personal Notes

- **Born in San Francisco, 1948**
- **Former stock broker**
- **Former chess champion**
- **Manages a log company**
- **Aspires to write a series of science fiction novels**
- **Resides between Oregon, Nevada, and California**

Dennis Waterman grew up in an Oregon logging family, where he worked in the forest as a timber feller from the age of thirteen. "I logged in the good weather," he says, "and I played poker in the bad weather." He followed that schedule, more or less, until he was 50. Dennis, however, did take some interesting detours during those years.

As a boy Dennis was very competitive. He started playing chess at age fourteen, and two years later earned the rank of Chess Master by winning tournaments all over the world. "There was no money to be made in chess," explains Dennis. "I'd sleep on the floor somewhere for three straight nights and play chess twelve hours each day for about $50." By the time Dennis quit the game, he ranked 12th in the United States and 100th in the world. "My highest rating was Senior Master," he adds.

In 1973, Dennis won the Brilliancy Prize in the American Open chess tournament that is played each year in Santa Monica, California. After an article was published about him in the *Los Angeles Times*, a business tycoon tracked him down. "I was living in the woods in Oregon," says Dennis, "and it took him nearly a year to find me, since I didn't even have a phone." Once found, Dennis was offered a job in Chicago. His offer: a membership on the Chicago Board of Trade, an enormous salary, two million dollars in cash and a $10 million line of credit.

"So I went to Chicago," says Dennis. "As a result, I pretty much had to give up chess." The theory behind the generous job offer was that exceptional chess players could logically apply their intelligence to the stock market and bring in millions. The theory proved true with Dennis Waterman. After experiencing success in Chicago, he moved on to New York City. "I was good at solving the practical problems that come about in a corporate environment," he remembers. "I made a lot more money than I could imagine at the time."

"You have to be hungry, and even if you play cheap you want to set your sights high."

-Dennis Waterman

In New York, he took the millions he'd made in Chicago and set up four new companies. "I was trying to make hundreds of millions of dollars," he admits, "and I went broke." That's when he returned to playing poker on a regular basis. From 1981 he played hold'em in Oregon and Nevada. When it became legal in California in 1986, he moved on to play in Los Angeles. He was back in the logging business again at this point, and returned to his old schedule: logging in the good weather, poker playing in the bad weather. "I have three sisters who inherited three estates with a lot of forest land," he says, "so I manage the land for them now."

Dennis plays both cash games and tournaments, but it's tournaments that he really enjoys. "For some reason there's an emotional intensity in tournament play that is unsurpassed," he says. Although he's won some 200 "brick and mortar" tournaments over the years, losing is still devastating for Dennis Waterman. "Even when I finish third, I'm really disturbed."

In addition to playing poker, Dennis has also worked as a consultant for several casinos. But he has other interests too, much outside the domains of logging and poker. "I teach meditation now," he explains. "I am interested in a kind of meditation that is called 'self-liberation.' I'm interested in working with energy, which includes working with light and sound." Dennis also says he has a grand plan to write a series of neo-spiritual books that proselytize his philosophy of life through a science fiction format. All of this he says, can be beneficial to playing poker. Considering that the psychology of the game comes together with mathematical aspects, he observes, "if you can master yourself, you can master your situation, and master the game."

Age, however, is more difficult to master. Dennis believes that poker is a young man's game in terms of the tremendous amount of energy, devotion and attention required. "You have to be hungry," he says, "and even if you play cheap you want to set your sights high." Realizing that he's not as young as he used to be and recognizing that he has many other interests, Dennis Waterman says he expects to concentrate much less on playing poker in the years to come, but doesn't think he'll ever leave the game totally behind.

Major Poker Accomplishments

2003, Second place, California State Poker Championship, No Limit Hold'em event

2003, Fourth place, WSOP, Pot Limit Hold'em

2003, 23rd place, WSOP, No Limit Hold'em Championship

2002, Player of the Year, Pot Limit Hold'em

2002, First place, Five Diamond World Poker Classic, No Limit Hold'em event

Robert Williamson III 

"Poker is just like any other sport except that we use our mental faculties rather than our biceps."

Personal Notes

- **Born in Granbury, Texas, 1970**
- **Graduate of Angelo State University**
- **Owned ten Pancake Kettle Houses in four states**
- **Retired real estate investor and ticket scalper**
- **Hosts an annual golf tournament in Costa Rica**
- **Resides in Dallas, Texas**

Born on 11/7/70, Robert Williamson III says he was born to gamble: "I've been around gambling my whole life, but I didn't pick up poker until I was ten." By the time Robert was a teenager he was playing regularly—and for high stakes! At Granbury High School, an hour southwest of Dallas, he and his friends gambled high. "Plenty of those kids had a whole lot of money. In high school I probably played for more than most people play in their entire life."

It wasn't just poker. Robert and his friends would shoot pool for $1,000 a game. They played air hockey for $500 a puck. "You could make a six figure income from the gambling I was around," he says when asked how much his high school gambling habits netted him. "I used to win between $2,000 to $3,000 from a good night of poker."

Robert's father was also a gambler, and he encouraged his son. During high school Robert would take a couple weeks off two or three times each year to go to Vegas. "My parents would arrange for me to be on 'educational field trips,'" he explains, "and they'd make sure I fulfilled all the requirements for school. I wrote papers on Hoover Dam and the Grand Canyon, for example." The highlight of his trips, of course, was his casino gambling. Robert's father took him to the casinos and let him loose. "We didn't play in the same areas of the casino," he says, "because I never wanted the heat to come back to him."

Robert played his share of casino poker when he was just 15 and 16 years old—more than five years underage by Nevada state law. "Everybody thought I was a lot older because I carried a large bankroll with me. When you see a 15-year-old pull out a wad of $10,000, you don't perceive him to be fifteen."

"I never saw a poker player's money that I did not like."

-Oklahoma Johnny Hale

Robert didn't earn all of that money through gambling. As much as he was a gambler, he was even more an entrepreneur. He started with summer lemonade stands and a lawn-mowing service. In high school he ran a food service company with a partner. "We would go around to town fairs and festivals and set up concession stands," he explains.

At the same time, Robert was known as a classy scalper, reselling tickets for all the major concerts and sporting events in and around Dallas. "People came to me when they wanted good seats," he says. "I prided myself on dealing only with the high-end tickets—only the best seats in the house."

By the time Robert graduated from college, he owned ten Kettle Pancake Houses in four states and was making a six-figure income in the business world alone. "It was a lot of work," he remembers. "I was working—literally—a hundred hours a week." The only time he took off was one weekend a month to go to the Horseshoe Casino in Tunica, Mississippi, where he played poker.

Although Robert typically played cash games, he learned how to get far in the tournaments too. He had made it to a dozen final tables before he won his first big event at the age of 22, and the wins kept rolling in. By the time he was 29, he had burned out on the long hours in the restaurant business. He sold his stores and took to the tournament trail year round. "I figured if I just played poker, I could put enough money away to have fun in my free time instead of working hard," he says.

For the past four years Robert has done just that, traveling to poker tournaments all over the world. It gives him a chance, at times, to get away from the poker tables and the smoky casino atmosphere for a while "Now I'm on vacation for about a third or fourth of the year. After I play in a tournament, I might hang out there and relax. I can just lay by the pool for three or four days if I want to."

Major Poker Accomplishments

2004, Second place, WSOP, Pot Limit Omaha

2003, First place, Mid-American Classic, No Limit Hold'em event

2003, First place, World Poker Open, Pot Limit Omaha

2003, Third place, WSOP, Pot Limit Omaha

2002, First place, WSOP, Pot Limit Omaha

Photography Credits

Front Cover Photo courtesy of the Aviation Club of France
Back Cover Photo: © Image Masters Photography

© Image Masters Photography
Pages: 1, 2, 3, 7, 11 bottom, 12, 13 bottom, 14, 15, 16, 17 bottom, 18, 22, 23, 25 bottom, 26, 27 head shot, 28, 29, 30, 31 bottom, 32, 33, 34, 37 bottom, 38, 39 bottom, 40, 41, 42, 43 bottom, 44, 45 bottom, 46, 49 bottom, 50, 51, 52, 55, 56, 57 bottom, 58, 59 bottom, 60, 61, 62, 63, 64, 65, 66, 67 bottom, 68, 69, 70, 71 bottom, 72, 73, 74, 75, 76, 77 bottom, 78, 79, 80, 81 bottom, 82, 83 bottom, 84, 85, 86, 87, 88, 89, 90, 91 bottom, 92, 95, 96, 101, 102, 103, 105, 106, 107 bottom, 109 bottom, 110, 111, 112, 115, 116, 117 bottom, 118, 119 bottom, 120, 121 bottom, 122, 123, 124, 125 bottom, 126, 127, 128, 129, 130, 131, 132, 133, 134, 135, 136, 137 bottom, 138, 139 bottom, 140, 143, 144, 147, 149 bottom, 150, 151 bottom, 152, 153, 154, 155, 156, 157 bottom, 158, 159 bottom, 160, 161, 162, 163 bottom, 164, 165, 166, 169, 170, 171, 175 bottom, 176, 177 bottom, 178

© www.poker-images.com/Bill Burlington
Pages: 8, 9, 10, 24, 47 bottom, 48, 54, 93 bottom, 104, 114, 141, 142, 172, 173 bottom, 174

© Rose Productions, LLC
Head Shots on pages: 5, 7, 11, 13, 17, 19, 21, 25, 31, 37, 39, 43, 45, 47, 49, 57, 59, 67, 71, 77, 81, 83, 91, 99, 107, 109, 113, 117, 119, 121, 125, 137, 139, 145, 149, 151, 157, 159, 163, 167, 173, 175, 177
Pages: 5, 19, 20, 21 108,, 145, 146, 167, 168

© 2003 World Poker Tour
Page: 148

Courtesy of the Aviation Club of France
Pages: 4, 53

Courtesy of David Colclough
Page: 27 bottom

Courtesy of Bonnie Damiano
Pages: 35, 36

Courtesy of Christer Johansson
Pages: 93 head shot, 94